Making
CONNECTIONS 3

Skills and Strategies for Academic Reading

Third Edition

LRC (104)

I. TOPIC
A. Main idea
1 --
2 --
3 --

B. Main idea

GIA 151

Kenneth J. Pakenham | Jo McEntire | Jessica Williams
with Amy Cooper

CAMBRIDGE
UNIVERSITY PRESS

CAMBRIDGE
UNIVERSITY PRESS

University Printing House, Cambridge CB2 8BS, United Kingdom

One Liberty Plaza, 20th Floor, New York, NY 10006, USA

477 Williamstown Road, Port Melbourne, VIC 3207, Australia

4843/24, 2nd Floor, Ansari Road, Daryaganj, Delhi – 110002, India

79 Anson Road, #06–04/06, Singapore 079906

Cambridge University Press is part of the University of Cambridge.

It furthers the University's mission by disseminating knowledge in the pursuit of education, learning and research at the highest international levels of excellence.

www.cambridge.org
Information on this title: www.cambridge.org/9781107673014

© Cambridge University Press 2013

First published 2004
Second edition 2013
20 19 18 17 16 15 14 13 12 11 10

Printed in Dubai by Oriental Press

A catalogue record for this publication is available from the British Library

ISBN 978-1-107-67301-4 Student's Book
ISBN 978-1-107-65054-1 Teacher's Manual

Cambridge University Press has no responsibility for the persistence or accuracy of URLs for external or third-party internet websites referred to in this publication, and does not guarantee that any content on such websites is, or will remain, accurate or appropriate.

Layout services, page design, and photo research: Page Designs International, Inc.
Cover and book design: Studio Montage

TABLE OF CONTENTS

GLOBAL HEALTH   1

MULTICULTURAL SOCIETIES   63

ASPECTS OF LANGUAGE 125

SUSTAINING PLANET EARTH 189

Acknowledgments

Many people have helped shape this third edition of *Making Connections 3*. We are grateful to all of the supportive and professional staff of Cambridge University Press for the opportunity to create this new edition. There are many others who did so much to make this project successful, including Page Designs International – Don Williams, the page designer; and especially Bernard Seal, our project manager, who has provided guidance and wisdom for all of the *Making Connections* books.

Thanks to Poyee Oster, photo researcher; Mandie Drucker, fact-checker and copyeditor; Patricia Egan, proofreader; and as always, Karen Shimoda, freelance development editor, whose dedication and attention to detail know few limits. We would particularly like to thank Amy Cooper for her help in writing several of the readings.

Finally, textbooks are only as good as the feedback that authors receive on them. Many thanks to the following reviewers whose insights helped shape the new editions of the entire *Making Connections* series: Macarena Aguilar, Lone Star College-CyFair, Texas; Susan Boland, Tidewater Community College, Virginia; Inna Cannon, San Diego State University, California; Holly Cin, University of Houston, Texas; Stacie Miller, Community College of Baltimore County, Maryland.

Making CONNECTIONS

MAKING CONNECTIONS 3 is a high intermediate academic reading and vocabulary skills book. It is intended for students who need to improve their strategic reading skills and build their academic vocabulary.

SKILLS AND STRATEGIES 7

Identifying the Thesis of a Reading

In Skills and Strategies 1, you learned that each paragraph has one main idea, which consists of the topic and the writer's claim about the topic. Like paragraphs, a whole reading (an academic text, article, essay, etc.) usually has one *central* main idea – the thesis. Usually writers clearly state the thesis at the end of the introductory paragraph or paragraphs of a reading, and the main ideas of all of the paragraphs in the reading generally contribute to the thesis. It may be repeated in a new way in the final paragraph. In addition, each paragraph has a function and a specific relationship to the thesis. Understanding the thesis of a reading is an important academic skill.

> Each unit begins with an in-depth study of key skills and strategies for reading academic texts, helping students to learn how and when to use them.

Examples & Explanations

These are the main ideas from the six paragraphs of a whole reading:

① With 1.5 billion speakers, English is now a global language, but the numbers are not the most important issue.

② Languages become global when they gain official status in many countries.

③ Languages become global when they gain favored foreign-language status in many countries.

④ English is an official language in many countries that have no native speakers of English, and it is the most widely studied language in the world.

⑤ A large number of native speakers does not necessarily cause a language to become global.

⑥ The economic, military, and political power of the nations promotes their languages to global status.

The **topic** that connects the main ideas of all of these paragraphs is *global languages*. As you read, you should form a hypothesis about the writer's thesis: What does the writer want to say about global languages?

The main idea of paragraph 1 introduces the **thesis** with the topic and a **claim**, with English as an example.

The main ideas of paragraphs 2 and 3 are the ways in which a language may reach global status.

The main idea of paragraph 4 is that English is an example of the claims made in paragraphs 2 and 3.

The main idea of paragraph 5 is the common view: a factor that readers might think is important but the author claims is not.

Paragraph 6 provides the most fundamental reason for the global status of a language.

Together, the paragraphs support the writer's primary **claim**: *A language attains global status, not because of the number of its speakers, but because of the power of the nations in which its native speakers live.*

The main idea in paragraph 6 restates the central main idea – the thesis – that the writer wants to express in this reading.

Strategies

These strategies will help you identify the thesis of a whole reading.

- As you begin to read, ask yourself: *What is the topic?* The title often can help you decide.
- What claim do you think the writer will make about that topic? In other words, what do you think the thesis will be?
- Think about the main ideas of each paragraph that you read. Are they all related to this topic and the thesis?
- Pay attention to the first, second, and last paragraphs in the reading. Writers often state or restate the thesis of the reading in one of these places.

Skill Practice 1

Read the following lists of main ideas of each paragraph of a reading. Highlight the topic of the reading for each list. Then read the four possible claims below. Circle the claim you think best expresses the thesis of the reading.

1   **Language and Machines**

① Machine translation uses software to translate sentences from one language to another.

② Machine translation has a long history.

③ Early machine translation programs translated word for word.

④ Word-for-word translations are not satisfactory because they do not produce very natural texts.

⑤ New methods of machine translation are different because they rely on huge databases of real language samples.

⑥ Machine translation has improved a lot in the last few decades.

⑦ Humans often still have to clean up machine-translated texts.

   a The crucial difference between machine translation of the past and machine translation today is the use of massive databases.

   b There have been tremendous improvements in machine translation in recent years.

   c Machine translation has improved a lot, but it still usually requires human involvement.

   d It is still better to use human translators than machine translators because machines cannot really understand language.

2   **Signed Languages**

① Signed languages use facial expressions, as well as hand and body positions and movements, rather than sounds to express meaning.

② Signed languages are equivalent to spoken languages in their ability to express a wide range of meaning.

③ Signed languages have their own grammars.

> Students learn strategies for approaching academic texts and skills for consciously applying the strategies.

WHAT'S NEW

- Critical thinking skills
- More recycling of skills and strategies
- Study of the Academic Word List

- Updated readings
- Enhanced unit navigation

Before You Read

Connecting to the Topic

Discuss the following questions with a partner.

1 Do you think babies can understand language before they can speak? Why or why not?

2 At what age do you think language learning begins?

3 Think about how you began to learn your *second* language. Do you think babies begin the process in the same way? Explain your answer.

4 How do people become bilingual (able to speak two languages well)?

Previewing and Predicting

> Reading the title and first sentence of each paragraph is a quick way to predict what a reading will be about.

A Read the title and the first sentence of each paragraph in Reading 1. What do you think this reading will be about? Put a check (✓) next to the topic or topics that you think will be included in the reading.

_____ A Research methods in the study of child language learning

_____ B A baby's first sentences

_____ C Bilingual education

_____ D Early bilingual language learning

_____ E Language learning before birth

_____ F How infants begin to understand the sounds of language

B Compare your answers with a partner's.

While You Read

As you read, stop at the end of each sentence that contains words in **bold**. Then follow the instructions in the box in the margin.

Predicting the content of a text is critical for reading college books, and students practice this skill extensively before beginning each reading.

Each unit contains 5 readings, providing students with multiple opportunities to practice applying the skills and strategies.

Students learn how to use the skills and strategies by applying them to each text while they read it.

READING 1

When Does Language Learning Begin?

1   By the time children have reached the age of about five, they have accomplished something that few of us give much thought to but is actually quite extraordinary: They have learned how to speak their native language. They have perfect pronunciation, and they have learned most of the grammar necessary to speak and understand their language. Language acquisition takes place regardless of whether the children are born into educated, prosperous families in a society that uses advanced technology or into uneducated, even illiterate, poor families in a developing country. It occurs regardless of the disparities in individual children's intellectual abilities or their motivation. It also begins far earlier than scientists once thought.

2   This remarkable achievement, which takes place without formal teaching, has fascinated scientists for centuries. Once children begin to verbalize, with words or simply with sounds, scientists can study the language acquisition process fairly easily. However, the more mysterious part of the process takes place before that time, when a baby begins to perceive the sounds of language and understand their connection to meaning. How do babies begin this language acquisition **process**?

3   Recent research indicates that this process begins before babies are even born. From inside the uterus, fetuses cannot hear individual sounds, but they can perceive the rhythm patterns and tones of the language that they hear. Once they are born, babies use this fetal auditory experience to accomplish three crucial tasks. First, they recognize their mother's voice; second, they distinguish between language sounds and non-language sounds; and third, they differentiate between basic contours of their own language – the rhythm and tone patterns – and those of other languages. They can do all of these things within days of birth.

> **WHILE YOU READ** 1
>
> What do you think the topic of this reading is?
> a) How babies learn language
> b) The earliest stages of language learning
> c) The most important factors in language learning

Children recognize their mothers' voices very early.

"Reading is an interactive process, in which readers use their knowledge of language, text organization, and the world to understand what they read."

"Reading is goal-oriented and strategic; good academic readers know when to use the right reading skills."

---

6 Why do some scientists prefer the term *sensitive period* rather than *critical period*?
a They are not really sure if the critical period applies to everyone.
b People are especially sensitive to any exposure to a second language when they are children.
c The loss of language learning ability is gradual rather than sudden.
d Animals as well as human beings share this important developmental period.

Skill Review

In Skills and Strategies 7, you learned that most readings have a central thesis that the writer wants to express. Identifying the thesis of a reading is an important academic skill.

A Review Reading 2, and then answer the questions below.

1 What is the topic of the reading?

2 What claim is the writer making about this topic?

3 Is there a sentence that contains the thesis? If so highlight it.

B With a partner, match the function of each paragraph in the right hand column with the correct paragraph. Write the paragraph left hand column.

PARAGRAPH NUMBER	FUNCTION OF PARAGRAPH
	Shows more specific application to *second language*
	Provides scientific explanation for thesis
	Shows broad application of thesis
	Presents thesis
	Discusses importance of main idea for teaching
	Provides evidence for thesis
	Shows specific application to language learning

Students continually review the skills and strategies, helping them build up a valuable set of tools for reading academic texts.

Students expand their vocabularies by studying key words from each reading and academic words from each unit.

Vocabulary Development

Definitions

Find the words in Reading 2 that are similar to the definitions below.

1 opposing (*adj*) Par. 1
2 argu... Par. 1
3 to be...
4 some...
5 most...
6 to re...
7 to go...
8 to re...
9 some...
10 relate...
11 a gro...
12 comp...
13 wild...
14 to tr...
15 exac...

Words in

Complet...

| attain |
| counter |

1 U.S...

proble...

begin...

ever...

educa...

nation...

2 Edu...

perfor...

people...

who work hard but have average abilities. They admit, however, that this is simply a generalization and that it is always possible to find _____ to this
general _____ .
           i

Academic Word List

The following are Academic Word List words from Readings 1 and 2 of this unit. Use these words to complete the sentences. (For more on the Academic Word List, see page 256.)

| acquisition (*n*) | attain (*v*) | distinctions (*n*) | fundamental (*adj*) | utilize (*v*) |
| approximate (*v*) | conflicting (*adj*) | exposure (*n*) | perceive (*v*) | visual (*adj*) |

1 She listened to the teacher and tried to _____ his pronunciation.
2 _____ information is processed in both hemispheres of the brain.
3 There are _____ arguments about the best way to learn an additional language.
4 It is a common belief that language _____ becomes easier with the third and fourth language, but scientists are not sure that this is true.
5 Research has demonstrated that it is easier to _____ sounds in women's speech than in men's speech.
6 Language learning scholars _____ advanced technology in their research.
7 _____ to print material in the home, such as books and newspapers, is an important predictor of a child's reading performance.
8 Some people with extraordinary abilities can _____ a high level of proficiency in a new language after a very short period of study.
9 Speakers of English have difficulty hearing the _____ between tones in languages such as Chinese and Vietnamese.
10 Reading is a skill that is _____ to success in modern life.

THE APPROACH

The *Making Connections* series offers a skills-based approach to academic reading instruction. Throughout each book, students are introduced to a variety of academic reading and vocabulary-building skills, which they then apply to high-interest, thematically-related readings.

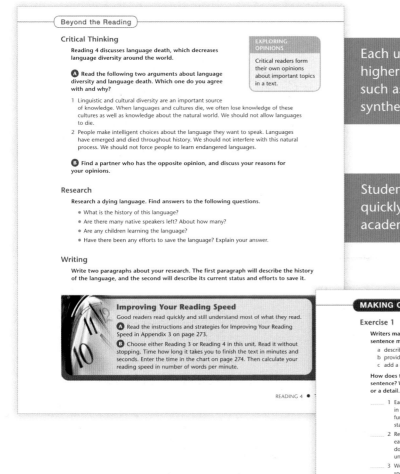

Beyond the Reading

Critical Thinking

Reading 4 discusses language death, which decreases language diversity around the world.

EXPLORING OPINIONS

Critical readers form their own opinions about important topics in a text.

A Read the following two arguments about language diversity and language death. Which one do you agree with and why?

1 Linguistic and cultural diversity are an important source of knowledge. When languages and cultures die, we often lose knowledge of these cultures as well as knowledge about the natural world. We should not allow languages to die.

2 People make intelligent choices about the language they want to speak. Languages have emerged and died throughout history. We should not interfere with this natural process. We should not force people to learn endangered languages.

B Find a partner who has the opposite opinion, and discuss your reasons for your opinions.

Research

Research a dying language. Find answers to the following questions.

• What is the history of this language?
• Are there many native speakers left? About how many?
• Are any children learning the language?
• Have there been any efforts to save the language? Explain your answer.

Writing

Write two paragraphs about your research. The first paragraph will describe the history of the language, and the second will describe its current status and efforts to save it.

Improving Your Reading Speed

Good readers read quickly and still understand most of what they read.

A Read the instructions and strategies for Improving Your Reading Speed in Appendix 3 on page 273.

B Choose either Reading 3 or Reading 4 in this unit. Read it without stopping. Time how long it takes you to finish the text in minutes and seconds. Enter the time in the chart on page 274. Then calculate your reading speed in number of words per minute.

READING 4 •

> Each unit develops students' higher level thinking skills, such as exploring opinions and synthesizing information.

> Students also learn to read more quickly, a valuable skill for extended academic texts.

> The units end with a study of how writers make connections across sentences, helping students learn how to navigate dense academic text.

MAKING CONNECTIONS

Exercise 1

Writers may connect ideas between sentences in many different ways. The second sentence may:

a describe a **result** of what is reported in the first sentence
b provide a **contrast** to what is described in the first sentence
c add a **detail** or details to support the more general information in the first sentence

How does the second sentence in each pair of sentences below connect to the first sentence? Write *a*, *b*, or *c* on the line depending on whether it is a result, a contrast, or a detail.

_____ 1 Early critical period studies of language acquisition contained a number of flaws in their research design and methods. Later studies avoided some of these fundamental weaknesses by using real language samples and powerful statistical analysis.

_____ 2 Researchers analyzed overgeneralization errors that children make, such as "I eated everything," and "My mommy brang me a cookie," which have been documented extensively in the child language literature. This helped them to understand some of the most basic principles of language acquisition.

_____ 3 We can define linguistic competence, or knowledge, as the ability of the native speaker to comprehend and produce novel utterances. One of the components is phonological competence, that is, knowledge of the sounds of the language and the rules for combining those sounds in appropriate ways.

_____ 4 As children, we all attain a uniform level of competence in our first language, apparently with little effort, just by interacting with native speakers in our environment. For most adults, however, learning a second language seems to be a fundamentally different process, which involves considerable effort and produces widely varying outcomes.

_____ 5 When immigrants come to a new country, it is usually their children that acquire the language of the host country most rapidly. Because their knowledge of the new language is superior to their parents, the children often have to translate for them at stores, hospitals, and government offices.

Exercise 2

Make a clear paragraph by putting sentences A, B, and C into the best order after the numbered sentence. Write the letters in the correct order on the blank lines.

1 Bilingualism has clear practical advantages, but recent research indicates that it also has significant cognitive benefits. _____ _____ _____

A They also found that learning and maintaining a second language can delay some of the effects of aging on the brain.

B Since that time, researchers have shown that bilinguals are often better at focusing their attention and performing complex tasks.

C This view is in contrast to the perspective of 50 years ago, which characterized bilingualism as a barrier to cognitive development and academic progress.

MAKING CONNECTIONS • 187

1

GLOBAL HEALTH

SKILLS AND STRATEGIES

- Identifying Main Ideas
- Cause and Effect
- Managing Unknown Vocabulary

Identifying Main Ideas

The main idea is the most important idea that a writer expresses in a paragraph. The writer supports this idea with details, such as examples, facts, numbers, and reasons. Although the main idea can appear anywhere in a paragraph, it most often appears in the opening one or two sentences. Sometimes, it is not stated directly; instead, the reader must infer the main idea by reading the whole paragraph. To emphasize the main idea, a writer may repeat it at the end of the paragraph. The writer may also refer to the main idea at the beginning of the next paragraph to provide a smooth transition between the paragraphs. Identifying the main ideas of each paragraph will help you better understand academic texts.

Examples & Explanations

①Medicine can transform a serious disease from a death sentence to a treatable condition. ②Yet this medicine often becomes available many years after a disease is discovered. ③This is because it takes years to carefully develop and test a new drug. ④Basic research begins in the lab, where scientists search for compounds that will fight the disease but not harm the patient. ⑤If a promising compound is found, it is further tested until the scientists believe it is safe to test on human volunteers in a clinical trial. ⑥If the new drug successfully completes this stage, the developing company applies to the government for permission to market it. ⑦Independent scientists review the research and approve the drug, which can now be sold. ⑧The total process is time consuming but necessary.

①Because of this long and careful process, antiretroviral drugs that treat HIV / AIDS became available years after that disease was discovered.

A main idea has two parts: a topic and a claim. Good readers ask two questions to find main ideas as they read a paragraph.

- What is the topic, or general subject?
- What claim does the writer make about the topic?

Sentence 1 introduces *medicine* as a possible topic.

The reader then looks for the claim the writer makes about this topic. Sentence 2 gives more information about a new drug, but it is too general to be the claim. It provides background information to the topic of medicine.

Sentence 3 explains that new drugs require careful development and testing. Together, these two sentences could be the claim – *that new drugs take a long time to become available*. The reader now looks for supporting details.

Sentences 4–7 provide reasons why it takes a long time for a new drug to be available. These reasons support the main idea in sentences 3 and 4.

Sentence 8 summarizes and comments on the main idea.

Sentence 1 of the next paragraph refers back to the main idea of the previous paragraph. This helps the reader remember the most important ideas and make connections between the two paragraphs.

Strategies

These strategies will help you identify main ideas.

- As you begin each paragraph, ask yourself: *What is the topic? What claim does the writer make about that topic?*
- Writers sometimes introduce background information in the first two or three sentences. This information is helpful to understand the paragraph, but it is not the main idea.
- Remember that the main idea is not always stated directly. You may need to infer it from the whole paragraph.
- As you read the other sentences in the paragraph, ask yourself if the information in the sentences supports the main idea.
- Writers often repeat the main idea in the last sentence of the paragraph.
- Pay attention to the first sentence of the next paragraph, which may refer back to the main idea of the previous paragraph.

Skill Practice 1

Read the following paragraphs. As you read, highlight the topic and underline the claim. Then read the four possible main ideas below. Circle the one you think best expresses the main idea of the paragraph.

1   When people think about illnesses, they usually think of physical illnesses. However, mental illnesses are on the rise in many developed countries. A 2011 study in the United States, for example, found that the number of Americans who could not perform ordinary, daily routines because of a mental illness nearly doubled between 1987 and 2007. This huge growth has raised many important questions about mental health. Some health experts believe that the increase in mental illnesses is due to better diagnosis of this disease. They argue that doctors today are trained to recognize mental illnesses such as depression. These experts also believe that people are more comfortable talking about their problems today, whereas in the past, a mental illness was seen as a weakness. Other researchers, however, think that life is becoming more stressful and that this stress leads to more people suffering from this type of illness. With 1 in 10 Americans taking drugs to fight mental illnesses, it is clear that more research needs to take place before these important questions are answered.

a The number of people suffering from mental illness is increasing in developed countries.
b The increase in mental illness is raising serious questions among mental health experts.
c Ten percent of Americans take a drug to fight some type of mental illness.
d Many health experts believe that better diagnosis of mental illness explains the increase in numbers.

2   There are several possible treatments for heart disease. If the disease is caught early, a change of diet and lifestyle is sometimes enough. When the condition is serious, medication may be needed. In the most critical cases, surgery becomes a possible solution. In many cases, heart surgery is lifesaving. However, this practice also raises important medical issues. First, focusing on research involved in heart surgery may move attention away from preventing the disease. Next, this research attracts money that could be used for programs to educate the public about the factors that contribute to heart disease – smoking, lack of exercise, and the fat in our diet. Finally, the emphasis on surgical treatment of heart disease may lead to doctors performing unnecessary surgeries. In a hospital that has the equipment and the medical expertise needed for this kind of surgery, the presence of that equipment and expertise creates a lot of pressure to perform heart surgeries.

Topic:
Heart
surgery

claim:
Raised
important
medical
issues

a   Heart disease is one of the most serious problems faced by the western world. *too general*
b   There are several ways doctors can treat heart disease. *Background*
c   The use of heart surgery has raised several significant medical issues.
d   Research clearly shows that smoking, lack of exercise, and a high fat content in our diet contribute to heart disease.   *detail*

3   Annually, millions of children in developing countries die before the age of five from infectious diseases such as measles, whooping cough, and simple diarrhea. Emphasizing the prevention rather than the treatment of these diseases could reduce the number of deaths. Some of these diseases can be prevented by vaccines, which are simple yet effective to use. A child usually needs only several doses of a vaccine. After the vaccination, the child has a natural protection against the disease. On the other hand, treating the diseases after they occur is often not effective; it is expensive and requires drugs, hospitals, and medical expertise, which are not available in all areas of developing countries.

a   Diseases like diarrhea are more common in developing countries than in developed countries.
b   In developing countries, millions of children die before their fifth birthday because of measles, whooping cough, and diarrhea.
c   Vaccines are an effective yet simple method to prevent many serious diseases.
d   If the health systems of developing countries emphasized disease prevention, they could reduce the number of deaths in young children.

Topic – Infectious Diseases
claim – emphasizing prevention rather than treatment could reduce deaths

Skill Practice 2

Read the following paragraphs. The main ideas are given to you. Find the supporting details in the paragraph, and write them on the blank lines.

1   What can be done to fight cardiovascular disease (CVD)? The surgical treatment of heart disease continues to benefit patients in countries where the necessary expertise, equipment, and resources are available. However, this surgical approach to CVD is not enough to win the fight against the disease. One reason is that surgery is very expensive, even for rich nations. Many countries simply do not have the resources to provide this type of treatment. In addition, even where resources for surgical treatment are available, this type of treatment is not always successful for all patients. A 2011 study in the United States showed, for example, that 10 percent of CVD patients suffer complications from heart surgery.

Main idea: A surgical approach is not enough to defeat CVD.

Supporting detail: Many countries simply don't have

Supporting detail: 10% of CVD patients suffer complicatioin from heart surgery

2   A number of developing countries have shown that low-cost health-care programs can be successful. The disease polio provides an example of the effectiveness of these programs. In 1985, the World Health Organization (WHO) worked to end this disease in North, South, and Central America. In 1991, nearly 2 million children in Peru were vaccinated just one week after polio was diagnosed in a two-year-old boy. The boy recovered and proved to be the last case of polio in the Americas. This disease was also common in India, with 150,000 cases in 1985. The government there partnered with WHO and began regular National Vaccination Days that aimed to vaccinate 170 million children under the age of five. The effort has been so successful that the last case of polio in India was reported in January 2011.

Main idea: The treatment of polio illustrates the effectiveness of low-cost health care programs.

Supporting detail: The boy recovered and proved to be the last case

Supporting detail: WHo worked to end this disease

Supporting detail: In 1991 nearly 2 million children were vaccoyed

Connecting to the Topic

Discuss the following questions with a partner.

1 What does it mean to be healthy?

2 What are some things you can do to be healthy?

3 It is the responsibility of an individual to stay healthy. Is it also the responsibility of a government to try to make sure its citizens are healthy?

4 What steps can a government take to improve the health of its citizens?

Previewing and Predicting

> You will understand a reading more easily if you can get an idea of its organization and content before you start reading. A quick way to do this is to read the first sentence in each paragraph. This can help you predict what the reading will be about.

A Read the first sentence of each paragraph in Reading 1, and think of a question that you expect each paragraph to answer. Then choose the question below that is most like your question. Write the number of the paragraph next to that question. The first one has been done for you.

PARAGRAPH	QUESTION
5	How does the way you live affect your life expectancy?
	What is meant by the term *life expectancy*?
	How healthy is the world today?
	Why is it important for all people to think carefully about their health?
	What are some of the causes of premature death?
	What is the connection between mortality rates and world health?

B Compare your answers with a partner's.

While You Read

As you read, stop at the end of each sentence that contains words in **bold**. Then follow the instructions in the box in the margin.

The State of the World's Health

1   Individuals regularly make decisions about their physical and mental health. They do this partly because a serious illness can have a devastating effect on a person and on his or her family. Similarly, just as the health of a family is connected to individuals within that family, the health of a nation is clearly connected to the health of its people. A country's economic strength depends on a healthy, productive workforce. Therefore, it is in the interest of governments to monitor the health of their populations and to examine the connections between such factors as health and lifestyle. Using statistics from governments, international organizations such as the World Health Organization (WHO) then try to answer an important question: How healthy is the world?

2   The WHO uses two indicators – life expectancy and mortality rates – to assess the health of large **populations**. Life expectancy is the average age a person is expected to live. Since the beginning of the twentieth century, most countries have seen a significant increase in life expectancy. Today, the average global citizen can expect to live 27 years longer than his relatives in the 1900s. Some nations have experienced even more dramatic increases; the average Japanese person, for example, lives 38 years longer than his or her counterpart lived 100 years ago. As Figure 1.1 indicates, even the

> **WHILE YOU READ** 1
>
> As you read this paragraph, highlight the topic.

Figure 1.1 Life Expectancies 1970–2015

COUNTRY	LIFE EXPECTANCY 1970–1975	LIFE EXPECTANCY 2010–2015
The World	58.3	68.5
Australia	71.7	82.0
Bangladesh	45.3	66.2
Brazil	59.5	74.7
Canada	73.2	81.4
China	63.2	74.0
Egypt	51.1	72.6
India	50.7	66.7
Saudi Arabia	53.9	73.8
United Kingdom	72.0	80.1
United States	71.5	78.9

Source: Earthtrends.org

Children's health is an important indicator of a country's health.

last 40 years has seen considerable increases worldwide. Therefore, using this indicator of life expectancy, the world at the start of the twenty-first century is significantly healthier than at the start of the previous **century**. (Mortaility)

3   The second indicator of world health is mortality rates, defined as the number of deaths within a specific geographic **region**. Mortality data is connected to life expectancy, with experts focusing on the number of premature deaths; in other words, the number of people who die before the average life expectancy within that area. In order to measure the health of a specific region, the WHO focuses on child mortality, since this accounts for more than 20 percent of all premature deaths. Unlike statistics for life expectancy, mortality rates provide a less optimistic picture of world health. Globally, child mortality is down by 30 percent since 1990, which is particularly encouraging since rates have fallen in all world regions. However, beneath this promising trend lie serious disparities between nations and between individuals living within a nation. Mortality rates are falling much more rapidly in wealthier countries, and within a wealthy country, mortality rates are falling more rapidly for those with higher incomes. Therefore, although there are reasons to be hopeful about mortality rates worldwide, there are still areas of concern.

4   The goal of most governments is, of course, to reduce mortality rates, and to do this, experts target the many causes of premature death. While there has been significant progress in the way medicine treats and even eradicates infectious diseases, these diseases are still responsible for millions of deaths every year, particularly in developing countries. For example, HIV / AIDS, virtually unknown until 30 years ago, has killed approximately 30 million people worldwide. At first, many nations were slow to deal with HIV / AIDS because of the social stigma surrounding the disease. In fact, some governments did not want to accept that HIV / AIDS was a health problem in their countries. Today, however, most countries are working toward HIV / AIDS prevention. As a result of these efforts, new infections are declining – 16 percent globally between 2000 and 2008. The development of new drugs, and particularly combinations of drugs, has also led to a decline in the number of HIV / AIDS deaths associated with this disease.

Infectious Disease

WHILE YOU READ ❷

Quickly reread paragraph 2. What claim does the writer make about the topic? Highlight the claim.

WHILE YOU READ ❸

As you read this paragraph, highlight the sentence that contains the main idea.

5   One factor that clearly affects both life expectancy and mortality rates is **lifestyle**. For instance, just as eating too little is unhealthy, so is eating too much. Severe obesity can reduce life expectancy by as much as 20 years. It can also lead to diabetes, one of the fastest growing diseases today. Smoking is another lifestyle choice that has serious health consequences. Although the number of smokers is decreasing in developed nations, it is growing in developing ones. The Center for Disease Control (CDC), an organization based in the United States, estimates that there are a billion smokers worldwide and that 80 percent of them live in developing countries. Every year, six million people die from tobacco-related products, including those who contract diseases from second-hand smoke, that is, smoke inhaled by nonsmokers. Such lifestyle choices lead to poor health, both for individuals and countries.

WHILE YOU READ ④

As you read, highlight details that support the main idea of this paragraph.

world
health
status
and
solutions

6   Information about life expectancy, mortality rates, and lifestyle can begin to address the question: What is the state of the world's health today? The answer is a mixed one. Because life expectancy is increasing globally, most people can expect to live a longer life. However, infectious diseases and poor lifestyle choices still lead to millions of deaths, especially in developing countries. This clearly demonstrates the need for nations to continue to work on improving health worldwide. Providing jobs and increasing incomes is an important part of this effort since there is a direct correlation between income level and health. There is also a strong connection between education and health. People who are better educated are less likely to contract serious diseases and are more likely to recover when they get sick. Knowledge allows people to make healthy lifestyle choices, get better jobs, eat healthier food, and pass these advantages to their children. With increasing access to good education as well as the ability for people to support themselves, the world's health will no doubt improve.

Healthy lifestyle choices are important.

Main Idea Check

Here are the main ideas of paragraphs 2–6 in Reading 1. Match each paragraph to its main idea. Write the number of the paragraph on the blank line.

___5___ A There is a clear connection between lifestyle and health.

___2___ B Life expectancy has been increasing in the last 100 years.

___4___ C Infectious diseases are still responsible for millions of deaths, especially in developing countries.

___3___ D Research shows both good and bad news about mortality rates.

___6___ E Nations need to continue to improve the overall health of their citizens.

A Closer Look

Look back at Reading 1 to answer the following questions.

1 Why is it important for governments to monitor the health of their populations?
   a The WHO needs this information in order to assess global health.
   b Ill health can have a serious effect on a person and a family.
   c There is a clear connection between the health of a country's workers and the strength of its economy.
   d There is a direct relationship between a healthy lifestyle and good health.

2 Which statement is true according to Paragraph 2 and Figure 1.1?
   a One hundred years ago, an average Japanese man lived to almost the same age as he does today.
   b Life expectancy in Bangladesh changed from being one of the lowest in 1970 to being one of the highest 30 years later.
   c Between 1970 and 2010, China and Saudi Arabia saw almost the same increases in life expectancy.
   d An average Egyptian lived approximately 21 years longer in 2010 than an average Egyptian lived 30 years earlier.

3 Which statement is not true according to the reading?
   a Children account for one fifth of all premature deaths.
   b Mortality rates show that health is improving for everyone in the world.
   c The number of people dying from premature deaths is decreasing worldwide.
   d There is a connection between national and individual wealth and mortality rates.

4 What does the reading suggest about the early attitude of some countries to HIV/AIDS?
   a Some governments did not realize the seriousness of this disease.
   b Not all countries had the necessary resources to deal with this disease.
   c Some countries did not immediately address HIV/AIDS because they did not want to admit this disease was in their country.
   d Many countries were slow to deal with HIV/AIDS because they did not know how to prevent it.

5 According to paragraph 4, the number of new HIV/AIDS cases fell between 2000 and 2008 because of changes in lifestyle. **True or False?**

6 Which statement is true according to the reading?
   a Diabetes, which is closely connected to obesity, is growing more quickly than any other disease worldwide.
   b Annually, 6 million people die from tobacco-related products throughout developed countries, including the United States.
   c Although smoking is increasing in developing countries, the majority of smokers today live in wealthier countries.
   d The news about smoking is mixed because the number of smokers in developed nations is decreasing while the number of smokers in developing countries is increasing.

Skill Review

In Skills and Strategies 1, you learned that each paragraph has a main idea, and that writers express the main idea in different places in a paragraph. Finding the main ideas of each paragraph will help you better understand academic texts.

A Look over Reading 1 again, and review the Main Idea Check. Where did you find the main ideas of paragraphs 2–6? Put a check (✓) in the correct columns to show where you found the main ideas. Some paragraphs may have more than one column checked.

PARAGRAPH	FIRST SENTENCE	SECOND SENTENCE	WHOLE PARAGRAPH	REPEATED AT THE END OF THE PARAGRAPH
2	✓		✗	✗
3		✓	✗	✗
4	✓	✗		
5	✗			
6			✗	

B Compare your answers with a partner's.

Definitions

Find the words in Reading 1 that are similar to the definitions below.

1 a signal that makes something clear (*n*) Par. 2

2 to decide the quality or importance of something (*v*) Par. 2

3 a person who has the same position as someone else in a different place or time (*n*) Par. 2

4 hopeful (*adj*) Par. 3

5 general direction of changes or developments (*n*) Par. 3

6 to focus on (*v*) Par. 4

7 to destroy something completely (*v*) Par. 4

8 a bad opinion of something because society does not approve of it (*n*) Par. 4

9 an excess amount of body fat, 20 percent or more over a person's ideal weight (*n*) Par. 5

10 to deal with a question or a problem (*v*) Par. 6

Words in Context

Complete the sentences with words from Reading 1 in the box below.

accounts for	contracted	devastating	monitored	statistics
considerable	correlation	disparities	promising	virtually

1 The child _____ the disease from drinking dirty water.

2 When scientists studied _____ from a recent study, they were surprised to see that the number of people receiving medicine for mental illnesses has sharply increased in the last few years.

3 New combinations of drugs to treat HIV/AIDS are having _____ results; more people are living healthier lives today because of these drugs.

4 Even though the connection between smoking and lung cancer is well known, there has been a/an _____ increase in the number of teenage smokers.

5 There is a clear _____ between smoking and heart disease.

6 The doctor _____ the patient's progress very carefully.

7 Not having access to clean drinking water can have _____ effects on young children.

8 Because of vaccines, polio is _____ nonexistent today.

9 Smoking _____ approximately 20 percent of all male deaths in India, according to a 2010 study.

10 There are wide _____ in pay between health-care workers in developed countries and those in developing countries.

Critical Thinking

Reading 1 states that life expectancy is increasing worldwide. The writer, however, does not explain why this is happening.

Discuss the following questions with a partner.

1 Why do you think life expectancy is increasing throughout the world today?

2 Women tend to have a longer life expectancy than men. What might explain this?

3 Do you think life expectancy will continue to increase in the future? How long might the average person live in the next century?

> **ANALYZING INFORMATION**
>
> Critical thinking involves thinking carefully about important topics that the writer has not completely explained.

Research

Choose a country that is not mentioned in Reading 1. Find answers to the following questions.

- What is the life expectancy of men and women in that country today?
- How does it compare to the average world life expectancy of 68.5 years? Is it higher or lower?
- Why do you think the life expectancy in that country is higher or lower?
- What is the government of that country doing to improve life expectancy?

Writing

Write two paragraphs. The first paragraph will explain why life expectancy is increasing generally throughout the world. The second paragraph will use your research to describe what is happening to life expectancy in the country you selected.

Connecting to the Topic

Read the definition of *cardiovascular disease*, and then discuss the following questions with a partner.

> **cardiovascular disease** (*n*) an illness relating to the heart and the blood vessels that run through the heart

1 Do you think the number of people suffering from cardiovascular disease is increasing or decreasing? Explain your answer.

2 What are some causes of cardiovascular disease?

3 What can people do to prevent this disease?

Previewing and Predicting

> Reading the first sentence in each paragraph can help you predict what a reading will be about.

A Quickly read the first sentence of each paragraph in Reading 2. Decide what the topic of the paragraph will be. Then read the following topics. Write the number of the paragraph (*1–7*) next to the topic that best describes it. The first paragraph has been done for you.

PARAGRAPH	TOPIC
7	Promising results in many countries from changes in attitudes
	Connection between daily lives and cardiovascular disease
	Negative news about CVD
	Positive effects from changes in attitude
	Behavioral changes and CVD
	Government attempts to decrease CVD
	Better medical understanding and treatment

B Compare your answers with a partner's.

While You Read

As you read, stop at the end of each sentence that contains words in **bold**. Then follow the instructions in the box in the margin.

Changing Attitudes Toward Cardiovascular Disease

1   In the middle of the twentieth century, medical research showed that there was a clear association between cardiovascular disease, or CVD – which includes heart disease, high blood pressure, and stroke – and lifestyle. This awareness initiated a shift in attitudes toward health care. Health experts began to emphasize the idea that people could take control of their own health instead of relying on medical help. By paying attention to factors such as smoking, stress, nutrition, and exercise, everyone could reduce their chance of having CVD. People listened. As a result, many more people now recognize the correlation between a healthy – or unhealthy – heart and lifestyle.

2   Various behavioral changes demonstrate this shift in **attitude**. Many people are no longer depending on doctors for advice and treatment; instead they are focusing on preventive measures and taking responsibility for their own health. A greater understanding of the connection between diet and health has led many to reduce or even eliminate food high in fat and cholesterol from their diets. Similarly, people are also becoming more serious about reducing stress, a known risk factor for CVD. An increasing number of people understand that regular and frequent aerobic exercise like walking, running, and swimming reduces stress. This is because aerobic exercise not only increases physical fitness but also releases endorphins, a natural substance that helps people reduce stress and feel better.

3   These changes in attitudes and behavior have had a positive effect. Deaths from CVD first began to fall in western countries in the 1960s, and this trend continues today. In the United States, the death rate from this disease fell by more than 35 percent between 1980 and 1997 and then by another 26 percent between 1999 and 2005. In 2010, 6 percent of adults suffered from some form of CVD, down from 6.7 percent in 2006. However, it should be noted that this research conducted by the U.S.-based Center for Disease Control (CDC) indicates that although the occurrence of CVD has decreased significantly, less-educated citizens suffer from this disease at rates well above the national averages. Other western countries have found similar patterns among their **populations**.

4   Another reason for falling mortality rates from CVD is better diagnosis and treatment. Advances in technology and medical science make early detection possible, which is key in allowing doctors to better treat the disease. Moreover, new drugs are more effective in lowering blood pressure and cholesterol and are becoming more accessible to people worldwide. This is one cause for optimism about the future of this disease.

5   However, the news about CVD is not all positive. In spite of the fall in death rates, CVD is still much too frequent in most western countries. In Europe, for example, CVD remains the leading cause of death, claiming

WHILE YOU READ 1

As you read, highlight details that support the main idea of this paragraph.

WHILE YOU READ 2

Look back over paragraph 3. Highlight the sentence that best expresses the main idea.

the lives of more than 4 million Europeans every year. The second piece of bad news is that CVD has also become much more prevalent in developing countries, with 80 percent of all CVD deaths now occurring there. Rapid social change in these areas has led to risk factors that are associated with CVD, factors including a decrease in physical activity, an increase in smoking, and a shift to a less healthy diet. By 2010, CVD had become the single greatest cause of death in the developing world, and the WHO projects this will continue for at least the next two decades.

6   What are governments doing to fight this terrible disease? The global effort to inform people of the benefits of a healthy lifestyle continues. As people become better educated, they can choose lifestyles that avoid high CVD risk. Governments are also introducing specific changes aimed at reducing unhealthy lifestyles. The British government collaborated with industries to reduce the amount of salt in manufactured food by 25 percent. In Mauritius, a government program encouraged the nation to switch from palm oil, high in saturated fat, to healthier soybean oil. In Japan, the government has created programs to reduce salt intake and to increase early detection of CVD. As a result, stroke rates have fallen by 70 percent in Japan since the 1970s.

7   Changes in attitudes toward personal health and a greater understanding of the link between health and lifestyle have had promising outcomes in many countries. However, little doubt remains that a global strategy to fight CVD is necessary since the disease still accounts for more deaths than any other disease. Governments need to do more to control the use of tobacco and to reduce the intake of foods high in fat, sugar, and salt. Individuals also need to take more control of their own health and make healthy lifestyle choices when possible. These changes would lead to benefits at individual and national **levels**.

WHILE YOU READ ❸

Look back over paragraph 7. Highlight the sentence that best expresses the main idea.

Figure 1.2 Death Rates per 100,000 for Men

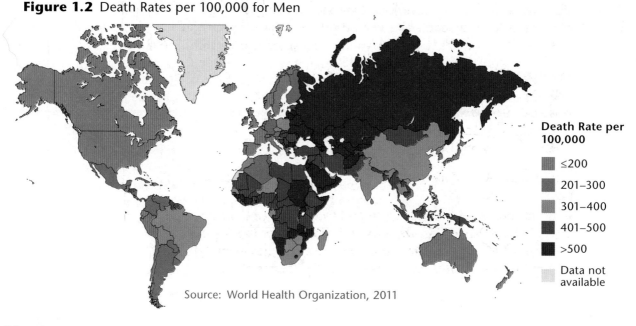

Death Rate per 100,000

■ ≤200
■ 201–300
■ 301–400
■ 401–500
■ >500
■ Data not available

Source: World Health Organization, 2011

Main Idea Check

Match the main ideas below to five of the paragraphs in Reading 2. Write the number of the paragraph on the blank line.

_3_ A As a result of changes in attitudes and behavior, mortality rates from CVD are decreasing.

_6_ B Governments in many countries have introduced programs aimed at lowering CVD.

_4_ C Accurate diagnosis and better treatment also explain falling death rates from CVD.

_2_ D People have changed their lifestyle in order to lower their risk of CVD.

_5_ E CVD remains a serious problem in both developed and developing countries.

A Closer Look

Look back at Reading 2 to answer the following questions.

1 CVD is a medical term that describes a number of heart diseases. **True or False?**

2 What factor does the writer *not* associate with cardiovascular disease?
   a Unhealthy food
   b Cigarettes
   c Poverty
   d Lack of regular exercise

3 The writer suggests that in the early twentieth century, doctors did not generally encourage their patients to live a healthy lifestyle including exercising and not smoking. **True or False?**

4 What change in attitude does the writer describe?
   a An increasing number of people now believe that medical science can cure CVD.
   b Many people are realizing that they should take better care of their health.
   c More and more people understand the need for an expert doctor.
   d Research shows that a decreasing number of people are dying from CVD.

5 According to the reading, what are more people doing to reduce stress?
   a Taking responsibility for their own health
   b Refusing to seek treatment from their doctors
   c Eliminating food high in saturated fat and salt
   d Exercising regularly

6 Which reason is *not* given to explain the fall in death rates from CVD in developed countries?
   a Better drugs, early diagnosis, high-tech equipment, and expert surgeons
   b Rapid social change in western countries such as the United States
   c The public's readiness to make significant changes in lifestyle
   d A public that understands more about the causes of CVD

7 The government of Mauritius has encouraged people to change from using palm oil to soybean oil in cooking. What does this suggest?

   a Soybean oil is cheaper than palm oil.

   b There are more health benefits connected to using soybean oil.

   c Soybean oil is more easily available than palm oil.

   d Palm oil is more difficult to produce than soybean oil.

8 The writer suggests that individuals and their doctors are the only people responsible for their health. **True or False?**

Skill Review

> In Skills and Strategies 1 you learned that a paragraph has a main idea supported by specific details. The main idea can appear in different places within a paragraph. Identifying the main idea in a paragraph will help you better understand academic texts.

A **Reread the following paragraph from Reading 1. As you read, highlight the sentence or sentences that best express the main idea. Then choose the statement below the paragraph that best summarizes the main idea.**

In the middle of the twentieth century, medical research showed that there was a clear association between cardiovascular disease, or CVD – which includes heart disease, high blood pressure, and stroke – and four factors in people's daily lives: smoking, stress, poor nutrition, and insufficient physical exercise. This awareness initiated a shift in attitudes toward health care. Health experts began to emphasize the idea that everyone can reduce their own chance of having CVD by paying more attention to these four factors. People listened. As a result, many more now recognize the correlation between a healthy – or unhealthy – heart and lifestyle.

   a By the middle of the twentieth century, research showed that CVD includes diseases such as high blood pressure, stroke, and heart disease.

   b Smoking, stress, poor nutrition and lack of exercise may lead to health problems.

   c By the middle of the twentieth century, people understood more clearly the connection between CVD and unhealthy lifestyles.

   d People began to pay more attention to their doctors.

B **Compare your answers with a partner's.**

Definitions

Find the words in Reading 2 that are similar to the definitions below.

1 a sudden change in blood flow to the brain, sometimes resulting in death (*n*) Par. 1

2 a change in focus or direction (*n*) Par. 1

3 to state that something is especially important (*v*) Par. 1

4 to show that something is true; to prove something (*v*) Par. 2

5 to get rid of something completely (*v*) Par. 2

6 a fatty substance found in the body (*n*) Par. 2

7 to carry out and organize an activity (*v*) Par. 3

8 the act of finding or discovering something (*n*) Par. 4

9 available; able to be used (*adj*) Par. 4

10 existing commonly; over a wide area (*adj*) Par. 5

11 to estimate an amount or number for the future (*v*) Par. 5

12 to work with someone for a special purpose (*v*) Par. 6

13 to change from one thing to another (*v*) Par. 6

14 a connection (*n*) Par. 7

15 a long-term plan to achieve a goal (*n*) Par. 7

Words in Context

Complete the passages with words from Reading 2 in the box below.

advances	aimed at	diagnosis	initiates	outcome
aerobic	awareness	effective	key	preventive

1   Early _____ of a serious illness is extremely important.

    a

    _____ in technology allow doctors to identify diseases earlier than in

    b

    the past. Once the disease has been identified, the doctor _____ the

    c

    treatment, and then carefully monitors the patient. If the treatment is

    _____, patients today can live a longer and healthier life than was

    d

    possible for previous generations.

2   Doctors recognize, however, that stopping an illness before it even begins

    produces a better _____ than treating someone who has already

    e

    contracted a disease. For this reason, doctors are trained in _____

    f

    medicine. This approach, which is _____ increasing the public's

    g

    understanding of the connection between lifestyle and health, appears to be

working. Research shows that _____ of this connection leads to
h
changes in behavior. A doctor might suggest a more healthy diet or more

_____ exercise, for example. In fact, educating patients about better
i
health is now a/an _____ part of a doctor's duties and responsibilities.
j

Academic Word List

You have already studied the words in the box in Vocabulary Development exercises
for Readings 1 and 2 of this unit. These are particularly important words to study
because they come from the Academic Word List – a list of words that frequently
appear in academic texts. (For more on the Academic Word List, see page 256.) Use
these words to complete the sentences.

accessible (adj)	correlation (n)	emphasize (v)	monitors (v)	strategy (n)
considerable (adj)	detected (v)	indicator (n)	shift (n)	target (v)

1 There is a clear _____ between eating food high in saturated fat and
getting heart disease.

2 Scientists are trying to develop drugs that specifically _____ the virus
that causes HIV/AIDS.

3 There is _____ research to show that when someone quits smoking, he
or she will suffer fewer respiratory illnesses.

4 The United Nations believes that health care should be _____ to
every person.

5 We need a global _____ to fight serious but preventable diseases
like CVD.

6 The World Health Organization _____ changes in life expectancy as one
method to assess the health of large populations.

7 The United Nations uses individual average incomes as a/an _____ of
the strength of the global economy.

8 When researchers tested the new drug, they _____ a serious problem.

9 The _____ from home-cooked meals to fast food resulted in higher
numbers of people with heart disease.

10 Doctors _____ the importance of vaccines for young children.

Critical Thinking

Reading 2 emphasizes the importance of lifestyle choices and how these choices affect our health. One important lifestyle choice for good health is our diet – what we eat each day. The United States Department of Agriculture (USDA) issues the following daily dietary recommendations for an average healthy adult living a moderately active lifestyle.

PERSONALIZING

Thinking about how new information applies to your own life can help you understand a text better.

A Read the USDA recommendations and think about your own diet.

B Discuss the following questions with a partner.

1 How often do you eat fruit, vegetables, and dairy products?

2 Do you drink the recommended amount of water? What else do you drink when you are thirsty?

3 What changes could you make in order to improve your diet?

RECOMMENDED SERVINGS

Fruit and vegetables: 5 servings a day
Dairy products – milk, cheese, yogurt: 3 servings a day
Water: 6–8 cups a day
Seafood: 2 servings a week

Research

There are many online sites that offer personal health assessments. Go online and take a health quiz. Then analyze the results. What can you do in order to have a healthier lifestyle? Make a list of steps you can take to achieve this goal.

Writing

Write two paragraphs. The first paragraph will explain the correlation between lifestyle and health. The second paragraph will describe steps people can take in order to be healthier. Use information from your research as examples.

Improving Your Reading Speed

Good readers read quickly and still understand most of what they read.

A Read the instructions and strategies for Improving Your Reading Speed in Appendix 3 on page 273.

B Choose either Reading 1 or Reading 2 in this unit. Read it without stopping. Time how long it takes you to finish the text in minutes and seconds. Enter the time in the chart on page 274. Then calculate your reading speed in number of words per minute.

Cause and Effect

Writers often need to show cause-and-effect connections in academic texts. They do this in several different ways. Writers use nouns, verbs, and verb phrases as cause-and-effect markers within sentences. They may also use connectors to show cause-and-effect relationships between clauses and sentences. It is important to recognize and understand language that signals these connections. Recognizing the signals of cause and effect can improve your comprehension of academic texts.

Example & Explanations

①In 2008, there was a serious outbreak of food-borne infectious diseases in the United States. ②The government quickly **attributed** the outbreak **to** contaminated tomatoes sold in restaurants and grocery stores. ③The government later discovered that **the cause** of the outbreak was in fact a different vegetable – contaminated peppers. ④According to health officials, these peppers contained high amounts of bacteria. ⑤As **a result**, thousands of people became ill when they ate these contaminated vegetables.

Sentence 1 contains an event. The rest of the paragraph explores the cause of this event.

In Sentence 2, the verb *attributes* tells readers to expect a causal connection.

Sentence 3 contains the actual cause of the event. The noun *cause* is also a cause-and-effect marker. According to the government, the connection is as follows:

contaminated peppers (cause)
↓
outbreak of food-borne infectious disease (effect)

Sentence 4 gives the details of the more general cause-and-effect connection.

Sentence 5 contains a result of the effect in sentence 4. The sentence connector as a result explains the connection between the two sentences.

high amounts of bacteria (cause)
↓
thousands of people became ill (effect)

The Language of Cause and Effect

Here is a list of cause-and-effect markers. Review them and start learning those that are new to you.

CAUSE-AND-EFFECT MARKERS				
Nouns		**Verbs / Verb Phrases**		
cause	influence	to affect	to bring about	to lead to
consequence	origin	to attribute to	to cause	to play a part in
effect	outcome	to be a factor in	to contribute to	to produce
factor	reason	to be associated with	to give rise to	to result from
impact	result	to be responsible for	to have a role in	to result in
		to blame	to influence	

Here is a list of cause-and-effect connectors. These are used to form a phrase, to connect clauses, or to connect sentences.

CAUSE-AND-EFFECT CONNECTORS		
To Form a Phrase	**To Connect Clauses**	**To Connect Sentences**
as a result of [+ cause]	as [+ cause]	As a result [+ effect]
because of [+ cause]	because [+ cause]	Consequently [+ effect]
due to [+ cause]	if [+ cause], then [+ effect]	For this reason [+ effect]
on account of [+ cause]	since [+ cause]	Hence [+ effect]
thanks to [+ cause]	so that [+ effect]	So [+ effect]
(in order) to [+ effect]		Therefore [+ effect]
		Thus [+ effect]

Strategies

These strategies will help you identify and understand cause and effect while you read.

- Look for cause-and-effect markers and connectors to identify parts of a text that show cause-and-effect organization.
- Do not expect writers always to describe the cause first and the effect later.
- Make notes while you read. Use **C** and **E** to mark *cause* and *effect*, and draw arrows to illustrate which specific causes lead to which specific effects.

Skill Practice 1

In the following sentences, circle the cause-and-effect markers. Highlight each cause and mark it with a C. Underline each effect and mark it with an E. Then draw an arrow to indicate the direction of cause and effect. The first one has been done for you

1 Many infectious diseases (are caused by) unsafe water and unsanitary living conditions.

2 A recent drop in hospital visits is being blamed on the high cost of health care.

3 Air pollution contributes to many respiratory diseases, such as lung cancer and asthma.

4 The police have identified a number of factors that contribute to traffic accidents, including alcohol, speeding, and weather.

5 The spring rain has produced a record number of mosquitoes that carry dangerous diseases.

6 The high price of drugs is one factor in the rising cost of health care in the developed world.

7 Some human diseases have been associated with chemicals in the environment.

8 Two months ago, the town's only hospital shut down. This will have a major impact on public health in the region.

Skill Practice 2

As you read the following paragraphs, highlight the cause-and-effect markers and connectors, and look for the specific causes and effects. Then complete the cause-and-effect diagrams. Write the correct letter in each box.

1   In the 1970s, there was an encouraging drop in the number of people who were killed in accidents on U.S. highways. According to some experts, the most important factor in the decrease was the 55-mile-per-hour speed limit that was introduced in 1973. The original reason for lowering the speed limit was economic; the government was attempting to reduce gasoline use at a time when fuel prices were high.

A There was a decrease in the traffic deaths on U.S. highways in the 1970s.
B The country needed to reduce the amount of gasoline that people were using.
C The government introduced the 55-mile-per-hour speed limit.

2 Pregnant women who smoke often have babies with a low birth weight. Smoking slows the growth of the unborn baby and increases the risk of early delivery. Low birth weight can have serious and long-term consequences. It can result in serious health and learning problems for the child later in life.

$\boxed{} \rightarrow \boxed{} \rightarrow \boxed{} \rightarrow \boxed{} \rightarrow \boxed{} \rightarrow \boxed{}$

A Their babies are often born with low birth weight.
B Some women smoke during pregnancy.
C The children often have learning problems when they get to school.
D The unborn babies grow too slowly.
E The babies may have serious health problems.
F The babies are born too early.

Skill Practice 3

Use a cause-and-effect marker or connector from the box to complete each item below.

attribute	consequences	lead to	responsible for
bring about	contributed to	link	thanks to

1 Life expectancy increased during the period 1925–1940 when the economy was in a depression. To what can we _____ this increase?

2 Some diseases are often associated with people's behavior. Therefore, a basic question for preventive medicine is this: How can we _____ changes in lifestyle?

3 Research has shown that alcohol is _____ a large number of traffic deaths.

4 _____ advances in medical science, diseases that once killed millions of children a year are no longer a danger in many countries.

5 Improvements in diagnosis and treatment have _____ the falling death rate from cardiovascular disease.

6 Actions can have _____ we don't intend. For example, pesticides that have been used to kill harmful insects have entered the food chain and killed birds and other animals.

7 Research has shown the _____ between smoking and an increased risk of heart disease.

8 The new clean water supply is expected to _____ many improvements in the health of the villagers.

Connecting to the Topic

Read the definition of *genes*, and then discuss the following questions with a partner.

> **gene** (*n*) a basic unit consisting of DNA, which is received from one's parents and controls a particular characteristic in an animal or plant

1 Discuss some characteristics that genes control in humans.

2 What characteristics have you inherited from your mother? Your father?

3 You can also inherit bad characteristics or diseases. What are some genetic diseases that you are familiar with?

Previewing and Predicting

> Looking for key words can help you predict what a reading will be about.

A Read the first sentence of each paragraph in Reading 3. Decide whether you think the paragraph will be about progress or problems in genetic research. Put a check (✓) in the *Progress* or the *Problems* column. If you think the paragraph will contain both progress and problems, put a check (✓) in both columns. Then look for key words that helped you decide. List them in the third column. Paragraph 1 has been done for you.

PARAGRAPH	PROGRESS	PROBLEMS	KEY WORDS
1		✓	*serious diseases, birth defects*
2			
3			
4			
5			
6			
7			
8			
9			

B Compare your answers with a partner's.

While You Read

As you read, stop at the end of each sentence that contains words in bold. Then follow the instructions in the box in the margin.

Medicine and Genetic Research

1   Scientists have long known that specific genes are associated with a number of serious diseases and birth defects. Scientists have used this knowledge to develop tests to identify defective genes, which are the result of *mutation*, a natural process that alters the genetic material. Researchers have identified a large number of genes that are responsible for life-threatening conditions, such as cystic fibrosis, a disease that shortens peoples' lives by attacking their lungs, and Huntington's disease, a fatal brain condition. Once these genes are identified, genetic tests for many such diseases become available. These tests can indicate if a person has a specific defective gene. By 2011, researchers had developed more than 2,000 genetic tests, which allow doctors to inform patients if they have inherited these genes and if they risk passing them on to their children.

2   These tests are a significant milestone in genetic research, because they provide people who have genetic defects with important information. However, the tests also introduce complex ethical issues. If patients find out that they have a dangerous genetic defect, they may not know what to do. Their decision will depend on several factors. First, in some cases, identification of the gene only suggests the likelihood that the patient will develop the disease associated with that gene. For example, women who have inherited the harmful BRCA gene mutation have a much higher chance of developing breast cancer than other women do. (See Figure 1.3.)

Figure 1.3 The Chance of Developing Cancer in Women with the BRCA Gene Mutation Compared to Women Without the Mutation

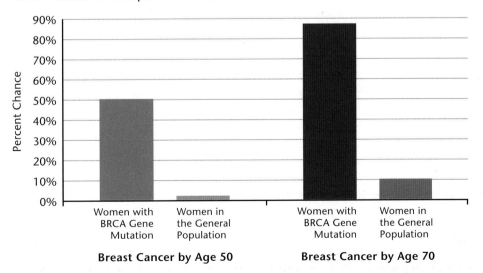

Source: Myriad Genetics

Thus, it is likely that women with the genetic mutation will develop cancer, but it is not certain. A second important factor in the decision is whether there is a treatment, and if so, what kind of treatment. In the case of the BRCA gene mutation, a frequent treatment is major surgery before the cancer develops. Women who test positive for the mutation must decide between this treatment and the possibility of dying of cancer.

3   Unfortunately, for some genetic diseases, there is no treatment, which gives rise to even more complex ethical issues. Would patients want to know that they are going to die young or become very sick if there is no treatment? Some may want to know so they can prepare themselves. If there is a chance they could pass the disease to their future children, they may decide not to have children. For others, however, the news could ruin their lives. They might prefer not to know about their condition and enjoy their lives while they are healthy so they may decide not to get genetic tests at all. There are also possible negative consequences if this private health information becomes **public**. It could be more difficult for patients with genetic conditions to obtain insurance.

WHILE YOU READ ①

Scan ahead to find the negative consequences. Highlight them.

4   Genetic testing is the first step in conquering diseases caused by defective genes. Most researchers hope that the next step will be gene therapy that repairs or replaces the defective gene. This would mean, for example, that BRCA patients would not face such a difficult decision. Instead, they could receive a treatment that actually changes their genetic material. More people would probably decide to take genetic tests if they knew that treatments were **available**.

WHILE YOU READ ②

Where is the main idea of paragraph 4?
a) The first sentence
b) The second sentence
c) The last sentence

5   At the end of the twentieth century, researchers began to develop treatments for a variety of life-threatening genetic diseases. The early results seemed very encouraging, and, consequently, people with genetic diseases became hopeful that they would soon see a cure. In 2000, for example, French doctors successfully treated babies who had a rare genetic disease that affected their immune systems. They injected the babies with a healthy replacement gene. Ten months later, the children's immune systems appeared completely normal.

6   Along with these early achievements, however, there were considerable problems and limitations. Success occurred in only a small number of patients with rare conditions, and even those results were mixed. Sometimes the therapy caused more problems than it solved. Three patients have died from effects of gene therapy. In addition, enthusiastic researchers sometimes underestimated the time it would take discoveries in the laboratory to become practical therapies, often leading to disappointment and a loss of confidence in the field of gene therapy.

7   In spite of these setbacks, many scientists pursued their research in gene therapy. They believed this form of treatment still held great potential. However, three basic technical challenges stood in the way of their progress. First, gene therapy is not like other kinds of treatments in which a patient can take a pill that sends medicine throughout the body. It must

be introduced into specific genes. Second, scientists need a way to deliver the therapy directly into the cell. In many cases, they have used a virus to do this, but they have to be sure that the virus will not harm the patient. Finally, they have to be sure that the new or repaired gene will not "turn off" after it is introduced into the **cell**.

WHILE YOU READ **3**

What is the main idea of paragraph 7? Highlight it.

8   After years of research and trials, scientists had made considerable progress in solving these problems. In the first years of the twenty-first century, positive results began to emerge, arousing renewed interest in the field. In a small clinical trial in 2007, patients with Parkinson's disease received genes for production of an important protein that they lacked. All 12 patients experienced an improvement in their condition with no negative effects. In 2011, researchers successfully treated patients with hemophilia, a disease that prevents blood from clotting, by injecting them with the healthy form of a defective gene. These were major achievements, but they are particularly exciting because the treatments are for major diseases that affect large numbers of people.

Figure 1.4 Gene Therapy

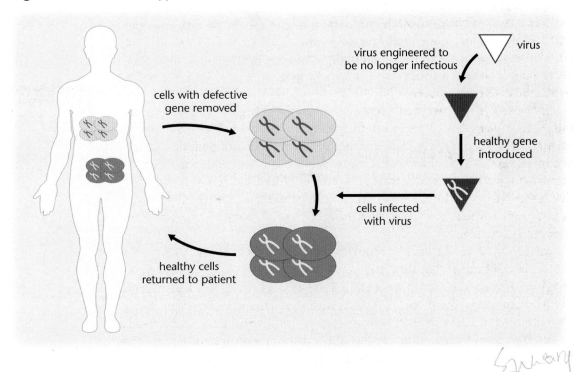

9   All of these positive results have revived the public's interest in gene **therapy**. Many researchers and scientists have renewed their belief in its enormous potential to treat killer diseases like cancer, diabetes, cystic fibrosis, and CVD. However, they are now more careful to warn patients and the public that many effective genetic therapies may still be years, or decades, in the future.

WHILE YOU READ **4**

Look back in paragraph 8 to find the main idea that this sentence refers to. Highlight it.

Main Idea Check

Match the main ideas below to five of the paragraphs in Reading 3. Write the number of the paragraph on the blank line.

_____ A Researchers who pursued gene therapy have faced several challenges.

_____ B Researchers are working on therapies that would change or replace defective genes.

_____ C Scientists must identify defective genes before they can develop tests for genetic diseases.

_____ D Recently, there has been important progress in gene therapies for major diseases.

_____ E Tests for genetic diseases that have no treatment create complex ethical questions.

A Closer Look

Look back at Reading 3 to answer the following questions.

1 How do genetic tests help people who have inherited defective genes?
   a They help them make informed decisions about having children.
   b They have resulted in technology that can repair the defective genes.
   c They solve complex ethical problems.
   d They have led to the elimination a number of previously incurable genetic diseases.

2 All women who have inherited the BRCA gene mutation will develop cancer by age 70. **True or False?**

3 What are some of the practical challenges that genetic researchers face in developing therapies? Circle all that apply.
   a They have to find a good way to introduce the therapy into the cell.
   b They have to make sure that the new or repaired genes remain active.
   c They have to be sure that the patients' blood clots after injuries.
   d They have to be sure that the viruses that deliver the therapy are not harmful.
   e They have to convince doctors to provide therapy to the patients with genetic diseases.

4 At the end of the twentieth century, some genetic researchers did not realize how long it would take to develop practical therapies from their research. **True or False?**

5 What does this reading suggest about the state of gene therapy today?
   a It has been so successful that many treatments have become widely available.
   b It has been successful enough that we can look forward to the availability of more genetic treatments in the future.
   c There have been enough failures to cause serious doubts about the overall value of gene therapy.
   d It is likely that only patients with rare genetic diseases will ever benefit from genetic research.

6 Review Reading 3. What are the basic steps in developing gene therapies? Place the correct letter in each box.

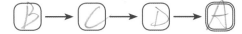

A Repair or replacement of defective genes
B Identification of the defective gene
C Development of genetic tests to identify people with defective genes
D Development a delivery system for gene therapy

Skill Review

In Skills and Strategies 2, you learned that academic writers often describe the connection between causes and their effects. Remember that writers use cause-and-effect markers and connectors to signal cause-and-effect relationships. Recognizing these signals can improve your reading comprehension.

A Reread the following sentences from paragraph 5 in Reading 3. For each sentence, highlight the cause or effect marker or connector. Then write *C* above the cause and *E* above the effect.

1 The early results seemed very encouraging and, consequently, people with genetic diseases became hopeful that they would soon see a cure.

2 Sometimes the therapy caused more problems than it solved.

3 In the case of the French children, it caused a type of cancer in several of the children, one of whom died.

B Reread paragraph 3. Find four cause-and-effect relationships. Highlight the effects.

   Unfortunately, for some genetic diseases, there is no treatment, which gives rise to even more complex ethical issues. Would patients want to know that they are going to die young or become very sick if there is no treatment? Some may want to know so that they can prepare themselves. If there is a chance they could pass the disease to their future children, they may decide not to have children. For others, however, the news could ruin their lives. They might prefer not to know about their condition and enjoy their lives while they are healthy, so they may decide not to get genetic tests at all. There are also potential negative consequences if this private health information becomes public. It could be more difficult for patients with genetic conditions to obtain insurance.

Definitions

Find the words in Reading 3 that are similar to the definitions below.

1 imperfect, containing a mistake (*adj*) Par. 1

2 an important event in the development of something (*n*) Par. 2

3 related to moral beliefs (*adj*) Par. 2

4 to get (*v*) Par. 3

5 a treatment to help a person get better (*n*) Par. 4

6 protected against disease (*adj*) Par. 5

7 to think or say that something is less or lower than it really is (*v*) Par. 6

8 something that causes a delay or stops progress (*n*) Par. 7

9 to appear; come out (*v*) Par. 8

10 a possibility not yet reached. (*n*) Par. 9

Word Families

Word families are different *parts of speech*, or word forms, that have similar meanings. Some parts of speech are *verbs*, *nouns*, *adjectives*, and *adverbs*. When you learn a word, learn the other words in its word family, too.

A The words in **bold** in the chart are from Reading 3. The words next to them are from the same word family. Study and learn these new words.

B Choose the correct form of the words from the chart to complete the following sentences. Use the correct verb tenses and subject-verb agreement. Use the correct singular and plural noun forms.

NOUN	VERB
achievement	*achieve*
conquest	*conquer*
inheritance	*inherit*
pursuit	*pursue*
revival	*revive*

1 My son wants to _____ his interest in art.

2 The architect considered the new building his finest _____.

3 This new discovery will _____ earlier interest in genetic medicine.

4 Her sons _____ her bright red hair.

5 Researchers have worked for years in their _____ of a cure for cancer.

6 Although we have not _____ cancer, we have come a long way in treatment.

7 In the future, genetic researchers may _____ success with other major diseases.

8 She received a diamond ring as part of a/an _____ from her grandmother.

9 Discoveries in basic science can lead to the _____ of dangerous diseases.

10 During the war, there was a/an _____ of interest in home gardens.

Critical Thinking

In Reading 3, you learned about research in and therapy for genetic diseases. You also learned that genetic testing introduces complex ethical questions.

A Imagine a new test has become available for a genetic disease that causes muscles to weaken. People with the disease lose many physical abilities. A positive result on the test predicts that a person is likely, but not certain, to develop the disease. There is also evidence that people with the disease usually pass it on to their children. The disease is not fatal but there is no cure for it.

Work in a small group and discuss why or why not it would be a good idea for the following people to be tested to see if they carry the gene.

1 A 25-year-old unmarried man: No one in his family has ever had the disease.

2 A 40-year-old mother of two: Her uncle has the disease.

3 A 15-year-old girl: Her mother has the disease.

4 A 50-year-old unmarried woman with no children: No one in her family has ever had the disease.

5 A 30-year-old married man: His father and one brother have the disease.

B Would your answers be different if there were a cure for the disease?

Research

Look in the newspaper or online for a personal story of a patient with a genetic disease.

- What is the disease?
- What are the symptoms?
- Is there any therapy available for this disease? Surgery? Medication? Gene therapy?
- What happened to the patient?

Writing

Write a short report on the patient's life story.

Connecting to the Topic

Discuss the following questions with a partner.

1 What do you know about the disease malaria?

2 Is this disease common today?

3 Where do you think cases of malaria are most likely to be found?

4 How do you think malaria spreads from one person to another?

5 Do you think it can be prevented, treated, or cured?

Previewing and Predicting

> Reading the title and the first sentence in each paragraph can help you predict what a reading will be about.

A **Read the title of Reading 4 and the first sentence of each paragraph. Then put a check (✓) next to the topics you think will be included in the reading.**

_____ A How malaria can be prevented

_____ B What organizations are doing to conquer malaria

_____ C The economic effects of malaria

_____ D Malaria and lifestyle choices

_____ E Genetics and malaria

_____ F Treating patients with malaria

_____ G The scientist who discovered the cause of malaria

_____ H How malaria spreads

B **Compare your answers with a partner's.**

While You Read

As you read, stop at the end of each sentence that contains words in bold. Then follow the instructions in the box in the margin.

Malaria: Portrait of a Disease

1   Medical science continues the fight against many infectious diseases. However, in the past 100 years, science has made tremendous progress in conquering an array of diseases, particularly infectious diseases, such as smallpox, typhoid, polio, and measles, which killed thousands of people in past centuries. Scientists now understand how these diseases are transmitted and how they can be prevented and treated. These preventable diseases have now almost disappeared from the developed world; however, they remain a major cause of mortality in the developing world. Malaria is one of these diseases.

2   Someone dies of malaria every 30 seconds. Malaria is fifth among leading causes of death among infectious diseases in the world. Long ago, malaria was prevalent in many areas of the world. In ancient Rome, it was so common that it was called Roman Fever. Until very recently, there were more than 300 million cases of malaria every year. Today, half of the world's population is at risk for malaria, with its impact concentrated primarily in one place – sub-Saharan Africa, one of the poorest areas in the world. Other affected areas include parts of South and Southeast Asia and the Amazon basin. This disease, which is both preventable and curable, pervades every part of the lives of the people who live in these areas.

3   Malaria is spread by mosquitoes, which are host to the parasites that cause the disease. Just one mosquito bite can lead to a malaria infection. When a mosquito bites a person with malaria, it draws blood filled with parasites. The parasites continue to multiply inside the mosquito. Later, when the mosquito bites a healthy person, it introduces parasites into that person's blood. In one week or up to several months after the mosquito bite, the person may develop symptoms of malaria, including fever, headache, vomiting, and extreme fatigue. Not everyone who is bitten develops malaria, and people who have had the disease develop some level of immunity. Children, pregnant women, and travelers without any immunity are the most vulnerable to the disease. Eighty-five percent of all malaria deaths are children who are younger than five.

4   The spread of malaria can usually be attributed to two features of the environment. It is most likely to spread in conditions where lots of people live close together and where mosquitoes can live and breed. Mosquitoes

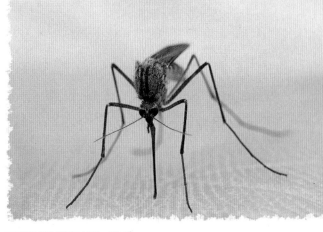

Mosquitoes spread malaria.

thrive in warm, wet climates, and most of them lay their eggs in standing water. The best way to stop the spread of malaria is to prevent it. The first line of defense in malaria prevention is eradication of the mosquito population. There are two strategies for eradicating mosquitoes: eliminating the places where they lay their eggs and killing the mature insects. The first strategy is relatively straightforward. Even small pools of standing water, for example, pots that collect rainwater, can become breeding grounds for mosquitoes. Elimination of all of these pools can bring about a significant reduction in the number of mosquitoes.

5   The second eradication strategy is more **complicated**. The mosquito population can be controlled by spraying insecticide indoors, where people live and sleep. After the walls of a home have been sprayed with insecticide, mosquitoes that land on these walls will die. However, the spray is not effective for very long, so homes must be sprayed every three to six months to maintain effectiveness. In addition, insects can develop

WHILE YOU READ ❶

Look back to paragraph 4 to find the first strategy that this sentence refers to. Highlight the strategy.

Spraying insecticide can reduce the spread of malaria.

resistance to these insecticides so they are no longer effective, eventually requiring stronger and stronger chemicals, which may have other serious negative effects on **health**.

6   The next line of defense is to stop the mosquitoes from biting people. Because mosquitoes bite mostly at night, sleeping under a net can offer protection. Treating the nets with insecticides significantly enhances their effectiveness. All of these are relatively inexpensive measures, yet even they are out of reach of the poorest populations. As a result, in spite of the fact that these methods of malaria prevention are well known and available, an estimated 216 million people contracted the disease in 2010, according to the World Malaria Report. Like many diseases, malaria disproportionately affects the poor, especially those who live in remote, rural areas.

WHILE YOU READ ❷

What is the main idea of paragraph 5? Highlight it.

Sleeping under a net offers protection from mosquitoes.

7   Treating malaria is more difficult and more expensive than preventing it, but early diagnosis and treatment are major factors in a patient's chances of recovery. The problem is that in areas where malaria is the most prevalent, many people have little or no access to health care, so early diagnosis and treatment are often not **possible**. There are several types of effective treatment, but again, the problem is access and cost. From some villages, it can take a day of travel on bad roads to reach the nearest clinic. Furthermore, the parasites are beginning to develop resistance to some of the medicines that have been used to treat malaria.

WHILE YOU READ ❸

Look back in the sentence to find a cause-and-effect relationship. Highlight the cause.

8   Philanthropic and health organizations are making progress against the disease. They have supported mosquito eradication programs, the training of health-care workers who travel to remote villages, and the distribution of nets treated with insecticide. Between 2001 and 2011, the use of nets in affected areas rose from 3 percent to 50 percent. During this period, the number of fatal malaria cases dropped by 25 percent. The World Malaria Report estimates that there were 655,000 malaria-related deaths in 2010. However, this estimate may be low. The British medical journal, *Lancet*, claims the number is closer to 1.2 million.

9   Whatever the correct figure, most experts believe that although these measures are useful and important, it is unlikely that the disease will be conquered until there is a vaccine. Researchers have been working toward this goal for many years. A preliminary vaccine for children and babies is now being tested; however, it will not offer full immunity. Researchers estimate the immunity level will only be about 50 percent. Therefore it will be crucial to continue prevention and treatment efforts even after the vaccine program begins.

10   In countries where a large percentage of the population is at risk for malaria, the impact of the disease is broad and deep, affecting individuals,

families, communities, and the nation. It is both a cause and effect of poverty. First, there are the costs of prevention and treatment. Adults with malaria cannot work, leading to a loss of productivity for their families and for the nation as a whole. One study estimated that in countries that are heavily affected, malaria is responsible for a 1.3 percent reduction in economic growth every **year**. Furthermore, the symptoms of malaria often linger for years, making physical labor difficult long after the patient has recovered. Children with malaria cannot go to school, often for weeks. According to the World Health Organization, an African child in affected areas will have between 1.6 and 5.4 episodes of malaria fever every year. In severe cases, the disease may leave children with cognitive impairment. If this happens to a large number of children, it can affect the level of educational achievement of the entire country.

WHILE YOU READ 4

Look back at the sentence to find a cause-and-effect marker. Highlight it.

11   Finally, widespread malaria depresses all areas of economic development. Businesses are reluctant to invest in countries where employees are likely to become ill. Tourism cannot develop because travelers, most of whom have no immunity, are unwilling to risk travel in countries where they may contract the disease. Many infectious diseases, like malaria, are both preventable and treatable. Nevertheless, they remain pervasive in some parts of the world, where they perpetuate a cycle of poverty and disease that is difficult to break.

Figure 1.5 Malaria Around the World

Malaria free
Eliminating malaria
Controlling malaria

Source: *The Lancet*

Main Idea Check

Match the main ideas below to five of the paragraphs in Reading 4. Write the number of the paragraph on the blank line.

_9_ A The final solution to malaria will require a vaccine.

_5_ B Spraying insecticide can kill mosquitoes and stop the spread of malaria.

_7_ C Malaria is spread by mosquitoes that carry infected blood from one person to another.

_10_ D Diseases such as malaria have an effect on productivity and education.

_6_ E Mosquito nets are an effective and inexpensive preventive measure.

A Closer Look

Look back at Reading 4 to answer the following questions.

1 In which of the following places would malaria be most likely to spread?
   a A hot desert town
   b A densely populated tropical city on the banks of a river
   c A densely populated city that is cold in winter and hot in summer
   d Dense tropical forest with small villages 10–15 miles apart

2 What steps can help to prevent the spread of malaria, according to the reading? Circle all that apply.
   a Give vaccinations to all children.
   b Spray insecticide in places where there are a lot of mosquitoes.
   c Sleep under mosquito nets.
   d Eliminate the places where mosquitoes live.
   e Make sure everyone gets regular health checks.

3 Why does malaria affect the poor most of all? Circle all that apply.
   a Most poor people live in hot wet places.
   b Poor people often live in countries where the government cannot provide health care.
   c Poor people don't understand how malaria spreads.
   d The poor often cannot afford prevention strategies.
   e Many poor people don't have access to adequate health care.

4 Once the malaria vaccine becomes available, it is likely that malaria will soon disappear as a health problem. **True or False?**

5 Between 2000 and 2011, the number of fatal malaria cases fell by 50 percent.
   True or False?

6 According to Figure 1.5, where is malaria *not* a problem?

    a South America

    b Australia

    c China

    d Sub-Saharan Africa

Skill Review

> In Skills and Strategies 2, you learned that academic writers often describe the connection between causes and their effects. Remember that writers use cause-and-effect markers and connectors to signal cause-and-effect relationships. Recognizing these signals can improve your reading comprehension.

A Reread paragraphs 3–7 and highlight the cause-and-effect markers and connectors.

B Work with a partner to decide on the cause-and-effect relationships in infections and death from malaria. Place phrases A–D in the correct order in each box of the cause-and-effect chain below to show the cause-and-effect relationships.

    A Growing mosquito population

    B Malaria deaths

    C Standing pools of water

    D Malaria infections from mosquito bites

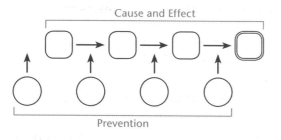

C With your partner, discuss how the cause-and-effect chain can be broken. How can each step in the chain be prevented? Place phrases E–H in the correct order in each circle in the chart below to show how malaria infection and death can be prevented.

    E Early diagnosis and treatment

    F Elimination of standing water

    G Insecticide spraying

    H Use of mosquito nets

Definitions

Find the words in Reading 4 that are similar to the definitions below.

1 to send; to move from one location to another (v) Par. 1 *trashutte d.*

2 most important (adj) Par. 2

3 to spread through all parts (v) Par. 2 *impact*

4 a plant or animal in which another plant or animal lives (n) Par. 3

5 a plant or animal that lives on or in another animal or plant (n) Par. 3

6 easily hurt (adj) Par. 3

7 to reproduce (v) Par. 4

8 to send out liquid in very small drops (v) Par. 5

9 a chemical that kills insects (n) Par. 5

10 too much or too little compared to other things (adv) Par. 6

11 related to helping others through gifts of money (adj) Par. 8

12 to remain longer than expected (v) Par. 10

13 related to thinking (adj) Par. 10

14 a weakness or an inability (n) Par. 10

15 to cause something to continue (v) Par. 11

Synonyms

Complete the sentences with words from Reading 4 in the box below. These words replace the words or phrases in parentheses, which are similar in meaning.

depressed (v)	fatigue	primarily	remote	straightforward
enhance	preliminary	reluctant	rural	thrive

1 Tourists are often (hesitant) _____ to visit places where there is a lot of disease.

2 Mining and other industries are located (mainly) _____ in the south of the country.

3 There is a (simple) _____ solution to the problem.

4 Children (do well) _____ in classrooms that are filled with interesting activities.

5 A good education will (improve) _____ your chances of getting a good job.

6 After you recover from a serious illness, you may still feel some (tiredness) _____ .

7 People from (country) _____ villages are sometimes frightened of cities.

8 This is just a/an (beginning) _____ idea. We will develop something more detailed later.

9 The war has (reduced) _____ prices for wheat and oil.

10 He lived in a (faraway) _____ village so he had to travel for 2 days to reach a doctor.

Academic Word List

The following are Academic Word List words from Readings 3 and 4 of this unit. Use these words to complete the sentences. (For more on the Academic Word List, see page 256.)

achievements (n)	enhances (v)	obtain (v)	primarily (adv)	transmit (v)
emerged (v)	ethical (adj)	preliminary (adj)	reluctant (adj)	underestimated (v)

1 You can _____ diseases by coughing or sneezing.

2 The newspaper reported on government workers who did not follow _____ principles when they took public money for their own use.

3 We _____ the cost of my father's surgery. It was more expensive than we predicted.

4 The discovery of the structure of atoms was one of the most important scientific _____ .

5 The natural light _____ the beauty of the new building.

6 Some new health problems _____ after her heart surgery.

7 The hospital's costs are paid _____ by philanthropic organizations.

8 The research study provided only _____ answers to the cause of the disease. More research will be needed.

9 If you want to visit China, first you will have to _____ a visa.

10 The manager was _____ to talk about the project before it was complete.

Critical Thinking

In Reading 4, you read that two respected publications, *The World Malaria Report* (WMR) and *The Lancet*, the British medical journal, have given very different estimates of the number of deaths worldwide from malaria in 2010. *The Lancet* estimate is almost twice as high as the WMR estimate.

ANALYZING INFORMATION

Critical thinking involves thinking carefully about important topics that the writer has not completely explained.

With a partner or group, make a list of factors that might explain why the two publications came to different conclusions. Use the questions below to guide you.

- Where do most of the deaths occur?
- How easy is it to get accurate information about malaria deaths?
- Who are the people who most frequently die from malaria?
- How are deaths from malaria reported? Who reports them?
- For whom are these figures important?

Research

Choose another infectious disease, such as polio, HIV/AIDS, tuberculosis, or influenza. Find answers to the following questions.

- Where is this disease most prevalent, and what populations are most affected by it?
- Can it be prevented? Can it be cured?
- Have there been efforts to eliminate it? How successful have they been?

Writing

Write two paragraphs about your research. The first paragraph will describe the disease, and the second will address prevention and treatment efforts.

Improving Your Reading Speed

Good readers read quickly and still understand most of what they read.

A Read the instructions and strategies for Improving Your Reading Speed in Appendix 3 on page 273.

B Choose either Reading 3 or Reading 4 in this unit. Read it without stopping. Time how long it takes you to finish the text in minutes and seconds. Enter the time in the chart on page 274. Then calculate your reading speed in number of words per minute.

Managing Unknown Vocabulary

When you read, you will encounter many new words and phrases. If you stop to look up every unknown item in a dictionary, it will interrupt your reading and make reading comprehension more difficult. Your goal is to understand the *key* vocabulary that allows you to comprehend the main ideas and supporting details of a reading. Some vocabulary is not crucial to your comprehension of a reading, so you can learn to skip these words and phrases. Often, an approximate understanding of a new word or phrase is enough for you to keep reading. You can also choose strategies for using context – words and ideas near the unknown word or phrase – to help you read without interruption.

Examples & Explanations

CVD has grown at an **astonishingly** rapid rate in the developing world.

Skip unfamiliar words: Although the word *astonishingly* may be unfamiliar to you, understanding the meaning of this word is not important for understanding the meaning of the sentence. *Rapid rate* gives you enough information so you can skip *astonishingly*.

Medical research requires a great deal of money. Most of the **funding** comes from the government.

Look for context clues: Sometimes there are clues to the meaning of an unknown word in the surrounding context. Here, you can guess that *funding* means about the same thing as *money*.

Diseases that affect the lungs and breathing are referred to as **respiratory diseases**.

Look for a definition: If the writer thinks that a word might be unfamiliar to readers, he or she often provides a definition using signal words, such as *is referred to, is called, is known as, is defined as, that is,* or *in other words*.

Heart disease occurs more often in people who lead **sedentary** lives than in people who are physically active.

Look for a contrast: Sometimes the context offers a contrast. In this case, there is a contrast between *sedentary* and *physical exercise*. So you can guess that *sedentary* means *inactive*.

The **hazards** of smoking include CVD, lung cancer, and other diseases.

Guess from examples: You may be able to guess the meaning of a word from examples that the writer provides. In this sentence, several diseases are given as examples of *hazards*, so you can guess that *hazard* means something bad – a *danger*. There may be signal words such as *for example, for instance,* or *such as* before the examples.

Smallpox was once one of the world's most **deadly** diseases.

Connect to a word you know: You may be able to guess the meaning of a word by connecting it to a word you already know. You know the word *dead*, so you can guess that *deadly* is related to *death*. Something that is *deadly* causes *death*.

Strategies

These strategies will help you to read effectively when you encounter an unknown word or phrase.

- If you understand the text, even if you do not understand every word or phrase in it, ignore the unknown items.
- Do not stop reading. Continue reading until the end of the sentence, even into the next sentence. By doing this, you will see the full context of the unknown word or phrase.
- Look for signals of context clues such as definitions, examples, and contrast in the context to help you figure out the meaning of unknown words and phrases.
- Use your understanding of context to make a guess about the meaning of the unknown word or phrase.
- If an unknown word looks like a word you already know, use that knowledge to guess the meaning of the unknown word.
- Combine strategies to guess meaning.

Skill Practice 1

As you read the following sentences, think about whether you need to understand the words and phrases in bold in order to understand the sentences. If you do not need to understand the words or phrases, write *A* on the blank line. If you need to understand the words or phrases, write *B* on the blank line. Then look for context clues to help you understand their meanings. Highlight the context clues that helped you. The first one has been done for you.

A = I can generally understand the sentence so I can ignore the word(s) in **bold**.
B = Context clues can help me understand the meaning of the word(s) in **bold**.

_B_ 1 The surgeon used a sharp instrument to cut a small **incision** in the patient's chest.

_A B_ 2 The typical western **diet** contains too many foods with animal fat, such as meat, eggs, and cheese. *foods with animal fat*

_A_ 3 Smokers **tend** to have more health problems, such as heart disease and lung cancer, than nonsmokers.

_B_ 4 We can delay the less serious health care problems for a while, but we must *less serious* work on the most **urgent** problems immediately.

_A_ 5 We have made **substantial** progress in preventing and treating many of the most dangerous infectious diseases around the world.

_A_ 6 The World Health Organization has suggested that health facilities **utilize** simple, early diagnostic tests.

_A B_ 7 Local programs to help the earthquake victims were already **under way** in Haiti, *these ongoing efforts* when teams of doctors from Europe and North America arrived to join these ongoing efforts.

_A B_ 8 Patients with heart disease require care from a doctor with **expertise** in CVD. *care from a doctor*

Skill Practice 2

Look back at the sentences in Skill Practice 1. Which strategies helped you guess the meanings of any unknown words and phrases in **bold**? Fill in the chart below for sentences 1–8 that you put a **B** next to in Skill Practice 1. Put a check (✓) next to the strategies that helped you. You may want to check more than one strategy.

STRATEGY	1	2	3	4	5	6	7	8
A definition								
A contrast								
An example								
Other words or context clues								
Similar to a familiar word								

Skill Practice 3

The following sentences contain words in **bold** that you may not know. Use the strategies you have learned to try to figure out their meanings. Write your answers on the blank lines. The first one has been done for you.

1 There have been many **obstacles** in the development of adequate health care in poorer countries; however, the most important is probably the lack of access to clean water.

  things that stand in the way of movement or progress

2 The doctors have not been able to **diagnose** the patient yet, so they are going to conduct some more tests to try to find out what is wrong.

3 During the night, the patient's condition **deteriorated** substantially, but by the following day, her heart and lung function began to improve.

4 Several months after the earthquake in Haiti, there was a cholera **epidemic**. There were over 500,000 cases of the infectious disease, and almost 7,000 people had died.

5 The earthquake caused a lot of damage but fortunately, there was only one **fatality**: a woman who was sleeping when her home collapsed.

6 Many household cleaning products are **toxic**. It is therefore very important to keep these poisonous products away from babies and young children who might try to drink them.

Connecting to the Topic

Discuss the following questions with a partner.

1 What are some different reasons that people get sick and are in need of health care?

2 Where do you go when you need health care?

3 Are you satisfied with the care you usually get? Why or why not?

4 Do some people in society get better health care than others? Explain your answer.

Previewing and Predicting

> When you preview a reading, look to see if the writer has divided the text into sections. Also, look to see if the sections have headings. Read the headings and think about why the writer divided the text in this way.

A Read the title and section headings in Reading 5. Then decide what content will be in each section. Write the number of the section (*I–V*) next to the topic that best describes it.

SECTION	TOPIC
	Problems related to getting good health care
	Worldwide recognition of the importance of good health care
	Financial concerns related to health care
	Various illnesses that countries are fighting
	Health-care challenges and the future

B Compare your answers with a partner's. Then, with your partner, discuss some examples that might be included in each section.

While You Read

As you read, stop at the end of each sentence that contains words in bold. Then follow the instructions in the box in the margin.

The Health Care Divide

اتباع نهج عالمي لتحسين الرعاية الصحية

I. A Global Approach to Improving Health Care

1   The health of a nation is dependent upon the health of its people. In turn, the health of the people is largely dependent upon the quality of the health care that they receive. When people have access to skilled health-care workers and essential medicines, they significantly increase their chances of living long, productive lives and of being contributing members of society.

2   It is therefore not surprising that the governments of both developed and developing nations have agreed to make health care a top priority in the twenty-first century. This agreement is reflected in the Millennium Development Goals (MDGs) set by the 193 members of the United Nations. The MDGs represent a shared commitment to saving millions of lives by combating disease and making health care accessible and affordable. As developed and developing nations work toward these goals, there are both differences and similarities evident in the challenges they face and in their strategies for dealing with them.

II. Combating Disease

3   In the past, infectious diseases, such as cholera, typhoid, and malaria, have been the greatest threat to human **health**. In the developed world, these diseases are largely under control, but they continue to plague

> **WHILE YOU READ** ❶
>
> Look back at this sentence and highlight the words that can help you figure out the meaning of *threat*.

Figure 1.6 NCD Mortality Rates

صحيح

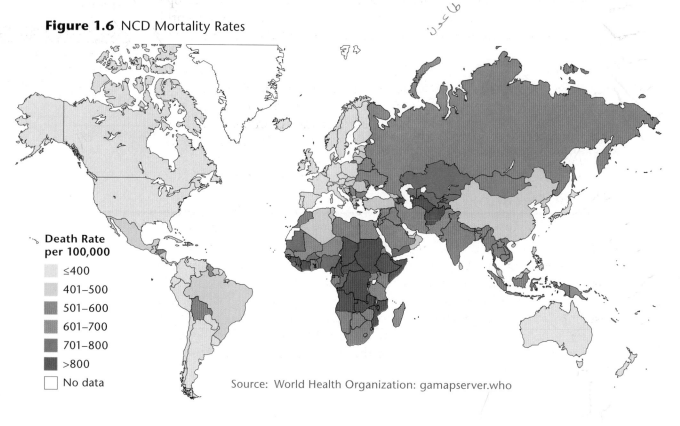

Death Rate per 100,000
- ≤400
- 401–500
- 501–600
- 601–700
- 701–800
- >800
- No data

Source: World Health Organization: gamapserver.who

developing countries. One reason for this discrepancy is the fact that access to clean water and sanitation is almost universal in the developed world, whereas in the developing world, contaminated water and unsanitary living conditions remain a problem in many regions. Almost 800 million people in the developing world use unsafe sources of water, and about 2.5 billion people lack adequate sanitation. Consequently, over one million people die each year from diarrheal diseases, with most of those deaths occurring among children in Sub-Saharan **Africa**. Improving access to clean water and sanitation is one of the MDGs, and countries are indeed making progress in this regard. However, considerably more work is needed to improve conditions for people in the poorest areas of the world.

4   In addition to infectious diseases, a new global health threat has emerged in the past century: noncommunicable diseases (NCDs), such as heart disease, cancer, and diabetes. In the developed world, NCDs have in fact become the leading cause of illness and death, even though these illnesses are largely preventable. In North America and Western Europe, for example, NCDs cause 85 percent of all deaths. In the developing world, where infectious diseases are still a major killer, **NCDs** are on the rise, as well.

5   The increase in NCDs in the developing world causes particular hardship. In these regions, NCDs tend to kill people during their most productive years. In parts of Africa and Asia, for example, almost 30 percent of NCD deaths occur in people under the age of 60. This loss of working-age people greatly hinders economic growth. By contrast, in the developed world, NCDs primarily claim the lives of the elderly. In North America and Western Europe, for example, only about 13 percent of NCD deaths occur in people under 60.

6   Between 2010 and 2020, the number of deaths from NCDs is expected to rise approximately 15 percent worldwide, with increases of over 20 percent in parts of Africa and Asia. Since the health-care systems in most developing countries were originally designed to handle infectious diseases, they are unprepared for the increase in NCDs. For instance, in Uganda, a country of 34 million people, there is only one cancer clinic. The rise in NCDs will put greater pressure on health-care systems in developed countries, as well. Clearly, all nations will need to increase their capacity to serve NCD patients and to ensure that they will be able to obtain the health care they need.

WHILE YOU READ ②

Look back at this sentence and the one before it. Find a cause-and-effect relationship. Highlight the cause-and-effect marker. Does it introduce a cause or an effect?
a) Cause
b) Effect

WHILE YOU READ ③

Look back over paragraph 4, and highlight the sentences that express the main idea.

Figure 1.7 Maternal Mortality Rates

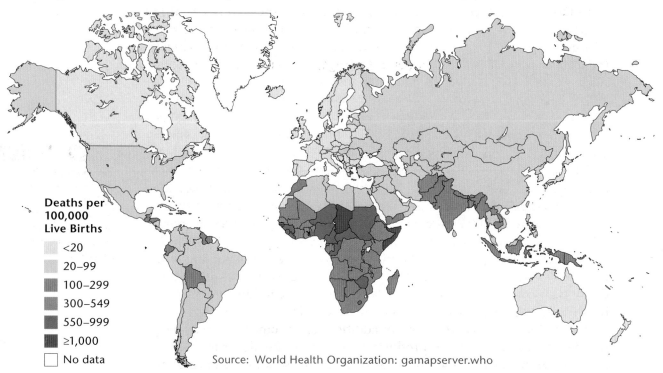

Deaths per 100,000 Live Births

	<20
	20–99
	100–299
	300–549
	550–999
	≥1,000
	No data

Source: World Health Organization: gamapserver.who

III. Access to Health Care

7   In the fight against disease, access to skilled health-care workers and essential medicines is critical. However, there are striking inequalities in the numbers of health-care workers and supplies of important medicines around the **world**. The World Health Organization (WHO) has identified more than 50 developing countries with significant shortages of health-care workers. This severely limits the ability of these nations to ensure basic life-saving services at critical times. In most Sub-Saharan African countries, for example, there are fewer than 2.3 health-care workers per 1,000 people as compared with 18.9 health-care workers per 1,000 people in Europe.

8   Maternal mortality rates clearly demonstrate the consequences of such **shortages**. Almost 300,000 women die each year – about 1,000 a day – from causes related to pregnancy and childbirth, and 99 percent of those deaths occur in the poorest, most remote areas of the developing world. If appropriate care had been available, most of those deaths could have been prevented. Improving maternal health is therefore one of the MDGs, and progress has been made in many areas, including North Africa and Southeastern Asia. However, for Sub-Saharan women, the risk of death before, during, or shortly after childbirth is 1 in 22 compared with 1 in 7,300 in developed regions, where a skilled health-care worker is present at almost every birth.

WHILE YOU READ 4

Look back at this sentence. Is the meaning of *striking* important for your understanding of this sentence?
a) Yes
b) No

WHILE YOU READ 5

Scan ahead and highlight the details that support the main idea expressed in this sentence.

9   In recent decades, the shortage of health-care workers in developing countries has worsened because thousands of doctors and nurses, attracted by greater employment opportunities and higher salaries, leave their countries every year to work in North America and Europe. Today, for example, there are more Ethiopian doctors in Chicago, Illinois, than there are in Ethiopia, the second largest country in Sub-Saharan Africa. This "brain drain" is damaging to nations that are already struggling to meet their people's health-care needs. Emigration results in understaffing of health-care facilities and reduces the number of medical school professors to train doctors for the future in the **developing world**.

10   The lack of essential medicines is another problem that affects both developing and developed regions. In the developing world, drugs are often unavailable because of inefficient supply and distribution systems, especially in remote locations where roads and transportation are poor. NCD drugs, in particular, are in low supply. For instance, several developing countries have no or extremely limited stocks of insulin, a drug that many diabetics need to survive. The developed world is experiencing drug shortages, too. For example, in North America and Europe, there are insufficient supplies of many life-saving cancer drugs, and this is having a profound effect on patient care. In addition, drug companies frequently decide to stop or limit the production of less profitable drugs, which reduces supplies all over the world. Recognizing the seriousness of all these problems, the United Nations has included improving access to medicines in one of the MDGs.

IV. The Cost of Health Care

11   In addition to shortages of health-care workers and medicines, there is the problem of rapidly rising health-care costs. One reason for the increase is that the health-care industry has invested heavily in developing new equipment and medicines. The increase in NCDs has had an effect on cost, as well. NCDs tend to be serious chronic conditions, meaning that patients will have the conditions for a long period of time, thus requiring higher expenditures for their care. Another major reason for the increased costs of health care is the aging of the global population. Since older people usually have more serious medical problems than younger people, they place a greater strain on health-care budgets in both developed and developing **countries**.

12   Rising health-care costs are creating serious consequences for the governments of developed countries. They are spending increasing amounts of money on health care and are concerned about how they will manage to cover costs in the future. Britain, France, and Germany, for example, all have extensive public health-care systems; however, costs are rising faster than these programs can be funded. In the United States, public and private spending on health care almost doubled during the first decade of the twenty-first century. Therefore, there is ongoing debate in developed

WHILE YOU READ 6

Look back at this sentence and find a cause-and-effect relationship. Highlight the cause-and-effect marker. Then highlight the effects.

WHILE YOU READ 7

Look back at this sentence and find a cause-and-effect relationship. Highlight the cause.

countries about how to cut costs and increase the efficiency of health-care systems without having to sacrifice quality and accessibility.

13   The immediate concerns of the governments of developing nations are somewhat different because they have significantly less money to spend on health care. Whereas annual health spending in Europe averages between $3,000 and $4,000 per person, many developing countries spend less than $30 per person each year. With such limited spending, developing countries are **struggling** to find ways to cover the costs of fighting infectious diseases and to provide medical help for the increasing number of people with NCDs, as well.

14   The high costs of health care can also have a devastating effect on individuals for whom even the cost of the medicines they need can be overwhelming. In developing countries, buying basic medicines can be a hardship for all but a handful of wealthy people. Since governments cannot often cover the costs of drugs, most people must pay for them out of pocket, that is, with their own money. Government stocks of drugs are often inadequate, so people must buy drugs from private pharmacies where the prices are usually higher. The most common drug treatment can cost a low-paid worker several days' wages. For instance, a family living on $1.00 a day in a developing country would need to spend about one-third to one-half of their monthly income at a private pharmacy to buy one small vial of insulin for a family member with diabetes. For diabetics, a continuous supply of insulin is critical, yet it is unaffordable for many.

WHILE YOU READ 8

Look back over paragraph 13. Highlight the words and phrases that can help you figure out the meaning of *struggling*.

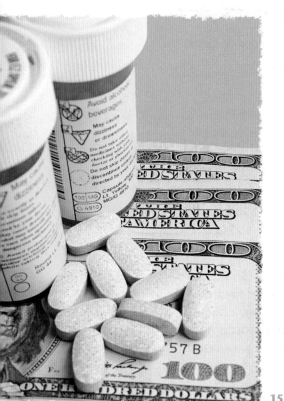

Affordable drugs are an important part of effective health care.

15   Highly priced medicines are also a problem in developed nations lacking universal health care, and they especially affect poor people. For example, a person with limited or no health insurance in the United States must pay for their drugs out of pocket. Some cancer drugs cost about $2,000 a month, which is more than many people's overall monthly budget. To address the prohibitive expense of some drugs, one MDG aims to make generic drugs more widely available. A generic drug is a copy of a brand-name drug that can be sold after the patent on the brand-name

drug expires. Generic drugs are generally much less expensive because drug manufacturers don't have to pay for developing and testing the **drugs**.

V. The Way Forward

16   There are significant differences in the health-care issues facing the developed and developing worlds, but their challenges are remarkably similar. Both developed and developing regions are trying to make health care more affordable and accessible at a time when NCDs are on the rise, costs are increasing, and medicines and health-care workers are in short supply.

17   The key solutions to the challenges are also similar for both developed and developing countries. For instance, emphasizing prevention is considered to be a highly effective way for all nations to improve health and lessen the strain on health-care systems. It is viewed as a particularly effective strategy for addressing NCDs. In both developed and developing countries, there are many examples of successful, cost-effective programs that help prevent NCDs by promoting good nutrition and physical exercise and by discouraging smoking. Prevention is also the developing world's best strategy for combating contaminated-water diseases. When more people have clean water and good sanitation, the number of these diseases will decrease.

18   The worldwide shortages of health professionals and affordable medicines can be addressed in similar ways in both developed and developing nations. Health-care experts recommend that every nation train its own people and provide them with incentives to stay in the country. Over time, this will ensure that countries have ample national workforces. Nations also need to continue collaborating with drug companies in efforts to increase the availability of generic drugs.

19   Countries all over the world are also taking a big step forward with both high-tech and nontechnological solutions to improve the accessibility and affordability of **health care**. For example, countries as different as Mexico and Finland are implementing Internet- or telephone-based services, which provide large numbers of people with health advice at a low cost. Other developing and developed countries are establishing community-based fitness programs, which provide easy and inexpensive ways for people to maintain their cardiovascular health. Continued expansion of these sorts of solutions would significantly improve health care worldwide.

20   The world is a long way from ensuring that all people have good health care and from achieving the MDGs. However, both developed and developing countries are making substantial progress as they respond to the immense challenges with strategies that are very much alike.

WHILE YOU READ 9

Look back over paragraph 15, and highlight the sentence that expresses the main idea.

WHILE YOU READ 10

Look back at this sentence and find a cause-and-effect relationship. Highlight the cause.

Main Idea Check

For sections II–V of Reading 5, match the main ideas to three of the paragraphs in each section. Write the number of the paragraph on the blank line.

SECTION II: Combating Disease

__6__ A In the future, there will be more cases of NCDs worldwide, and health-care systems will need to accommodate them.

__5__ B In developing countries, NCDs kill people during their most productive working years.

__3__ C Developing nations are still fighting infectious diseases.

SECTION III: Access to Health Care

__10__ A In developed and developing countries, people often can't get the drugs they need.

__8__ B In parts of the developing world, many women die giving birth because there aren't enough health-care workers to assist them.

__9__ C Developing countries are losing medical professionals who choose to work elsewhere.

SECTION IV: The Cost of Health Care

__13__ A It isn't possible for developing countries to spend as much money on health care as developed countries.

__12__ B Developed countries must pay more and more for health care these days, which is a matter of great concern.

__14__ C Paying for medicine can be a huge financial burden for many people in developing countries.

SECTION V: The Way Forward

__19__ A Various improvements in health care around the world include some that are based on technology and others that are not.

__16__ B Developed and developing countries have several health-care concerns in common.

__17__ C Taking preventive steps to guard against disease is an effective way for all nations to deal with their health-care problems.

A Closer Look

Look back at Reading 5 to answer the following questions.

1 Why does the writer mention the MDGs in paragraph 2?

   a To identify the members of the United Nations

   b To show the importance of high-quality health care

   c To identify the major health problems facing developed countries

   d To show that improving world health requires a global effort

2 Which statement about NCDs is *not* true according to the reading?

  a It is possible for people to protect themselves against most NCDs.

  b NCDs account for most of the deaths in developed countries.

  c Most countries have adequate facilities for treating NCD patients.

  d Experts project that the number of NCDs will increase in the future.

3 Why does the writer discuss age in paragraph 5?

  a To show that NCDs can affect both younger and older adults

  b To show that NCDs can have an effect on the development of a country

  c To show that NCDs are a major problem in the developed world

  d To show how NCDs affect North Americans and Africans alike

4 What is the point of the example of Ethiopian doctors in paragraph 9?

  a To show that the developing world has more health-care professionals than it needs

  b To show that some health-care professionals in North America are from Africa

  c To show that Chicago is a particularly attractive choice for health-care workers

  d To show that large numbers of health-care professionals from developing countries choose to work outside their home countries.

5 According to the reading, the governments of developing countries usually pay for the medicines people need. **True or False?**

6 Why does the writer mention generic drugs in paragraph 15?

  a To explain the process of how generic drugs are made

  b To explain why drug manufacturers don't often develop new drugs

  c To present an affordable alternative to expensive brand-name drugs

  d To give an example of a drug that health insurance doesn't cover

7 What are two examples of prevention as an effective health-care strategy?

  a Providing diagnosis and treatment over the Internet

  b Increasing access to clean water

  c Keeping drug costs low

  d Encouraging healthy lifestyle choices

8 Which two statements best express similarities in health care between the developed and developing worlds?

  a They both would benefit from more availability of generic drugs.

  b They both are trying to fight contaminated-water diseases.

  c They both have been successful in achieving all of the MDGs.

  d They both need to build national health workforces.

Skill Review

In Skills and Strategies 3, you learned to focus on key vocabulary and to skip over unknown words or phrases that are not crucial to your understanding of a text. You also learned some strategies for using context near the unknown words or phrases to help you get an approximate understanding of the meanings. Reading without interruption will help you better understand academic texts.

The following sentences or parts of sentences from Reading 5 contain words in bold that you may not know. Use the strategies you learned to try to figure out their meanings. Write your answers on the blank lines. Then highlight the words that helped you. The first one has been done for you.

1 The MDGs represent a shared commitment to saving millions of lives by **combating disease**, and making health care accessible and affordable.

 fighting

2 **Maternal** mortality rates clearly demonstrate the consequences of such shortages. Almost 300,000 women die each year from causes related to pregnancy and childbirth, . . .

3 For instance, several developing countries have no or extremely limited stocks of **insulin**, a drug that many diabetics need to survive.

4 NCDs tend to be serious **chronic** conditions, meaning that patients will have the conditions for a long period of time, thus requiring higher expenditures for their care.

5 Since governments cannot often cover the costs of drugs, most people pay for them **out of pocket**, that is, with their own money.

6 . . . that every nation train its own people and provide them with incentives to stay in the country. Over time, this will ensure that countries have **ample** national workforces.

Definitions

Find the words in Reading 5 that are similar to the definitions below.

1 something that is considered more important than other matters (*n*) Par. 2

2 a promise to do something (*n*) Par. 2

3 easily seen; obvious (*adj*) Par. 2

4 an unexpected difference that suggests that something has to be explained (*n*) Par. 3

5 enough or satisfactory for a particular purpose (*adj*) Par. 3

6 to make it difficult for something to happen (*v*) Par. 5

7 the ability to do something (*n*) Par. 6

8 to put money into something to make a profit or achieve a result (*v*) Par. 11

9 the quality of working well without wasting time or resources (*n*) Par. 12

10 to give up something for something else considered more important (*v*) Par. 12

11 so expensive that it prevents people from doing something (*adj*) Par. 15

12 the legal right to be the only one who can make, use, or sell an invention for a certain number of years (*n*) Par. 15

13 things that encourage a person to do something (*n pl*) Par. 18

14 to put a plan or system into operation (*v*) Par. 19

15 the increase of something in size, number, or importance (*n*) Par. 19

Words in Context

A Use context clues to match the first part of each sentence to its correct second part and to understand the meaning of the words in **bold**.

_____ 1 The people were warned that the river nearby is

_____ 2 Health experts from all over the world are participating in

_____ 3 Tuberculosis and measles still

_____ 4 Having enough food and clean water is

_____ 5 A major concern in the developing world is

_____ 6 The doctor did a blood test to

_____ 7 If drugs are too expensive, people

_____ 8 MRI scanners are expensive, and they

_____ 9 People need doctors who are

_____ 10 Eradicating smallpox was

a **critical** for the survival of all living things.

b **plague** some developing nations.

c **ongoing** discussions about how to improve health care.

d **contaminated** with chemicals.

e require large **expenditures** of hospital funds.

f an **immense** challenge, but the effort was successful.

g easy to get to and whose fees are **affordable**.

h **ensure** that the baby was healthy.

i the lack of medical and sanitation **facilities** in remote areas.

j **tend** to avoid buying them.

B Compare your answers with a partner's. Discuss what clues helped you match the parts of the sentences and helped you understand what the words in **bold** mean.

Same or Different

The following pairs of sentences contain vocabulary from all the readings of this unit. Write *S* on the blank lines if the two sentences have the same meaning. Write *D* if the meanings are different.

_____ 1 There is some **promising** new research showing improvement in people's **cognitive** ability when they play math games.

Researchers are **optimistic** about new studies showing that playing math games can help people think and reason better.

_____ 2 The world will not be able to **conquer** infectious diseases unless nations **collaborate** with each other.

Eradicating infectious diseases will only be possible if countries **aim** toward the same goals.

_____ 3 The most serious effect of the HIV virus is the **impairment** of the **immune system**.

The HIV/AIDS virus causes the **immune system** to become **defective**, and this is the greatest threat to a person's health.

_____ 4 **Preventive** measures, such as getting a little exercise and not smoking, are **affordable** ways to guard against cardiovascular disease.

Doing daily **aerobic** exercise and avoiding cigarettes are **key** ways to protect the heart and lungs.

_____ 5 People who suffer from **obesity** are more **vulnerable** to diabetes.

Diabetes is especially **prevalent** among people who are extremely overweight.

_____ 6 Lung diseases still **plague** the developed world, where they **account for** millions of deaths each year.

Lung diseases are still **devastating** illnesses in developed countries, where they kill millions of people each year.

_____ 7 The drug can be an **effective** way to treat **fatigue** and muscle soreness.

That medicine might cause a **setback** in people who suffer from muscle aches and tiredness.

_____ 8 Despite recent **advances** in medical science, there are still huge **disparities** between people who benefit from new research and those who do not.

Even though medical researchers have made progress in recent years, there is still an enormous **discrepancy** between people who benefit from new discoveries and people who do not.

Academic Word List

The following are Academic Word List words from all the readings of this unit. Complete the sentences with these words. (For more on the Academic Word List, see page 256.)

awareness (*n*)	conduct (*v*)	ensure (*adj*)	implementing (*v*)	priority (*n*)
capacity (*n*)	demonstrate (*v*)	expansion (*n*)	outcome (*n*)	project (*v*)
commitment (*n*)	disproportionately (*adv*)	facilities (*n*)	potential (*adj*)	pursue (*v*)

1 Population experts _____ that the number of older adults in the world will double by 2030.

2 The poorest regions of the world have the fewest hospitals, clinics, and other health-care _____.

3 The medical students were encouraged to _____ their research on obesity in China next semester.

4 Scientists are testing a new drug, which has the _____ to cure certain types of diabetes.

5 It is difficult for parents to _____ that their children are eating healthy foods while their children are away from home.

6 Health experts are trying to increase public _____ of the dangers of texting while driving.

7 The new city hospital has an immense _____; it can to treat 1,000 patients at one time.

8 Reducing maternal mortality rates is a high _____ for the World Health Organization.

9 The researchers won't know the results of the experiment for several months; however, they are hoping for a positive _____.

10 The rapid _____ of cell phone use in Africa is improving people's access to health information throughout the continent.

11 Some schools in the United States are _____ programs that teach children how to grow their own healthy food.

12 Mortality rates among children are _____ high in locations where living conditions are unsanitary.

13 The biologist is planning to _____ an experiment to test the effects of sugar on mice.

14 They asked the technician to _____ how a cell phone can be turned into a simple microscope.

15 Even though she is extremely busy, she made a/an _____ to volunteer at the clinic once a week.

Critical Thinking

In Unit 1, you learned about some of the challenges related to health and health care that the world is facing today. Fighting various infectious diseases and non-communicable diseases (NCDs) is one of the most critical of these challenges.

> **SYNTHESIZING**
>
> Critical thinking includes connecting information you have learned among several readings.

A With a partner, think of some specific examples of infectious diseases and NCDs discussed in this unit. Choose one of each and write them in the top row of the chart below. Then, using information from all the readings in Unit 1, fill in as much information as you can about the two diseases you chose.

	INFECTIOUS DISEASE:	NONCOMMUNICABLE DISEASE (NCD):
Cause of the disease		
Regions with the most cases		
Preventive measures		
Possible treatment		
People affected		
Actions of governments and health organizations		

B Compare your charts with your class. Discuss which diseases you think need the most attention today.

Research

Many international organizations, such as Doctors without Borders or Partners in Health, play a key role in the fight against diseases today. Research one of these organizations. Find answers to the following questions.

- What are some examples of diseases that they are focusing on?
- Where are the organizations working to combat these diseases?
- What specific things are they doing to combat the diseases?

Writing

Write two paragraphs. The first paragraph will describe one of the diseases you chose in the Critical Thinking task. The second paragraph will explain what the organization you researched is doing to combat a particular disease of concern.

Exercise 1

Writers connect ideas between sentences in many different ways. The second sentence may:

   a describe a **result** of what is reported in the first sentence

   b describe a better **response** to a problem than the response described in the first sentence

   c add a **detail** or details to support the more general information in the first sentence

How does the second sentence in each pair of sentences below connect to the first sentence? Write *a*, *b*, or *c* on the line depending on whether it is a result, a response, or a detail.

_____ 1 Heart disease is often associated with a person's lifestyle choices. Smoking, a poor diet, stress, and insufficient exercise are all factors that contribute to the development of the disease.

_____ 2 Experience has shown that we cannot afford to wait until heart disease and infectious diseases are established and then rely exclusively on drugs and surgery to fight them. We need to provide access to early diagnosis and to information on prevention.

_____ 3 Historically, mass vaccination has made it possible to control, and sometimes even eradicate, some infectious diseases. In countries where an effective vaccine has been available since the late 1950s, for example, there have been few or no cases of polio.

_____ 4 In the 1990s, governments, research institutions, biotechnology companies, and investors became aware of the significant potential of genetic research. This realization led to an enormous growth of interest in, and financial support for, the research.

_____ 5 For many years patient records have been a headache for both patients and doctors because they were kept in physical files. Increasingly, health professionals are now shifting to digital records, including doctor's notes, test results, and digital images such as X-rays.

Exercise 2

Make a clear paragraph by putting sentences A, B, and C into the best order after the numbered sentence. Write the letters in the correct order on the blank lines.

1 The death rate from cardiovascular disease (CVD), which includes heart disease, high blood pressure, and stroke, has been falling since the 1960s, with a decrease of 35 percent in the last 20 years. _____ _____ _____

A A second factor is the considerable improvement in the detection and treatment of CVD	B To what can we attribute this encouraging trend?	C One crucial factor is people's willingness to make lifestyle changes in order to reduce their risk of CVD.

2 Although many patients benefit from advances in heart surgery, critics give two reasons for why an overemphasis on the surgical treatment is the wrong strategy for reducing heart disease. _____ _____ _____

A The main reason is that it takes financial resources away from the prevention programs and research on other types of therapy.	B To recover these enormous costs of expertise and equipment, hospitals raise their charges for all patients.	C It has also lead to increasing costs of health care.

3 In 2000, French doctors demonstrated success with a procedure in which they introduced a normally functioning gene into three children who suffered from a fatal deficiency in their immune systems. _____ _____ _____

A A few years after this preliminary success, another team of researchers reported the promising outcome of gene therapy for patients who were suffering from hemophilia.	B These kinds of results have led to cautious optimism about the potential of gene therapy.	C Ten months later, the children's immune systems appeared to be functioning normally, evidence that the normal gene had taken over the work of the defective one.

4 Many experts argue that one of the primary aims of public health in the United States should be to improve preventive care. _____ _____ _____

A For the same reason, their children frequently do not complete their programs of vaccination.	B For many low-income Americans, annual physical examinations are not affordable, so, detection of serious diseases often comes late, when survival rates are lower.	C Both of these problems could be reduced by programs that make disease prevention a priority.

5 Studies show that chronic disease can have a lasting negative impact on a nation's economy. _____ _____ _____

A There is also a negative impact on workers' families. If parents cannot work because they are sick, often their children have to work instead of going to school.	B The primary impact is direct: the government has to spend precious resources on health care.	C There are also more indirect costs. When a nation's workers are plagued by chronic disease, productivity suffers.

2

MULTICULTURAL SOCIETIES

SKILLS AND STRATEGIES

- Continuing Ideas
- Point of View
- Reduced Relative Clauses

Continuing Ideas

Continuing ideas are ideas that a writer has introduced in an earlier sentence and then refers to again in a later sentence. Paying attention to continuing ideas will help you understand the connections between sentences and improve your academic reading.

Examples & Explanations

Last year there was continuous violence in several areas of the country. **This** caused many people to leave the country and look for a safer place for their families.

Writers often use the word *this* to repeat an idea from the sentence before.

This = violence in several areas of the country.

The state has decided to allow the children of illegal immigrants to go to public schools. **This decision** has angered a lot of people.

Here the writer uses *this* + **noun**. *Decision* is a noun from the same word family as the main verb (*decide*) in the earlier sentence.

This decision = the decision to allow children of illegal immigrants to go to public school.

According to new statistics, unemployment has fallen in the last six months. **These figures** suggest that the economy is improving.

Here the writer uses *these* + **synonym**. The noun *figures* is a synonym for the noun *statistics* in the earlier sentence.

These figures = the statistics about unemployment in the last six months.

In 2011, more than 60 African immigrants died off the coast of Italy when their boat ran out of fuel. Survivors say no one answered their call for help. **The tragedy** shocked the world.

The + **noun** does not always show a repeated idea, but here it does. In this sentence, the noun *tragedy* is a general word that describes something in the two earlier sentences. If you know the meaning of *tragedy*, the connection between the sentences is clear.

The tragedy = death of the African immigrants.

The government wants to increase the number of immigrants it allows into the country. However, **such a move** would be risky with an election in only six months.

Such + **noun** shows a repeated idea (*Such* = like this or like these).

Such a move = increasing the number of immigrants.

The Language of Continuing Ideas

Writers often use the words *this, these, the,* and *such* as continuing idea markers. They often follow these markers with a noun, either a synonym for the idea in the earlier sentence or a general word. Here is a list of general words that may follow continuing idea markers.

GENERAL WORDS FOR CONTINUING IDEAS			
For Things That Happen	**For Things That People Do**	**For Things That People Say or Write**	**For Things That People Think**
circumstances	achievement	claim	attitude
crisis	action	complaint	belief
development	behavior	criticism	idea
disaster	decision	objection	opinion
event	habit	offer	reaction
incident	move	request	view
problem	practice	statement	
situation	response	warning	
tragedy	tendency		

Strategies

These strategies will help you identify and understand continuing ideas while you read.

- Look for continuing idea markers: *this, this,* or *these* + repeated noun or synonym; *the* + repeated noun or synonym; *such* + noun.
- Ask yourself what the continuing idea marker refers to. If you are not sure, search for its meaning in the sentences before the marker.
- Use your knowledge of vocabulary: general words, synonyms, and word families.

Skill Practice 1

From the box below, find the noun that best continues an idea from the first sentence of each item. The first one has been done for you.

decrease	fact	possibility	requirement
discovery	opinion	prediction	response

1 Immigrants gave up a familiar life for a chance of success in the New World. This _possibility_ . . .

2 In 1968, a resident of Brooklyn, New York, found the remains of a nineteenth-century African American settlement. This _____ . . .

3 Some experts believe there will be 9 billion people in the world by 2050. This
   _____ prediction _____ . . .

4 In some countries, you must be able to speak the national language in order to
   become a citizen. This _____ requirement _____ . . .

5 In the nineteenth century, established immigrant groups often had a hostile reaction
   to new immigrant groups. This _____ response _____ . . .

6 About 1.5 million people of Japanese descent now live in Brazil. This
   _____ fact _____ . . .

7 Some people think that that western culture has had too much influence around the
   world. This _____ opinion _____ . . .

8 The number of immigrants arriving in the United States dropped considerably during
   the economic downturn. This _____ decrease _____ . . .

Skill Practice 2

**For each pair of sentences, circle the continuing idea marker in the second sentence.
Then answer the question that follows. The first one has been done for you.**

1 In the nineteenth century, the cost of travel across the Atlantic dropped considerably.
   (This) made the journey possible for many more people.
   What made the journey possible? *The lower cost of travel*

2 On many farms in Europe, the soil was thin and rocky. (This) made it harder for farmers
   to grow crops to feed their animals and families.
   What made it hard to grow crops? _____ soil was thin and rocky _____

3 After World War I, many countries began to limit the number of immigrants who could
   enter the country. (Such) restrictions resulted in a lower percentage of immigrants in
   the population.
   What decreased the percentage of immigrants in the population? _____ limit the number of many variable _____

4 The steel and cotton industry needed lots of workers to keep their factories running.
   (This) demand for labor was a major factor in immigration.
   What was a major factor in immigration? _____ need lots of worker _____

5 Starting in 1882, people from China were prohibited from immigrating to the United
   States. This practice continued until 1943.
   What continued until 1943? _____

6 Many developed countries now have immigration policies that are designed to attract skilled workers. These policies have attracted thousands of engineers and computer specialists.

What has attracted engineers and computer specialists? _____ *immigration policies*

Skill Practice 3

From the box below, find the noun that best continues an idea from the first sentence of each item. The words in bold will help you.

attempts	changes	crisis	statements
attitude	circumstances	move	views

1 The government has made several **modifications** to the university admission test. There is a new writing section and a longer vocabulary section. These _*changes*_ mean that high school students will have to practice different skills to prepare for the test.

2 Some politicians **believe** that the government needs to do a better job of controlling its country's borders. These _*views*_ are shared by many citizens.

3 For many years, scientists have **tried to find** a cure for HIV/AIDS. So far these _*attempts*_ have been unsuccessful, but scientists have had some success in finding ways to help people with HIV/AIDS live longer.

4 Some people want **the government to allow people who came to the country illegally to become citizens.** Others think that such a/an _*circumstances (move)*_ would be very unpopular.

5 Medical technology **can keep a patient alive** even when his or her brain has stopped working. In such _*crisis (circumstances)*_, many people believe that the life support equipment should be switched off.

6 In the nineteenth century, many people on the West Coast of the United States openly **expressed their prejudice against Chinese immigrants.** Such a/an _*attitude*_ would not be acceptable today.

7 The striking workers **have said** that the company has no interest in improving job safety. The employers **have complained** that the workers want to destroy the company. These _*move (statements)*_ have not helped the two sides reach an agreement.

8 Between 2009 and 2012, several major European countries were **unable to pay their debts.** This _*move (crisis)*_ had a negative impact on the global economy.

Connecting to the Topic

Read the definition of *immigration*, and then discuss the following questions with a partner.

> **immigration** (*n*) the process by which people come in to a foreign country to live

1 Why do you think people choose to immigrate?

2 Has there been a history of immigration in your country? Describe it.

3 Do you think immigration has a positive or negative effect on a country?

Previewing and Predicting

> Looking at illustrations and graphic material (pictures, photos, charts, tables, or graphs) can help you predict what a reading will be about.

A **Read the title of Reading 1, and look at the photograph and the graph (Figure 2.0). What do you think this reading will be about? Put a check (✓) next to the topic or topics that you think will be included in the reading.**

_____ A Historical immigrations trends

_____ B The lives of immigrants

_____ C Immigration to the United States and Canada today

_____ D Immigrants' journeys to the New World

_____ E Immigration laws and regulations

B **Compare your answers with a partner's.**

While You Read

As you read, stop at the end of each sentence that contains words in bold. Then follow the instructions in the box in the margin.

The Age of Immigration عن الهجرة

1   The period between 1830 and 1930 was a time of explosive immigration from the Old World to the New World – North, South, and Central
America. In the United States, for example, almost 15 percent of the
population was born outside of the country in 1890. (See Figure 2.1.)
For the first 60 years of this period, almost all immigration to the United
States was from Northwestern Europe, especially from Britain, Ireland,
Scandinavia, and Germany. Then, as the flow of immigrants from these
countries declined, large numbers of people began to make the journey
from countries in Southern and Eastern Europe. In addition, a smaller but
significant number of immigrants came to the United States from Asia,
particularly China and Japan. Finally, during the early part of this period,
there was forced migration of Africans as slaves to many places in the
New World.

2   The largest number of immigrants went to the United States, but substantial numbers also went to Canada. Initially, like the United States, most
immigrants to Canada came from Northwestern Europe; subsequently,
there was a shift to Southern and Eastern Europe as the primary sources of
immigration. In South America, Argentina and Brazil received the largest
number of immigrants during the same period. About 6.5 million immigrants went to Argentina, and about four and half million went to Brazil.
In Argentina, the majority came from Spain and Italy, and in Brazil, most
immigrants came from Portugal, Italy, and Germany.

Figure 2.1 Immigration to the United States* (1831–1930)
and Canada (1851–1930)

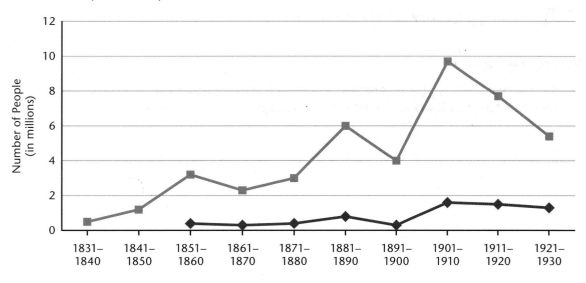

Source: Statistics Canada and U.S. Department of Commerce

*Figures do not include forced migration of slaves

What are the factors?

3   A number of factors lay behind immigrants' decisions to leave their home countries. Sociologists and economists generally **categorize** these as "push" and "pull" factors. Push factors are characteristics of the home country that make staying there less attractive. Pull factors are characteristics that make the new country more attractive, despite the hardship of giving up a familiar life and of taking a difficult journey. Although immigrants all had their own reasons for leaving home, one push factor – economic hardship – was behind most of the decisions to risk an uncertain future in the New World.

4   In nineteenth-century Europe, economic hardship affected workers of all kinds. Both agriculture and industry were in transition. The old agricultural system that depended on large numbers of unskilled workers was disintegrating and had left many farm workers unemployed. The farm work that remained available was difficult and uncertain. When a harvest failed, there was not enough to eat. The persistent failure of the potato harvest in Ireland (1845–1852) caused widespread starvation and

Harvest failure potato

WHILE YOU READ 1

Use context and your knowledge of a related word to guess the meaning of *categorize*. Does it mean (a) to make categories, (b) to put into categories, or (c) to find categories?

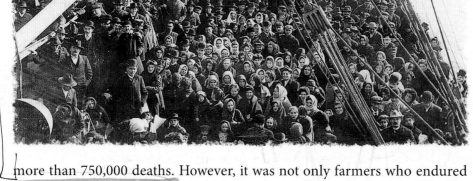

In the nineteenth century, most immigrants came from Europe.

more than 750,000 deaths. However, it was not only farmers who endured **such difficult conditions**. Industrialization was drawing large numbers of people into the cities. This growing supply of workers depressed wages, so often jobs did not pay enough to support a family. Many people could not find work at all.

5   In contrast, life in the New World offered several pull factors that attracted immigrants. For farmers, good land in the New World was

WHILE YOU READ 2

Look back in paragraph 4 to find what *such difficult conditions* refers to. Highlight the earlier idea that this continuing idea marker refers to.

inexpensive. The governments in many countries, including the United States and Canada, encouraged immigrants by offering land at low prices or in some cases, at no cost to farmers who were willing to build homes and communities. Many countries in the New World also had a large and growing demand for non-farm labor. Companies sent representatives to countries all over Europe to recruit both skilled and unskilled workers, offering higher wages than European factories. With the invention of the steamship, travel time from Europe fell from several months to just two weeks, making the option to immigrate more attractive. Finally, the countries that experienced the highest rates of immigration – the United States, Canada, Argentina, and Brazil – also offered political stability. These push and pull factors combined to fuel a colossal immigration wave that peaked between 1900 and **World War I.**

① land inexpensive

② demand labor
high wage

③ steamship save time

④ political stability

6   During this period, the strongest demand for labor in the New World was for the most difficult jobs: building subways and railroads, harvesting sugar cane, picking fruit, and mining precious metals. Such **robust** demand led many countries to turn to the system of contract labor. In this system, a company paid the cost of the immigrants' journey to the New World. The companies profited in two ways: first, the immigrants had to work for the company, usually for low wages; and second, they had to pay back the cost of the journey plus interest. Many Asians, pushed by poor economic conditions in their own countries, came to the New World under this system. In South America, many Chinese and Japanese went to Peru, and to a lesser extent, Brazil, during this period. There was also substantial immigration from Asia to the United States. More than 400,000 Chinese immigrated to the United States during this period, including about 50,000 to Hawaii, which was not yet part of the United States. About 380,000 Japanese came to the United States, 200,000 of them to Hawaii. Some, though not all, came as contract laborers.

M.I what was the strongest demand

WHILE YOU READ ③

What is the main idea of paragraph 5? Highlight it.

WHILE YOU READ ④

Look back in the previous sentence for a word that means the same thing as *robust*. Highlight the word.

① contract system
② company profit.
1. low wage
2. employee pay back

M.I.

7   Finally, a large number of laborers were brought to the New World against their will. The slave trade began in the seventeenth century and reached its height before the age of immigration. Brazil was the last country in South America to abolish slavery in 1888, by which time, between 9 and 10 million Africans had been brought to the New World. Only about five percent went to the United States. The majority of slaves were taken to South America and the Caribbean, with the largest number going to Brazil. In many countries, including the United States, slaves worked in physically demanding jobs for which it was difficult to find enough paid laborers.

① Slave in Brasil
② slave status

8   The age of immigration, which closed with the beginning of World War II, prepared the way for a multicultural New World. Following the war, immigration continued, but patterns and directions of immigration changed. In addition, although the number of immigrants remained high in some countries, the percentage of immigrants in the population has never been as high as it was during the Age of Immigration.

restate

Main Idea Check

Match the main ideas below to five of the paragraphs in Reading 1. Write the number of the paragraph on the blank line.

_____ A Life was very difficult in nineteenth-century Europe.

_____ B The contract labor system was the result of high demand for labor in the New World.

_____ C Slaves worked in sectors where it was difficult to find paid workers.

_____ D Push and pull factors can explain decisions to immigrate.

_____ E Life in the New World had many attractions.

A Closer Look

Look back at Reading 1 to answer the following questions.

T 1 In the beginning of the period described in the reading, most of the immigrants were German, Irish, British, and Scandinavian. **True or False?**

2 When did immigration reach its highest point?
   a Between 1881 and 1890
   b In the decade before World War II
   c In the decade before World War I
   d Immediately after World War I

3 In Paragraph 4, why does the writer describe the economic hardship and difficult living conditions of workers in Europe?
   a To show the improvements that occurred in immigrants' lives in the United States
   b To show the sacrifices that immigrants made to establish new lives in the United States
   c To show how much immigrants suffered
   d To illustrate the role push factors played in immigrants' decisions

4 What did the governments of some countries in the New World do to attract immigrants?
   a They offered free land.
   b They paid for immigrants' families to join them.
   c They promised jobs for new immigrants.
   d They offered immigrants a free place to live for their first year in the country.

5 Put a check (✓) in the blank before the four countries that received the largest number of immigrants during the Age of Immigration.

   ✓ Canada   _____ Peru
   ✓ the United States   ✓ Brazil
   _____ Mexico   ✓ Argentina

6 Who benefitted the most financially from the contract labor system?
   a Asian laborers
   b South American countries where laborers settled
   c The companies who paid the laborers passage
   d The shipping companies who brought the laborers to the New World

7 More slaves went to the Caribbean than the United States. True or False?

Skill Review

In Skills and Strategies 4, you learned that writers often make connections between ideas by using continuing idea markers, such as *this*, *these*, and *such*, as well as general nouns. Learning these signals of continuing ideas can improve your reading comprehension.

A **Reread the following sentences from Reading 1. Highlight the continuing ideas that the words in bold refer to.**

1 A number of factors lay behind immigrants' decision to leave their home countries. Sociologists and economists generally categorize **these** as "push" factors and "pull" factors. (Par. 3)

2 These push and pull factors combined to fuel a colossal immigration wave that peaked between 1900 and World War I. During **this** period, the strongest demand for labor in the New World was for the most difficult jobs: building subways and railroads, harvesting sugar cane, and mining precious metals. (Par. 5)

3 During this period, the strongest demand for labor in the New World was for the most difficult jobs: building subways and railroads, harvesting sugar cane, picking fruit, and mining precious metals. **Such** robust demand led many countries to turn to the system of contract labor. (Par. 6)

4 Such robust demand led many countries to turn to the system of contract labor. In this system, a company paid the cost of the immigrants' journey to the New World. Then, the immigrants had to work for the company, usually for low wages, until they had paid it back plus interest. Many Asians, pushed by poor economic conditions in their own countries, came to the New World under **this** system. (Par. 6)

5 In many countries, including the United States, slaves worked in physically demanding jobs, for which it was difficult to find enough paid laborers. **These** included sugar cane, cotton, and tobacco farming, as well as mining. (Par. 7)

B **Compare your answers with a partner's.**

Definitions

Find the words in Reading 1 that are similar to the definitions below.

1 a difficult and unpleasant situation (*n*) Par. 3

2 a process of change (*n*) Par. 4

3 to become weaker or destroyed by falling into small pieces (*v*) Par. 4

4 lack of food for a long period of time (*n*) Par. 4

5 someone who speaks or acts for another person or group (*n*) Par. 5

6 to persuade someone to become an employee (*v*) Par. 5

7 when something stays the same and doesn't move or change (*n*) Par. 5

8 to reach the highest point (*v*) Par. 5

9 additional money that you must pay when you borrow money (*n*) Par. 6

10 requiring a lot of strength, energy, or attention (*adj*) Par. 7

Synonyms

Complete the sentences with words from Reading 1 in the box below. These words replace the words or phrases in parentheses, which are similar in meaning.

abolish	colossal	fueled	option	source
attractive	endured	initially	persistent	subsequently

1 Scientists identified a gene mutation for breast cancer and (later) _____, developed a test to identify people who carry the gene mutation.

2 Many immigrants believed that leaving home and looking for work in the New World was their only (choice) _____.

3 The discovery of gold in the Western United States (encouraged) _____ immigration to California.

4 The idea of a new life in a new country was very (appealing) _____ to many immigrants.

5 Many people would like the government to (end; eliminate) _____ the income tax, but this is unlikely to happen.

6 A/An (very large) _____ storm damaged the immigrant's farm.

7 The (origin) _____ of political discontent is often economic.

8 Many countries (at first) _____ welcomed immigrants because they needed workers.

9 The (continuous) _____ failure of national economic policies has forced many people to look for jobs in other countries.

10 The slaves who were brought to the New World (suffered) _____ terrible treatment and many of them even died.

Critical Thinking

In Reading 1, the author introduced the concepts of push and pull factors in immigrants' decisions to leave their home countries and start over in a new country.

A Think about the terms *push factor* and *pull factor*. Briefly define each term and use the chart below to make a list of the factors that are discussed in the reading.

PUSH FACTORS	PULL FACTORS

B With a partner, think of other push and pull factors in immigration that the writer did not mention. Add them to the chart.

C Considering push and pull factors is not limited to decisions about immigration. Many important decisions require you to go through a similar process, for example, to leave one job for a different one or to move to a new city. Think of a decision in your own life that involved push and pull factors.

Research

Research the importance of migration on the history of your country. Find answers to the following questions.

- Has there been substantial immigration *to* your country? When? From where?
- Has there been substantial emigration *from* your country to other places? When? To where?
- If there has been neither, find out if there have been any barriers to immigration or emigration in your country.

Writing

Write two paragraphs about your research.

Connecting to the Topic

Discuss the following questions with a partner.

1 Where do you think most of today's immigrants come from?

2 Where do you think most immigrants go?

3 In Reading 1, you considered why most people immigrate. Do you think their reasons are different from the reasons that immigrants had 100 years ago?

Previewing and Predicting

> Reading the title and the first one or two sentences of several paragraphs can help you predict what a reading will be about.

A Read the first two sentences of paragraphs 2–6 in Reading 2, and think about the title of the reading. Then read the following topics. Write the number of the paragraph next to the topic that best describes it.

PARAGRAPH	TOPIC
	Illegal immigration
	The reasons why people today choose to immigrate
	Non-economic factors in immigration decisions
	The economic needs of today's destination countries
	The destinations of today's immigrants

B Compare your answers with a partner's.

While You Read

As you read, stop at the end of each sentence that contains words in **bold**. Then follow the instructions in the box in the margin.

Who Are Today's Immigrants?

1   The world's population is more mobile today than ever before. In 2010, more than 200 million people left their home countries to live in a new country. This is about 3 percent of the total world population. Some experts believe that number will swell to 400 million by 2050. Rates of immigration have remained strong for the last 300 years, but patterns of immigration have changed since World War II. The backgrounds and experiences of today's immigrants are different from those of the typical European immigrant of the nineteenth and early twentieth centuries. Contemporary immigrants range from unskilled laborers to highly skilled professionals, and they come from and go to countries all over the world. (See Figure 2.2.)

2   In the nineteenth century and until World War II, immigration was primarily in one direction – from the Old World to the New World. This is no longer the case. Countries such as Russia and China, which have long been, and continue to be, significant source countries, are now also destination countries. There is also considerable mobility inside regions, such as from one European country to another, or among the countries of the former Soviet Union.

3   In spite of **such** differences, the push and pull factors for immigration remain essentially the same as they were 100 years ago. Most people move to another country because they want a better life. For the majority of immigrants, this means better economic conditions. As in past generations, a labor shortage in one country often draws workers from another country, especially if wages are significantly higher. In some small countries, for example, Qatar, United Arab Emirates, and Kuwait, there are more jobs

> **WHILE YOU READ 1**
>
> What is the continuing idea that *such* refers to? Highlight it.

Figure 2.2 Source and Destination Regions of Migrants, 2010

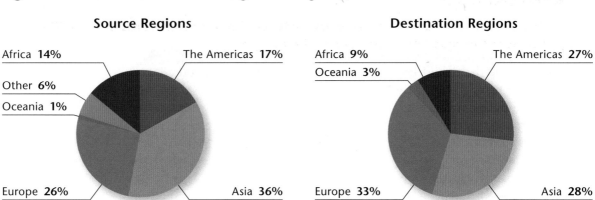

Source Regions

Africa **14%**
The Americas **17%**
Other **6%**
Oceania **1%**
Europe **26%**
Asia **36%**

Destination Regions

Africa **9%**
Oceania **3%**
The Americas **27%**
Europe **33%**
Asia **28%**

Source: Migration Policy Institute

than citizens. The demand for labor is so high that the majority of the population consists of foreign-born workers, ranging from highly skilled engineers and financial experts to domestic and construction **workers**.

4   In traditional destination countries, such as the United States, however, labor needs have changed. Today, although there is still demand for unskilled labor, there is increasing demand for people with a high level of skill and education. The need for less skilled labor has shifted to other countries. As work on farms and in industry in the United States and Canada once drew workers from all over the world, now work in factories in Taiwan and South Korea attracts workers from Vietnam, the Philippines, and Cambodia.

5   Most global immigration is legal; however, a large number of people also move across national borders illegally in pursuit of employment. Experts estimate that about 15 to 20 percent of immigrants worldwide are in their new countries illegally. The United States has the largest number of **these** immigrants, followed by South Africa, with significant numbers also in Northern and Western Europe and Mexico. These immigrants face particular challenges because they often must hide from the authorities who might deport them back to their home countries. Their illegal status also means that employers may take advantage of them by forcing them to work longer hours and paying them less than the legal minimum wage.

6   Although economics remains the most important motivation in all forms of immigration, other factors are also important. Some people decide to leave their home countries because their actions or political beliefs make it dangerous for them to remain. Others choose to leave because their home country has become too dangerous and unstable, often because of war or political unrest. They wish to find a place that is secure for themselves and their families. Education is also a significant factor for many modern immigrants. They want to raise their children in a place where they can get a good education, which, in turn, they hope will provide them with better prospects for the future. Finally, family and community ties also play a role in immigration **decisions**. As in the past, once a group of people from one country establishes a community in a new country, more people from that country are likely to follow.

7   The pattern, direction, and rate of immigration may change as the global economy changes. However, as long as life in a new country is more attractive than life in the old country, immigration will continue.

Some people become refugees because it is too dangerous to stay in their homes.

WHILE YOU READ 2

What is the main idea of paragraph 3? Highlight it.

WHILE YOU READ 3

What is the continuing idea that *these* refers to? Highlight it.

WHILE YOU READ 4

Look back in the previous sentence to find a cause-and-effect relationship. Highlight the cause.

Main Idea Check

Here are the main ideas of paragraphs 2–6 of Reading 2. Match each paragraph to its main idea. Write the number of the paragraph on the blank line.

_____ A A significant percentage of immigration occurs illegally.

_____ B Today immigrants come from and go to many different countries.

_____ C Although economic reasons are primary, there are other factors in immigration decisions.

_____ D Economic reasons remain the primary factor in making decisions about immigration.

_____ E The need for unskilled labor has shifted away from countries like the United States to countries such as South Korea.

A Closer Look

Look back at Reading 2 to answer the following questions.

1 Unskilled workers are no longer among today's immigrants. **True or False?**

2 Look at Figure 2.2. Which area of the world has the largest percentage of *net immigration*, that is, the percentage of people arriving minus the percentage of people who are leaving?
   a Europe   b Asia   c Africa   d The Americas

3 According to the reading, what are the patterns of immigration in China and Russia today?
   a They are major destination countries for immigrants.
   b They are major source countries for immigration.
   c Many people leave these countries, but many people also immigrate to them.
   d Some people immigrate to these countries but many more people leave them.

4 Why is the percentage of foreign-born workers so high in Kuwait, Qatar, and the United Arab Emirates?
   a These countries pay very high wages, so they attract many foreign workers.
   b There are not enough native-born workers in these countries so they must recruit workers from other countries.
   c It is very easy to immigrate to these countries.
   d These countries are very stable so many workers prefer to go there.

5 Compared to 100 years ago, there is a higher demand for skilled workers in the United States. **True or False?**

6 Why do some employers sometimes pay illegal immigrants less than the legal minimum wage?
   a They often do not speak good English.
   b Authorities might send illegal immigrants back to their home country.
   c Employers know that they will not complain about their wages to authorities.
   d Illegal workers often cause problems for employers.

7 What factors, other than economic opportunity, are offered in the reading to explain why people choose to immigrate? Circle all that apply.

a Education
b Religious freedom
c Political stability
d Freedom of expression
e Family and community connections

Skill Review

In Skills and Strategies 4, you learned that writers often signal connections between ideas with continuing idea markers, such as *these*, *this*, *that*, and *such*, as well as general nouns. Learning these signals of continuing ideas can improve your reading comprehension.

A **Reread the first three paragraphs of Reading 2. Find examples of *this* that signal continuing ideas. Write the ideas that these markers refer to.**

Par. 1 (this) _____

Par. 2 (this) _____

Par. 3 (this) _____

B **Read the sentences below. Then write a new sentence that continues the ideas that were introduced in the earlier sentences. Use a general word for continuing ideas to begin your sentence. Review the Language of Continuing Ideas box on page 65 if you need help.**

1 Often immigrants want to escape political oppression in their countries. Some groups were escaping widespread prejudice and violence against them, while others just wanted a good job. These _____

_____ .

2 Many immigrants to the United States have made important contributions in music, art, business, and especially technology. Jerry Yang founded Yahoo, Sergey Brin is a founder of Google, and Andrew Grove is a founder of Intel. These _____

_____ .

3 Some people say that immigrants take away jobs, increase crime, and don't learn the language of their new county. These _____

_____ .

Definitions

Find the words in Reading 2 that are similar to the definitions below.

1 to increase in size or amount (*v*) Par. 1

2 to vary (*v*) Par. 1

3 the place where someone is going (*n*) Par. 2

4 from an earlier time (*adj*) Par. 2

5 basically (*adv*) Par. 3

6 to be made of (*v 2 word*) Par. 3

7 related to the management of money (*adj*) Par. 3

8 related to the house and home (*adj*) Par. 3

9 the building of something (*n*) Par. 3

10 a group of people with official power to enforce rules or laws (*n pl*) Par. 5

11 a position or condition at a particular time (*n*) Par. 5

12 the lowest possible amount (*adj*) Par. 5

13 money paid for work (*v*) Par. 5

14 the reason why you are willing to do some thing (*n*) Par. 6

15 connections (*n pl*) Par. 6

Words in Context

Complete the passages with words and phrases from Reading 2 in the box below.

contemporary	mobility	secure	the case	unskilled
deport	prospects	take advantage of	unrest	unstable

1 When people are unhappy with the government and there is political

_____, the economy often becomes _____, as well. When
         a   b

this happens, in some countries, the government may _____ the
                                                                          c

situation and decide to _____ foreign workers. The government may
                                  d

claim that these steps are necessary in order to provide jobs for citizens and to keep

the economy _____.
                      e

2 The _____ workforce is very different from the workforce of 100
               f

years ago. Perhaps the most important difference is its _____. Workers
                                                                            g

frequently move to other countries for better employment _____. This
                                                                              h

is particularly _____ with technology experts, who are in great demand
                        i

all over the world. However, _____ workers also move across borders to

j

find work, often in factories or agriculture.

Academic Word List

The following are Academic Word List words from Readings 1 and 2 of this unit. Use these words to complete the sentences. (For more on the Academic Word List, see page 256.)

consist of (v)	minimum (adj)	options (n)	range (v)	subsequently (adv)
contemporary (adj)	motivation (n)	prospects (n)	source (n)	transition (n)

1 Every state in the United States establishes a/an _____ hourly wage. Employers may not pay workers less than this.

2 The reasons for a high mortality rate _____ from lack of access to adequate health care and clean water to poor sanitation.

3 Many immigrants name the education of their children as the primary _____ for leaving their home country.

4 _____ ideas about conquering killer diseases, such as the use of gene therapy, are very different from the ideas of the last century.

5 We are in _____ from the old system to the new system, so there may be some delays in the project.

6 College graduates have far better job _____ than people who have only a high school education.

7 Most computers _____ a central processing unit, a monitor or screen, and a keyboard.

8 He decided to take a job in Germany but _____ changed his mind and decided to stay in Japan instead.

9 The government offers several _____ for health care, but all of them are too expensive for the poorest people in the country.

10 The doctors are uncertain about the _____ of her infection. They believe she may have become ill on a trip she took last month.

Critical Thinking

Readings 1 and 2 were both about immigrants and immigration in different time periods.

A Work with a partner. Think about immigration during the Age of Immigration and about immigration today. How are these two periods similar or different? Use the chart below to list your ideas. The first row has been filled in for you.

> **SYNTHESIZING**
>
> Critical thinking includes connecting new information to information you learned in previous readings.

DURING AGE OF IMMIGRATION	TODAY
Immigrants came from the Old World	*Immigrants come from all over the world*

B Discuss your ideas with the rest of the class.

Research

Consider immigration in your own country or a country you know well. Find answers to the following questions.

- How large is the foreign-born population?
- Where do the largest number of immigrants come from?
- What are their reasons for coming? What kind of work do they do?

Writing

Write two paragraphs about your research. The first paragraph will describe the population, and the second will describe their reasons for coming to your country.

Improving Your Reading Speed

Good readers read quickly and still understand most of what they read.

A Read the instructions and strategies for Improving Your Reading Speed in Appendix 3 on page 273.

B Choose either Reading 1 or Reading 2 in this unit. Read it without stopping. Time how long it takes you to finish the text in minutes and seconds. Enter the time in the chart on page 274. Then calculate your reading speed in number of words per minute.

Point of View

Writers sometimes present two different points of view on an issue. They present a point of view that is commonly held by many people or by a specific group of people, and they present their own or some other opposing point of view. Usually writers then explain why one point of view is preferable. Recognizing and understanding a point of view is an important part of academic reading.

Examples & Explanations

①It seems to be a reasonable assumption that the health-care problems in developing nations are very different from those that face developed ones. ②However, we would be seriously mistaken if we accepted this assumption. ③In fact, the reality is that health-care systems throughout the world are facing many of the same general challenges and some of the same specific problems. ④HIV / AIDS, for example, is a major threat in both developed and developing countries.

Sentence 1 contains an idea about differences in health-care problems for developing and developed countries. The word *assumption* is a view marker, a word that tells readers that the writer considers what comes next to be an opinion, not a fact. Note that some view markers are more neutral than others. For example, *belief* is neutral, offering no judgment, whereas *assumption* suggests a mistaken or inaccurate opinion.

Sentence 2 begins with *However*, a contrast marker. It tells readers to expect the writer's disagreement with sentence 1. The word *mistaken* is an assessment marker, a word the writer uses to judge (here, negatively) the view that is expressed in the first sentence.

Sentence 3 offers a different view of health-care problems around the world – that they are often the same. The words *in fact* and *reality* emphasize that the writer believes in this view.

Sentence 4 contains an example to support the writer's point of view.

The Language of Point of View

Here are lists of commonly used view markers, contrast markers, and assessment markers used to express points of view.

VIEW MARKERS					
Verbs			**Nouns**		
to accuse	to conclude	to question	accusation	claim	notion
to allege	to consider	to regard	allegation	conclusion	opinion
to argue	to criticize	to seem	analysis	criticism	perception
to assume	to doubt	to suggest	argument	doubt	theory
to believe	to imagine	to think	assumption	idea	thought
to blame	to interpret	to view	belief	impression	view
to claim	to perceive		blame	interpretation	
			charge	judgment	

CONTRAST MARKERS	
but	on the other hand
however	yet
in theory . . . in practice	

ASSESSMENT MARKERS Words that indicate approval or disapproval of the common view					
Nouns			**Adjectives**		
accuracy	flaw	myth	defective	illusory	unconvincing
defect	illusion	shortcoming	erroneous	inaccurate	unjustified
error	(mis)conception	trap	false	incorrect	unreasonable
fallacy	misinterpretation	validity	faulty	invalid	unsound
fault	mistake	weakness	flawed	mistaken	unwarranted
			flawless	questionable	weak

Strategies

These strategies will help you recognize and understand texts that present points of view.

- Look for view markers. Use them to establish that you are reading about what the writer considers to be opinions not facts and to identify the common view.
- Look for contrast markers. Use them to identify where the first view ends.
- Look for assessment markers. Use them to identify the opposing view.

Skill Practice 1

The following sentences contain points of view. As you read them, underline the view markers and highlight the opinions. The first one has been done for you.

1 At the end of their analysis, the authors <u>conclude</u> that political oppression is increasing in some parts of the world.

2 The government would like you to believe that its programs are helping the economy to recover.

3 Most people who have not lived in cultures other than their own assume that the rules for polite speech and behavior are universal.

4 People who watch a great deal of television tend to perceive the world as more violent than it really is.

5 A frequent allegation that is made about people between the ages of 18 and 25 is that they have no interest in politics.

6 Using the latest statistics, which show an increase in the high school completion rates, the government claims that its programs have brought about improvements in education.

7 The tendency of immigrants to live in their own ethnic communities is sometimes interpreted as evidence that they do not wish to become integrated into U.S. society.

8 The researchers argue that much more information is needed before anyone can adequately describe how people adjust to life in a new culture.

9 Relations between the company and its workers worsened after the employees charged that the company wanted to destroy their union.

10 Among Americans, a common perception is that most immigrants enter the United States illegally.

Skill Practice 2

Read the following short texts. Underline the contrast markers and assessment markers. Then highlight the common view. The first one has been done for you.

1 There is a widespread belief that cardiovascular disease is a problem only in affluent societies and that it attacks mostly men. Studies from the 1990s, <u>however</u>, provide evidence that this view of CVD is <u>no longer valid</u>.

2 Some years ago, it was argued, usually by western experts, that overpopulation in developing nations was one of the main causes of widespread poverty. According to

more recent studies, however, this analysis of the relationship between poverty and overpopulation is seriously flawed.

3 There is a tendency among nonexperts to regard primary health care in developing countries as exclusively for the prevention of disease. Yet a closer look at specific programs offers evidence to correct this common misperception.

4 The fact that some first-generation immigrants continue to speak their first languages might suggest that these immigrants and their families are unwilling to become a full part of their new society. Studies by social scientists, on the other hand, cast doubt on the validity of this conclusion.

Skill Practice 3

Read the following paragraphs and look for view markers, contrast markers, and assessment markers. Underline the common view and highlight the writer's point of view.

1   There is a widespread belief that cardiovascular disease is a problem only in affluent societies and that it attacks mostly men. This was perhaps true in the 1950s, when CVD was first identified as a major health risk. However, more recent studies indicate that this view of CVD is questionable. In many parts of the world, CVD is the leading cause of death among women under 65. It is also becoming more common in less affluent countries and is expected to become a leading cause of death.

2   Many people assume that the rules for polite social behavior are universal. They claim that all societies have the same rules, for example, for how and when to thank others. Yet research on intercultural communication shows that this apparently reasonable assumption is unjustified. In fact, the rules for social behavior may differ, sometimes widely, from culture to culture. Studies have established, for instance, that some Asian cultures do not give or expect to receive thanks while shopping, but Americans do.

3   Even before a measles vaccine became available, people in the West considered measles to be a relatively minor childhood disease that was more of an inconvenience than a danger to health. But past and present experience shows that such an optimistic view of this highly infectious disease is unwarranted. Measles, with its many complications – including diarrhea and pneumonia – is, in fact, potentially fatal. Before the vaccine became widely available late in the twentieth century, measles killed an estimated 8 million children annually. In 2000, the disease caused an estimated 700,000 deaths in developing countries.

Connecting to the Topic

Discuss the following questions with a partner.

1 What does *culture* mean?

2 How does culture affect our lives?

3 What would you expect to see in a country that is described as "culturally diverse"?

Previewing and Predicting

> Reading the first sentence of each paragraph is a quick way to predict what a reading will be about.

A **Read the first sentence of each paragraph in Reading 3. What do you think this reading will be about? Put a check (✓) next to the topic or topics that you think will be included in the reading.**

_✓_ A The definition of assimilation

_✓_ B Positive effects of the process of assimilation

_____ C The history of immigration to North America

_✓_ D Canada's attitude toward diversity

_____ E Reasons why immigrants leave their home countries

_✓_ F The effect of multiculturalism on the United States

B **Compare your answers with a partner's.**

While You Read

As you read, stop at the end of each sentence that contains words in bold. Then follow the instructions in the box in the margin.

The Meeting of Cultures

1   In the last few decades, the world has become more culturally diverse than at any time in its history. Much of this diversity is the result of migration, both voluntary and involuntary. In Canada, according to census data, one in five people are foreign born, which is the highest proportion since the 1930s. In fact, between 2001 and 2006, the number for the foreign-born population increased by over 13 percent, 4 times faster than the Canadian-born population. Australia is another example, with 22 percent of the population originating from other countries. In the United States, the figure is 12 percent. Immigrants come to new countries from an array of different nations, bringing with them their hopes and dreams. They also bring their cultures. This meeting of cultures can add to the richness of a society, but it can also generate serious challenges.

2   Culture has been described as one of the most complicated concepts to explain. Generally, it refers to the entire way of life of a group of people. More specifically, material culture refers to language, clothes, and food, whereas symbolic culture refers to ideas, beliefs, and customs. Culture shapes the way people view their world. It is so closely connected to a sense of personal identity that it feels innate rather than **learned**. However, it is learned, and learned so gradually that people are unaware of the process. When exposed to another culture, however, a person can immediately identify differences. Within today's culturally diverse societies,

WHILE YOU READ ❶

Use context to choose the definition of *sense* in this sentence.
a) Good judgment
b) A feeling
c) Ability to see, hear, etc.

Figure 2.3 Percentage of Foreign Citizens

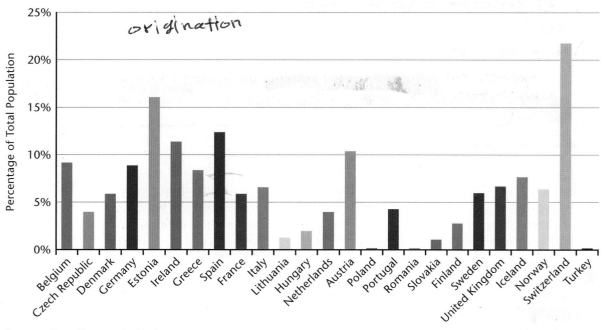

Source: Guardian.co.uk chart

the challenge facing everyone, from individuals to governments, is how different cultures can best interact with one another.

3   One approach to interaction among cultures is assimilation. This refers to a minority group that gradually changes so that it can absorb into the dominant culture. Assimilation is often explained through the "melting pot" metaphor. During the twentieth century, immigrants to the United States were eager to adapt to the American way of life. There was widespread assumption that this was a necessary step in realizing the economic rewards of the American **Dream**. Immigrants from Ireland, Italy, and Eastern Europe learned English, became citizens, and gradually merged into the dominant culture. Their children accelerated this process as they self-identified as American rather than as their parent's nationality.

WHILE YOU READ 2

This is a continuing idea marker. Highlight the idea it repeats from the previous sentence.

Learning the language of the new country can help immigrants assimilate.

4   Many people claim that there are advantages to the process of assimilation. Assimilation creates a national identity, a sense that regardless of racial or ethnic background, people feel part of the country in which they live. If everyone within a society belongs to the same group, then conflict will decrease. It can be argued that this sense of national identity has served the United States well for many years. In a country where 79 percent of the population is white, 16 percent Latino or Hispanic, 12 percent African American, and 4 percent Asian, this diverse group of people shares a strong sense of national identity. Although some conflicts between different cultural groups have occurred, this sense of national identity has allowed the United States to enjoy a relatively peaceful domestic history compared to many other countries.

5   However, not all ethnic groups are invited to assimilate into the mainstream culture. Laws have even restricted the rights of specific immigrant groups. In the United States, laws segregated African Americans from the white population, particularly in the southern states, until the Civil Rights

legislation of the 1960s corrected these unjustified practices. Another example is South Africa where, prior to 1994, the government believed that white South Africans were superior to black South Africans. Strict laws were passed to separate black South Africans from the dominant white culture. As a result of this belief, immigration was **limited** to only those who the government believed could successfully assimilate into the dominant culture. Since this culture was based on race (white) and language (English and Afrikaans), Africans from neighboring countries were prohibited from entering as immigrants. Instead, the government classified them as migrant workers and severely restricted their rights.

WHILE YOU READ 3

Reread the previous sentence. Highlight the reason why immigration was limited.

6   In the last few decades, people have begun to question the concept of assimilation, even when it is open to all. Many people have come to view assimilation as a flawed process since it assumes that the dominant culture is superior. People began to question whether assimilation was the best approach to diversity. As the number of immigrants has continued to rise in many countries and as globalization has encouraged more travel and openness between nations, the traditional image of the melting pot has been replaced by the metaphor of a "mosaic." A mosaic is comprised of hundreds of small pieces, which together make up a complete picture. This mosaic represents multiculturalism, an attitude that encourages people to embrace cultural differences rather than expecting minority cultures to assimilate into the dominant one.

7   Legal equality together with respect and tolerance of racial and ethnic differences are at the core of multiculturalism. Canada provides a good example. Canadians are among the most diverse populations worldwide. Its minorities include European, Chinese, Indian, and Middle Eastern immigrants as well as native people, the First Nations. It has two official languages, French and English. National and local governments have passed many laws aimed at encouraging multicultural harmony. In 1988, for example, the Canadian Multiculturalism Act declared equal access for all Canadians within economic, social, cultural, and political life.

8   This strong legal foundation for multiculturalism might suggest that Canada has fully embraced its diversity. Yet a 2010 poll reveals a different picture. In this poll, 30 percent of Canadians believed multiculturalism has been bad for Canada. In addition, 54 percent believed the melting pot was preferable to the mosaic, claiming that all cultures should merge into one Canadian **culture**.

9   In the United States, multiculturalism is also integrated within political, social, and economic life. In particular, it is closely connected to education. However, as in Canada, embracing cultural differences within schools is not without controversy, as history of bilingual education has shown. A bilingual education program uses the native language of immigrant children to teach them math, science, and social studies while they are learning English. These programs have caused disagreement both within immigrant communities and in the wider American public. Education in

WHILE YOU READ 4

Look back in this paragraph. Highlight the contrast marker and the view marker.

California has been at the heart of this debate. Before 1998, many English language learners there were taught in a mix of their native language and English instruction. Supporters of bilingual education claim that forcing immigrant children to learn all subjects in English causes them to fall behind in school. Opponents, however, argue that the best way to learn a new language is to be fully immersed in that language. In 1998, the issue was brought to a vote. The majority of Californians chose an English-only teaching policy. With many second language students still struggling in school, the controversy continues today. Bilingual education illustrates that multiculturalism in practice is not always easy.

10   Why is multiculturalism such a divisive issue? Some people argue that the poll results and votes against bilingual education are evidence of growing intolerance toward immigrants in Canada and the United States. However, such an interpretation appears unjustified since in both countries, the majority of citizens claim that immigration has been good for their countries. A more likely explanation may be the confusion around the term *multiculturalism*. One common interpretation of this term is that immigrants should retain their own culture and language and need not adapt to their new country. Canadians and Americans who define multiculturalism in this way oppose it. On the other hand, the majority of citizens interpret it differently. For them it means accepting American or Canadian cultural traditions and learning the new languages while retaining their own culture to enjoy in private and family life.

11   Migration has had a long history, and it is far from ending. A 2011 poll of people from 150 countries found that 630 million adults have the desire to move permanently to another country; another 1.1 billion wish to relocate for temporary work. It is very likely that in the future, countries will become even more culturally diverse as individuals and governments continue to work toward racial and ethnic equality, harmony, and respect.

WHILE YOU READ 5

Look back at the previous two sentences. Highlight the view marker and the common view.

Many immigrants become citizens of their new country.

Main Idea Check

Match the main ideas below to five of the paragraphs in Reading 3. Write the number of the paragraph on the blank line.

_____ A Assimilation has not been possible for all ethnic groups.

_____ B Bilingual education reflects the ongoing challenges of multiculturalism.

_____ C The concept of multiculturalism has replaced assimilation.

_____ D In the twentieth century, immigrants to the United States assimilated into American culture.

_____ E Assimilation builds a sense of national identity.

A Closer Look

Look back at Reading 3 to answer the following questions.

1 Which statement best defines *culture* according to the reading?
   a Culture refers to how people speak, the clothes people wear, and the food people eat.
   b Culture can be defined as the way that a group of people think.
   c Culture is a process that is learned slowly from childhood.
   d Culture can be described as the habits, behavior, and attitudes of a group of people.

2 Which of the following statements would the writer agree with?
   a Individuals have a clear sense of their culture.
   b It is easier to explain cultural differences than to describe one's own culture.
   c A person acquires culture through birth.
   d It is easy for cultures to live together in today's multicultural world.

3 Which of the following statements is correct according to the reading?
   a Although not a perfect solution, in the United States, assimilation helped unite a very culturally diverse society.
   b Assimilation benefited the children of immigrants but not their parents.
   c The process of assimilation worked well for all immigrants.
   d Like many other countries, the process of assimilation has caused conflict in the United States.

4 Before 1994, South African migrant workers had the same social, political, and economic rights as citizens. **True or False?**

5 According to the reading, which statement supports the writer's claim that multiculturalism is still a divisive issue in Canada?
   a The government passed the Canadian Multiculturalism Act, which provided equality for all Canadians.
   b The languages of the First Nations people are not among official languages of Canada.
   c In 2010, almost a third of Canadians doubted the benefits of multiculturalism.
   d Canadian immigrants come from all over the world including China, India, the Middle East and Europe.

6 Reread Paragraph 9. Which of the following arguments might be made by supporters of bilingual education?

   a Immigrants have always learned English best by speaking it at home and at work.

   b Learning all subjects in English is the most effective way to learn that language.

   c Forcing an immigrant child to learn entirely in English leads to failure in school.

   d A child is not capable of learning two languages at the same time.

7 Which statements support the writer's opinion that multiculturalism is still a divisive issue in North America? Check all that apply.

   a Votes and poll results in Canada and the United States indicate that citizens in these countries prefer assimilation to multiculturalism.

   b Most Canadians and Americans believe that immigration has had a positive effect on their countries.

   c Many citizens of Canada and the United States misunderstand the term *multiculturalism*, believing it to mean that new immigrants do not need to adapt to their new country.

   d The English-only teaching policy has not been successful in helping second language students succeed in school.

Skill Review

> In Skills and Strategies 5, you learned to identify points of view in a text. One way to identify them is to look for view markers that introduce these views. Recognizing different points of view will improve your academic reading.

A Reread the following sentences from Reading 3. Underline the view markers. Highlight the opinions that these markers introduce.

1 There was widespread assumption that this was a necessary step in realizing the economic rewards of the American Dream.

2 Many people claim that there are advantages to the process of assimilation.

3 It can be argued that this sense of national identity has served the United States well for many years.

4 Another example is South Africa where, prior to 1994, the South African government believed that white South Africans were superior to black South Africans.

5 Many people have come to view assimilation as a flawed process since it assumes that the dominant culture is superior.

6 Supporters of bilingual education claim that forcing immigrant children to learn all subjects in English causes them to fall behind in school.

B Compare your answers with a partner's.

Definitions

Find the words in Reading 3 that are similar to the definitions below.

1 to communicate; to spend time with someone (v) Par. 2 *interact*

2 to take in knowledge, ideas, and information (v) Par. 3 *absorb*

3 to combine or join together (v) Par. 3 *merge*

4 despite what has been said or done (adv) Par. 4 *regardless*

5 common or shared by most people (adj) Par. 5 *mainstream*

6 to accept something with enthusiasm (v) Par. 6 *embrace*

7 a willingness to accept behavior or ideas different from your own (n) Par. 7 *tolerance.*

8 the center; the most important part of something (n) Par. 7 *core*

9 people who disagree with something and speak against it (n pl) Par. 9 *opponents*

10 to be fully involved in an activity (v) Par. 9 *immersed*

Words in Context

A **Use context clues to match the first part of each sentence to its correct second part and to understand the meaning of the words in bold.**

_____ 1 Sometimes the bright colors of a rainbow are used as

_____ 2 In order to find out more about children's attitudes to race,

_____ 3 In Southern states in the 1950s, black students were

_____ 4 The government argued that

_____ 5 Immigrants often find it difficult to

_____ 6 Fewer employment opportunities and lower wages are examples of how

_____ 7 Because of the high percentage of Latino voters in the United States,

_____ 8 Research is beginning to indicate that

_____ 9 Indonesia is an example of a culturally diverse country where

_____ 10 Because the men were caught crossing the border illegally, they were

a **segregated** from white students and forced to study in usually inferior schools.

b this group of immigrants plays a **dominant** role in American politics.

c **severely** South African workers have been affected by large numbers of refugees arriving in the country.

d a **metaphor** to illustrate the beauty of diversity.

e some people are born with the **innate** ability to understand other people.

f people generally live in **harmony** with one another.

g **classified** as undocumented and sent back to their country of origin.

h criticism against the new immigration law was **unjustified**.

i researchers designed a **poll**.

j **adapt** to a new country, especially if they need to learn a new language.

B **Compare your answers with a partner's. Discuss what clues helped you match the parts of the sentences and helped you understand what the words in bold mean.**

Critical Thinking

In Reading 3, the writer presents the controversial topic of
bilingual education.

A Read the following statements. Then put a check (✓)
in the appropriate column if you agree or disagree with
the statement.

STATEMENT	AGREE	DISAGREE
The best way for children of immigrants to learn English is by teaching all subjects in English only.		
Young children of immigrants learn best overall if they receive intensive English training while continuing other subjects such as math and science in their native language.		
In order to create a truly multicultural society, all young children should be raised bilingual.		

B Compare your answers with a partner's. Explain your opinions.

Research

A community includes our home, neighborhood, school, and city. Think about
the community in which you now live. How diverse is it? Find answers to the
following questions.

- Are there many people from different countries living in your community?
- What languages are spoken?
- What kinds of ethnic restaurants are available?
- Are there any ethnic stores such as bookstores and grocery stores?
- Do primary and secondary schools offer English as a second language classes?

Writing

Write two paragraphs. The first paragraph will define culture and provide clear
examples as supporting details. The second paragraph will examine cultural
diversity within your community. How evident is this diversity (or lack of diversity)
in your everyday life?

Connecting to the Topic

Read the definition of *globalization*, and then discuss the following questions with a partner.

> **globalization** (*n*) the development of closer economic, cultural, and political relations among all the countries of the world as a result of travel and communication becoming easy

1 How has globalization affected cultures in different countries?
2 How has globalization affected you personally?
3 What role has technology played in globalization?

Previewing and Predicting

> Reading a title and looking at any illustrations or graphic material can help you predict what a reading will be about.

A Read the title of Reading 4, and look at the photograph. What do you think this reading will be about? Put a check (✓) next to the topic or topics that you think will be included in the reading.

_____ A Multiculturalism
_____ B The impact of advertising
_____ C Western influence on global cultures
_____ D Immigration
_____ E The international success of Coca-Cola

B Compare your answers with a partner's.

While You Read

As you read, stop at the end of each sentence that contains words in **bold**. Then follow the instructions in the box in the margin.

One World: One Culture?

1   A culture is a rich source of language, arts, fashion, music, ideas, and food. It is at the core of group identity, and while cultures have similarities, each is unique. All cultures are constantly changing and adapting to new influences. Today, the pace at which cultures are changing is increasing due to a number of factors. One factor is immigration. As immigrants enter a country, they bring new cultures, which then interact with the existing cultures. A second factor is globalization. As trade and technology build increasingly complicated connections among countries, sociologists are debating the effect this globalization will have on individual cultures.

2   Globalization can be defined as a system of very complex connections among countries. It happens at both an economic and cultural level. Vast multinational corporations, such as Shell, Samsung, and Mitsubishi, develop intricate relationships with different countries across the globe. As these huge corporations spread throughout the world, some sociologists believe that a process known as *cultural leveling* will occur because the companies distribute identical products everywhere. Cultures that were once distinct will become increasingly similar. Every shopping mall in every country will have the same stores; clothes will be the same brands; Toyota advertisements will be on every television; and a McDonald's will be on every corner. The result, these experts argue, will be a bland global culture, in which the rich variety of cultures will be diminished as standardization takes **over**.

3   Other sociologists dismiss the idea that individual cultures are so easily threatened by globalization. For one thing, nations are proud of their unique culture and as such, take steps to prevent the erosion of their culture by another. Soon after Starbucks opened in the 587-year-old

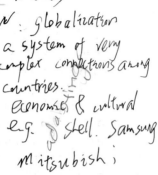

[handwritten margin notes:] thesis / CN: globalization / a system of very complex connections among countries. / economic & cultural / e.g. Shell, Samsung, Mitsubishi

Multinational companies sell their products all over the world.

Forbidden City of Beijing, the Chinese began to complain about this North American icon. The complaints were not about the quality of coffee; instead, people argued that it was inappropriate for Starbucks to be in such an important historical and cultural site. In the end, the Chinese government decided that Starbucks should not be in such close proximity to a historical site, and they closed the store. Starbucks remains in China, but in less culturally important locations.

4   Globalization not only influences culture by exporting products such as Starbucks but also by having a profound effect on individuals working for these multinational companies. Employees working for outsourcing services in India provide a clear picture of this effect. Outsourcing refers to the practice of sending some of the work of a company in one country to be done in another country. India provides 44 percent of outsourcing worldwide, largely due to its highly educated, English-speaking workforce, which is willing to work long hours for less money than workers in developed countries. Technology companies and financial institutions have set up numerous call centers throughout India. When American customers call their banks with questions, it is not unusual for them to speak to someone in Mumbai or Hyderabad. These companies want Indian employees to appear "American" to their customers. So they provide their employees with extensive training in living and behaving as Americans. In effect, to be successful at work, the employees have to adopt American culture.

5   It is often argued that globalization, and specifically outsourcing, has brought significant advantages to India. Its economy is strong, and a new Indian middle class is emerging. However, recent evidence is beginning to show that this progress is coming at a price. Before globalization, cultural changes happened slowly and incrementally. In contrast, the process of Americanization of employees in Indian call centers is extremely rapid. As Indian workers take on western names, wear western clothes, and even organize their workday around a western time zone, they can become alienated from their own culture. This results in what sociologists call a "hybrid culture": Indian by day, American by night. The high number of employees complaining of depression or quitting their jobs in these call centers reflect the stress of this **hybrid life**.

6   The media, with the United States as the dominant producer and exporter, has also had a profound effect on culture in other countries. Music, television, and movies communicate North American attitudes on sex, religion, gender, and politics. Because of this, the United States is sometimes accused of cultural bullying, or pushing other cultures to accept American values. This accusation seems unreasonable, however, since the demand for American movies and television has grown significantly in the last decade, resulting in huge profits for the American film **industry**. In 2003, domestic viewing brought in $9 billion according to the Motion Picture Association of America, while foreign revenue was $10.9 billion. By 2007, domestic revenue was almost unchanged at $9.6 billion, but overseas revenue had increased to over $17 billion. Demand for American television

WHILE YOU READ 2

Highlight the examples that provide context for the definition of *hybrid*.

WHILE YOU READ 3

Reread the previous two sentences. Highlight the contrast marker and the assessment marker.

programs has seen a similar increase. Ten years ago, most American programming shown overseas was relegated to late night viewing; today, American shows in many countries are broadcast in prime time when the largest numbers of television viewers are watching. This popularity of American media, therefore, indicates the flawed argument around this topic. The global public clearly wants access to American media.

In spite of global demand for western media, governments of some countries have attempted to limit it. For example, France has tried to protect French media against Hollywood's influence by restricting the number of American television shows and movies. In 2005, for example, a French movie was not allowed to enter a prestigious French competition because it was judged as "too American" despite being filmed in France with French actors and producers. The French organizers of the competition objected to the fact that the company was partly owned by Warner Brothers, a Hollywood company from California. However, the fact that American television shows, such as *CSI*, are more popular in France than in the United States shows that the French may support French filmmaking, but they still want the freedom to choose American shows.

Afghani rapper DJ Besho

8   Most countries welcome the influx of western media. Young people can listen to Lady Gaga in Bulgaria, surf western Internet sites in Vietnam, watch the television program *Friends* in China, and download the latest Hollywood movies in Afghanistan. Inevitably, the media communicates ideas and values of the culture of origin. This does not mean, however, that these values replace those of another **culture**. Rap music, for example, originated as an expression of African American street culture. Growing quickly in popularity, it spread throughout the United States and then globally. In 2006, rap came to Afghanistan in the form of a local artist, DJ Besho. While using the same distinctive rap beats, he raps in Dari, a local language, and he avoids the profanity that is characteristic of western rap. His songs speak of his love for Afghanistan. Like countless artists in different countries, DJ Besho has taken music from one culture and imprinted it with his own.

9   Culture is not static; it is living and dynamic. Indeed, the ability to change and adapt one's culture is an intrinsic part of human survival. So the influence of one culture upon another has been part of the story of humankind. What is new today is that globalization has increased the speed by which this process happens. However, the fear that increased internationalization will lead to the elimination of distinct cultures and the creation of one bland culture seems unfounded. It is more likely that as cultures interact, they will continue to adapt and change while maintaining their own unique **characteristics**.

WHILE YOU READ 4

Look back at the previous sentences. What idea does *this* refer to? Highlight it.

WHILE YOU READ 5

Which sentence best expresses the main idea of paragraph 9?
a) The second
b) The fourth
c) The last

Main Idea Check

Here are the main ideas of paragraphs 3–7 in Reading 4. Match each paragraph to its main idea. Write the number of the paragraph on the blank line.

_____ A Globalization has had a significant impact on employees working for multinational companies.

_____ B Increasing global demand illustrates the popularity of American media.

_____ C The fast pace of change has resulted in stressful conditions for Indian workers in outsourcing companies.

_____ D Countries are capable of protecting their cultures against globalization.

_____ E France has tried to restrict the influence of American media in France.

A Closer Look

Look back at Reading 4 to answer the following questions.

1 Which of the following are examples of cultural leveling as defined in Paragraph 2? Check all that apply.

   a People all over the world listen to Latin performers, such as Shakira and Enrique Iglesias, as well as their native pop music.

   b In Hong Kong and Vietnam, visitors find the same stores and products that they have in their home countries.

   c People from Africa to Asia to South America regularly buy McDonald's.

   d Reggae, a distinctive style of music from Jamaica, remains very popular today in that country.

2 Why does the writer provide the example of Starbucks in the Chinese Forbidden City?

   a It shows how globalization is a threat to distinct cultures such as the Chinese.

   b It demonstrates the strength of the Chinese government.

   c It shows the unpopularity of American companies in China.

   d It demonstrates that a country can limit some of the cultural effects of globalization.

3 Which statement is *not* true according to the reading?

   a The Indian workforce has benefitted financially from the practice of outsourcing.

   b Indian employees of outsourcing centers are comfortable with the rapid process of Americanization, which is part of their job.

   c Many workers quit their jobs at outsourcing centers because of stress.

   d The middle class in India is growing.

4 The influence of immigration, trade, and technology on culture continues to be one of slow and steady change. **True or False?**

5 Which statement best expresses the writer's point of view regarding the dominant role
   the United States plays in global media?
   a American media has had a negative effect on the cultures of other countries.
   b The increased demand for American movies and television shows is evidence of a
      global willingness to adopt American cultural values.
   c The United States uses its media as a means of cultural bullying.
   d Countries enjoy the benefits of American movies and television while at the same
      time they support media that reflect their own cultures.

6 The French government has successfully limited the amount of American television
   shows to French viewers. **True or False?**

Skill Review

In Skills and Strategies 5, you learned to identify points of view in a text. One
way to identify them is to look for view markers that introduce these views.
Recognizing different points of view will improve your academic reading.

A Reread the paragraphs in Reading 4 for each of the topics in the chart below.
Look for view markers. Then complete the statements in the chart about the
common point of view and the opposing point of view concerning the effect of
globalization on culture. Use view markers from the Language of Point of View on
page 85 to begin the opposing point of view. The first opposing point of view has
been started for you as an example.

TOPIC	COMMON POINT OF VIEW	OPPOSING POINT OF VIEW
The effect of globalization on cultures worldwide (Pars. 2 and 9)	Some sociologists believe that . . .	*Another point of view is . . .*
The effect of globalization on India (Par. 5)	It is often argued that . . .	
The exporting of American media (Par. 6)	The United States is accused of . . .	
American movies and television shows in France (Par. 7)	The French organizers of the competition objected to . . .	

B Compare your answers with a partner's.

Definitions

Find the words in Reading 4 that are similar to the definitions below.

1 huge; enormous (*adj*) Par. 2 *Vast*

2 having a lot of pieces arranged in a complicated way (*adj*) Par. 2 *intricate*

3 to spread over an area (*v*) Par. 2 *distribute*

4 separate; clearly different (*adj*) Par. 2 *distinct*

5 to reduce in size or importance (*v*) Par. 2 *diminished*

6 to decide something is not important or worth considering (*v*) Par. 3 *dismiss*

7 the gradual weakening of something (*n*) Par. 3 *erosion*

8 a symbol (*n*) Par. 3 *icon*

9 not right for a particular situation (*adj*) Par. 3 *inappropriate*

10 strong; extreme (*adj*) Par. 4 *profound*

11 to put someone or something at a lower rank (*v*) Par. 6 *relegated*

12 respected and admired (*adj*) Par. 7 *prestigious*

13 certainly (*adv*) Par. 8 *inevitably*

14 important principles and ideas (*n*) Par. 8 ~~characteristic~~ *value*

15 very many (*adj*) Par. 8 *countless*

Words in Context

Complete the sentences with words from Reading 4 in the box below.

alienated	brands	dynamic	influx	static
bland	debating	incrementally	profanity	unfounded

1 Some visitors to England find the local food to be rather _____ while Mexican food is often praised for its rich variety of spices and flavors.

2 Stories we heard about the dangers of living in the large city turned out to be _____; we feel very safe living there.

3 Art is an important form of cultural expression. Like culture, art is not _____; it is constantly changing.

4 When Ali first moved from Saudi Arabia to England, he felt very _____; the way of life in England was completely different from his life in his home country.

5 When singers in Islamic countries perform western songs, they often replace the _____ with different and less offensive words.

6 When we traveled to Vietnam, we were surprised to find the stores filled with the same _____ we find at home.

7 Educational experts are still _____ the advantages and disadvantages of bilingual education.

8 West African music is an example of a/an _____ style of music that is exciting and constantly changing.

9 When John started work, he learned that his salary would increase _____ over the next 5 years.

10 At the end of World War II, there was a/an _____ of refugees from all over Europe into the United States.

Academic Word List

The following are Academic Word List words from Readings 3 and 4 of this unit. Use these words to complete the sentences. (For more on the Academic Word List, see page 256.)

adapt (v)	distributed (v)	dynamic (adj)	inappropriate (adj)	interact (v)
distinct (adj)	dominant (adj)	erosion (n)	inevitably (adv)	unjustified (adj)

1 Different cultures have very _____ musical styles. Popular Egyptian music is very different from Chinese music, for instance.

2 Even when an immigrant carefully prepares for life in a new country, _____ there will still be surprises and even challenges.

3 Some people believe that the export of western music will lead to a/an _____ of the music from other less influential countries such as Morocco.

4 In Arab cultures, it is considered _____, even rude, to touch food with your left hand.

5 When the students first arrived in class, the teacher _____ a list of textbooks required for her course.

6 When Pierre moved from France to England, he found it quite easy to _____ because the lifestyles of the two countries are similar.

7 People use both verbal and nonverbal language in order to _____ with each other.

8 People often prefer to live in the city not only for employment opportunities but also because an urban lifestyle can be diverse, exciting, and _____.

9 The assumption that immigrants take jobs away from citizens is _____; in fact, newly arrived immigrants often take jobs that no one else wants to do.

10 In Chiapas, a region within Mexico, many people do not speak Spanish, the _____ language of the country. Instead, they speak languages native to their particular culture.

Critical Thinking

Reading 4 claims that immigration and globalization has influenced cultures in many parts of the world. It suggests that in some ways, cultures are becoming quite similar. However, the writer also argues that distinct cultures still exist.

Think about your own culture and the ways it has become more global or the ways it has remained unique. Complete the chart below. Then discuss your answers with a partner or the whole class. An example has been done for you.

PERSONALIZING

Thinking about how new information applies to your own life can help you understand a text better.

WAYS IN WHICH MY CULTURE HAS BEEN INFLUENCED BY OTHER CULTURES	WAYS IN WHICH MY CULTURE HAS REMAINED UNIQUE
I am Korean, but I eat different ethnic food, such as Mexican and Vietnamese.	*Young students should not look directly at their teachers.*

Research

Choose one aspect of your culture from the chart above, and find answers to the following questions.

- How has this specific aspect of your culture changed over the last generation?
- What has caused these changes?

Writing

Write two paragraphs about your research. The first paragraph will describe some traditional aspects of your culture, and the second will use an example to explain how your culture is changing.

Improving Your Reading Speed

Good readers read quickly and still understand most of what they read.

A Read the instructions and strategies for Improving Your Reading Speed in Appendix 3 on page 273.

B Choose either Reading 3 or Reading 4 in this unit. Read it without stopping. Time how long it takes you to finish the text in minutes and seconds. Enter the time in the chart on page 274. Then calculate your reading speed in number of words per minute.

Reduced Relative Clauses

> To add variety to their writing and to avoid having too many clauses that begin with *who*, *which*, or *that*, writers often use reduced relative clauses. Learning to recognize and understand these clauses will help your reading of academic English.

Examples & Explanations

Only a small percentage of **immigrants arriving** in the United States ever returned to live in their native countries.

Noun + verb-*ing*. To understand reduced relative clauses with this pattern, you can produce the full clause by making these changes:
- Before the verb *-ing*, add *that* or *who*.
- Drop the *-ing*.
- Give this verb the tense of the other verb(s) in the sentence.

*Only a small percentage of immigrants **who arrived** in the United States ever returned to live in their native countries.*

Today's immigrants are following the **patterns established** by earlier immigrants.

Noun + past participle. To understand reduced relative clauses with this pattern, you can produce the full clause by making these changes:
- Before the past participle, add *that* / *who*.
- After *that* / *who*, add *is* / *are* or *was* / *were*.

*Today's immigrants are following the patterns **that were established** by earlier immigrants.*

Many of **the drugs being used** in medicine today are extremely expensive.

Noun + *being* + past participle. To understand reduced relative clauses with this pattern, you can produce the full clause by making these changes:
- Before *being*, add *that* / *who*.
- After *that* / *who*, add *is* / *are* or *was* / *were*.

*Many of the drugs **that are being used** in medicine today are extremely expensive.*

The Language of Reduced Relative Clauses

Here are the markers for reduced relative clauses.

noun + verb -*ing*	***people** often **living** in poverty*
noun + past participle	***children** not **born** in the county*
noun + *being* + past participle	***immigrants being forced** to give up their culture*

↑
A negative or an adverb may follow the noun.

Strategies

These strategies will help you recognize and understand sentences that contain reduced relative clauses.

- Look for the markers of reduced relative clauses.
- Until you can easily understand reduced relative clauses, change them to full relative clauses. Use the Explanations shown on page 106.
- In most verbs, the past participle is the same as the simple past tense. So ask yourself, "Is this a main verb in the simple past or a past participle in a reduced relative clause?"

Skill Practice 1

In the following sentences, highlight the reduced relative clauses. Some sentences have more than one. The first one has been done for you.

1 The major problem facing health-care systems is the increasing cost of medical care.

2 In the nineteenth century, Europeans wanting to immigrate to the United States could do so as long as they were not criminals and did not have any infectious disease.

3 Stories told by new immigrants indicate the challenges they face as new arrivals to an unfamiliar land.

4 In the nineteenth century, the economic hardship created by the transition from agricultural to industrial economies was a major reason for European immigration to the United States.

5 Acquiring an adequate knowledge of English is one of the first tasks facing many immigrants coming to the United States and Canada.

6 Most democratic nations with diverse populations have laws intended to protect ethnic and religious minorities from discrimination.

7 In the 1980s, a large proportion of the immigrants settling in Los Angeles were from developing countries troubled by poverty and high unemployment.

Skill Practice 2

In the following sentences, highlight the reduced relative clauses. Then underline the verb of the main clause of the sentence. The first one has been done for you.

1 The economic hardships caused by the decline in agricultural economies created a huge increase in European immigration to the United States.

2 Economic hardship caused many nineteenth-century Europeans wanting a better life to immigrate to the United States.

3 The frustration resulting from an inability to communicate easily and effectively is a common experience among newcomers to the United States.

4 Research showing evidence of how second and third generations of recent immigrant groups learn a second language suggests that their experience is similar to that of nineteenth-century groups.

5 A complaint sometimes directed at immigrants is that they are unwilling to assimilate – to become full members of U.S. society.

6 One experiment showed that adults applying for jobs in England were less likely to be successful if they had non-English sounding names.

7 The sacrifices made by first-generation immigrants to the United States were sometimes greater than any immediate benefits they experienced.

Skill Practice 3

Rewrite the following sentences by replacing each reduced relative clause with a full relative clause. Some sentences have more than one relative clause. The first one has been done for you.

1 The government acknowledged that researchers had reported only 6 percent of the serious side effects experienced by patients in one type of gene therapy.

The government acknowledged that researchers had reported only 6 percent of the serious side effects that were experienced by patients in one type of gene therapy.

2 Gene therapy may be able to help people suffering from Parkinson's disease.

3 Refugees forced to leave their native countries often find it a long and difficult process to become legal immigrants in a new land.

4 Under a law passed in 1980, refugees are no longer counted in the annual total of immigrants admitted to the United States.

5 The procedures outlined by the National Institutes of Health are intended to make sure that researchers follow the rules requiring them to report all negative side effects observed in clinical trials.

Connecting to the Topic

Read the definition of *discrimination*, and then discuss the following questions with a partner.

> **discrimination** (*n*) the treatment of a person or a particular group of people in a way that is worse than the way people are usually treated

1 What is the most culturally diverse place you have ever lived in? Did people live in harmony with each other, or was there any type of conflict? Explain your answer.

2 Which group or groups of people are most often victims of discrimination in the world today?

3 Why do you think some people discriminate against other groups of people?

Previewing and Predicting

> Reading the title and section headings in a reading and looking at any illustrations and graphic material is a quick way to predict what a reading will be about.

A Read the title and section headings in Reading 5, and look at the photographs and the graph. Think of some questions that you expect will be answered in the reading. Then put a check (✓) next to the questions that are most like your questions.

_____ A What are some causes of discrimination?

_____ B Which groups of people in the world may be victims of discrimination?

_____ C Is it difficult to stop discrimination once it starts?

_____ D What are some countries doing about discrimination against older people?

_____ E What are some official regulations that help victims of discrimination?

_____ F Is there generally more discrimination against women or against men?

_____ G What are some of the consequences of discrimination?

B Compare your answers with a partner's. Discuss the reasons for your choices.

While You Read

As you read, stop at the end of each sentence that contains words in **bold**. Then follow the instructions in the box in the margin.

The Challenge of Diversity

I. The Roots of Discrimination

1   Migration has altered the character of almost every country in the world. Many nations that once had relatively homogeneous populations have become complex multicultural societies, and maintaining racial and ethnic harmony in those societies has become a considerable challenge. Often, the lack of understanding among people of different backgrounds has resulted in prejudiced attitudes and discriminatory behavior.

2   Sociologists generally define prejudice as a set of irrational judgments and bias about a certain group of people based only on their membership in that group. In today's world, some races, ethnicities, religions, and nationalities have become common targets of prejudice. Discrimination grows out of this prejudice and refers to the unequal treatment of people based on their group.

3   Discrimination generally increases in environments where the issues of cultural identity and economic security are at stake. This correlation is clearly evident in the experiences of indigenous people, long-time resident minority groups, and new **immigrants**.

II. Discrimination Against Indigenous People

4   Indigenous people are the descendants of the first people to inhabit a country or region prior to colonization. There are approximately 370 million indigenous people in the world today, and they are spread among 70 countries. Although their pasts are markedly different, what all indigenous people share is a history characterized by disruption of their ways of life caused by outsiders who arrive to establish new lives. Serious conflicts have arisen from cultural misunderstanding and the settlers' desire for land and other key natural resources. The experiences of indigenous people demonstrate how cultural clashes and discriminatory policies beginning hundreds of years ago can still have a detrimental effect on indigenous people's lives **today**.

5   The experience of Native Americans during the California Gold Rush (1848–1855) is just one example of the destructive effect of cultural conflict and competition on indigenous people. When gold was discovered in California, an estimated 300,000 people flocked there to seek their fortune and ensure their economic security. The 150,000 Native Americans in the area were vastly outnumbered. The mostly white, uneducated miners had no understanding of the indigenous people's traditions and relationships to the land. The native people were seen as an obstacle to the mining process and blamed for the disappointments and failures the miners encountered in their search for gold. Prejudice led to violence, and thousands of Native Americans were massacred. The U.S. government then forced Native Americans to move to specific areas of land, called reservations, for

WHILE YOU READ **1**

Look back at paragraph 3 to find the continuing idea marker *This correlation* refers to. Highlight the earlier idea.

WHILE YOU READ **2**

Look back at the previous two sentences to find two cause-and-effect relationships. Highlight the cause in each sentence.

Many Native Americans were forced from their lands during the California Gold Rush.

protection. However, reservation land was of poor quality for farming and was often contaminated with mercury, a poisonous substance used by the miners – a condition that persists to this **day**.

6   There are over half a million Native Americans living throughout the United States today, and about one-third live on reservations. The dispossession of their resources, along with inadequate social and economic support, has resulted in serious problems for Native American societies. Their problems are similar to those of other indigenous people, such as the Inuit in Canada, Aboriginal people in Australia, and the Maya in Guatemala. These and other indigenous groups often suffer from a higher degree of unemployment, less access to social services, and less political representation compared to other **groups**.

III. Discrimination Against Resident Minorities

7   There are numerous examples of prejudice and discrimination toward minority groups – especially visible minorities. Visible minorities are groups of people who are easily identifiable because of the color of their skin, their facial characteristics, their style of clothing, or their lifestyle and behavior. The effect of the prejudice and discrimination is the same for all visible resident minority groups: it impedes their social and economic integration and advancement.

8   In countries where the dominant population is white, people of African descent continue to suffer from the socioeconomic effects of discrimination. Unemployment rates in North America and Western Europe are a good indicator of this **situation**. In the United States, for example, despite the fight against workplace discrimination by the Equal Employment Opportunity Commission (EEOC), the unemployment rate among African Americans is disproportionately high compared to whites. In 2011, the

WHILE YOU READ 3

Look back at this sentence and highlight the reduced relative clause.

WHILE YOU READ 4

Look back at this paragraph and highlight the cause-and effect-marker. Then highlight the cause.

WHILE YOU READ 5

Look back at the previous two sentences to find what the continuing idea marker *this situation* refers to. Highlight the earlier idea.

Figure 2.4 U.S. Unemployment Rate by Race

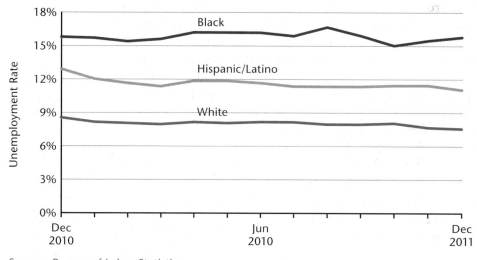

Source: Bureau of Labor Statistics

unemployment rate for whites fell from 8.5 percent to 7.5 percent, whereas it remained at 15.8 percent for blacks. Unemployment rates in Europe show similar trends. For instance, in 2012 in the United Kingdom, half of young black males (16–24 years old) didn't have jobs – roughly double the unemployment rate for whites. During an economic downturn, blacks are even more vulnerable because they become victims of additional discrimination, that is, discrimination against the unemployed. Employers are often reluctant to hire anybody who has been out of work for a long time.

9   The Roma people are another visible minority that has been victimized by years of deep-rooted prejudice and discrimination. The estimated 10 million Roma in Europe constitute its largest minority. The Roma originally migrated from Asia, with large numbers going to Eastern and Central Europe. For hundreds of years, their distinct nomadic lifestyle and culture have caused tension between them and the more stationary resident **populations**. Many Roma live in segregated, substandard housing, where they face the constant threat of possible eviction. Most are uneducated and unemployed.

WHILE YOU READ ⑥

Use context to figure out what *nomadic* means. Which strategy helped you?
a) Definition
b) Example
c) Contrast

The Roma are a visible minority.

10   In recent years, human rights groups have been putting pressure on governments to improve the plight of the Roma. This has led to more job training programs, better access to education, and increased political representation; however, there is still a long way to go. The negative stereotypes of the Roma that pervade European society still constitute a major obstacle to their integration into mainstream society. Such stereotyping may result in more discrimination and the continuing exclusion of the Roma from the economic, social, and political life of their countries.

The wearing of headscarves by Muslim women in Europe has caused controversy.

11   At times, something particular about a minority group creates controversy. In Europe, some Muslim women wear headscarves – *hijab* in Arabic. This highly visible article of clothing has sparked a great deal of controversy, and in France, the debate has been particularly heated. In 2004, a French law banned the wearing of all visible religious symbols, including the *hijab*, in state schools. At that time, most of the French public supported the ban, and agreed with the government's view that in a secular country, religion should be a private matter. According to this thinking, the ban would have a unifying effect since it would help prevent the splitting up of society into ethnic **communities**. It would better facilitate the integration of Muslims into French society. Critics of the ban argue, however, that it violates an individual's freedom of expression. They see it as discriminatory because it forces young Muslim women who choose to wear the *hijab* to leave state schools and attend private ones where the wearing of religious symbols is permitted. Furthermore, critics of the ban believe that it is an obstacle to the integration of Muslims into French society – just the opposite of what the government claims it intends to accomplish.

WHILE YOU READ 7

Look back at the previous two sentences to find out what the continuing idea marker *this thinking* refers to. Highlight it.

IV. Preferential Policies

12   There is no doubt that hundreds of years of racial and ethnic prejudice and discrimination have held back some minority groups both socially and economically. In order to help rectify these inequalities, some countries have instituted preferential policies with the goal of promoting equal opportunity for all in education, employment, business, and political life.

13   The preferential policies currently being used in India were established largely to benefit the **Dalit**. As members of the lowest group in the caste system (i.e., India's system of social stratification), the Dalit traditionally have been limited to segregated housing and schools and menial jobs. The preferential policies aim to increase opportunities by reserving a certain percentage of places for the Dalit in government-funded schools, government jobs, and political positions at the local, state, and national levels. Statistics show that, overall, these policies have helped many Dalit.

WHILE YOU READ 8

Use context and your knowledge of a related word to guess the meaning of *preferential*. Does it mean (a) harmful, (b) preliminary, or (c) advantageous?

14   Quota systems, such as the policies favoring the Dalit, are illegal in the United States, which outlaws any kind of race- or ethnicity-based numerical requirements in employment and **education**. The United States has used *affirmative action* programs to help remedy the inequalities that discrimination has caused for blacks and other minorities in housing, employment, and education. The goal of affirmative action is to ensure that minorities enjoy the same opportunities as all other people. For instance, it is legal for colleges and universities in the United States to consider race and ethnicity among the many factors that determine which students are selected for admission, scholarships, and financial aid.

15   Affirmative action is a highly controversial topic in the United States today. Those who oppose it claim it is a form of "reverse discrimination," which violates the rights of everyone, including the majority, to equal treatment under the law and decreases their opportunities for advancement. Opponents also argue that affirmative action ignores the importance of individual merit in a country that has always valued self-reliance. However, the weakness of this view is that it does not take into account the long history of discrimination in the United States and its **consequences**. For example, it seems unreasonable to ignore that, in the roughly 400-year history of blacks in North America, 245 years involved slavery, and 100 years involved legally sanctioned discrimination. Another questionable point about the critics' view is that it does not acknowledge the value of diversity within campuses and workplaces.

V. Discrimination Against New Immigrants

16   With the increasing mobility of the world's population, more and more people are choosing to live outside the countries where they were born. However, gaining permission to live and work in a destination country can be difficult, and would-be immigrants often face a host of governmental **barriers**. Such barriers, which usually reflect the attitudes of the native-born population, can discriminate against newcomers.

17   Stringent immigration requirements in the Netherlands suggest that attitudes toward immigrants have changed. For years, Dutch society was known for its promotion of multiculturalism and tolerance of different ethnicities. Yet, with the opening of internal borders in the European Union (EU) at the beginning of the twenty-first century, it became easier for both EU- and non-EU immigrants to move more freely within the EU. This ease of movement has resulted in particular concern in the Netherlands, where many Dutch people worry that a large influx of immigrants from non-EU countries would overwhelm the small country and affect its multicultural harmony. Therefore, many of the Dutch are generally in favor of the government's current stricter policies, which center on a set of tests that people wishing to immigrate to the Netherlands must take. The government claims the tests will encourage more rapid integration of new immigrants, and that is the hope of most Dutch people, who greatly value traditional Dutch cultural identity, social cohesion, and linguistic **unity**.

WHILE YOU READ 9

Use context to guess the meaning of *outlaw*. Which strategy or strategies helped you?
a) Definition
b) Similarity to familiar words
c) Other words in the context

WHILE YOU READ 10

Look back at the previous three sentences to find the contrast marker that shows where the writer's point of view begins. Highlight it. Then highlight the assessment marker and the writer's point of view.

WHILE YOU READ 11

Use context to guess the meaning of *a host of*. Does it mean (a) many, (b) few, or (c) unimportant?

WHILE YOU READ 12

Look back at the sentence and find the view marker. Highlight it. Then highlight the common view.

18   Japan is another country that tightly controls immigration, and its policies have led to a foreign-born population that is less than 2 percent of the total population. Its restrictive regulations are a subject of debate. Critics regard the controls as unwise at a time when Japan's population is aging and the number of working-age people is declining. They argue that continuing economic growth will depend largely on foreign labor. However, many Japanese are resistant to any loosening of the requirements. In a Japanese newspaper survey asking people how they felt about accepting more immigrants to "maintain economic vitality," 65 percent of the people polled opposed it. Those in favor of tight restrictions believe that cultural identity is more important than any impending economic problems.

19   In other developed countries, times of economic stress may lead some people to want to limit immigration. Their fear is that immigrants may be willing to work for lower wages, and therefore, take jobs away from native-born workers. This allegation is often combined with the charge that immigrants are likely to require government assistance and remain dependent on it for a long period of time. However, numerous studies contradict these concerns. In fact, the research suggests that immigrants actually contribute to economic growth. While official restrictions on immigration may ease feelings of economic insecurity among native-born people, the restrictions could, in fact, hinder a country's economic **growth**.

WHILE YOU READ 13

Look back at paragraph 19 to find the contrast marker. Highlight it. Then highlight the writer's point of view.

VI. Breaking the Vicious Cycle

20   Discrimination against newcomers and other minority groups, compounded by periods of economic stress, can lead to a vicious cycle, that is, a series of interrelated situations, which is hard to break. Consider, for instance, how an individual from a minority group could get caught in a cycle of poverty. That person may have to work while he or she goes to school and, therefore, may have less time for studies. If limited school time results in poor performance or inadequate education, it could lead to fewer job opportunities. If a person can only get a low-level, low-paying job, he or she will find it difficult to obtain the things necessary for a healthy, satisfying life. The majority society may evaluate a victim of poverty according to its own measures of cultural success and, therefore, consider that person to be inferior. This could lead to further prejudice and discrimination, which would limit the person's access to exactly what he or she needs most – better education, employment, and **health care**.

WHILE YOU READ 14

Which sentence expresses the main idea of paragraph 20?
a) The first
b) The third
c) The last

21   Prejudice and discrimination toward minority groups, such as indigenous people, resident minorities, and new immigrants, are being addressed with laws and policies; however, sanctions cannot change people's ways of thinking. A more harmonious multicultural world will be possible when there is wide recognition that individuals from different cultures are a great asset to a country. They are a valuable source of cultural enrichment, and as workers and consumers, they make an important contribution to the overall economic growth of nations.

Main Idea Check

For sections II–V of Reading 5, match the main ideas to three of the paragraphs in each section. Write the number of the paragraph on the blank line.

SECTION II: Discrimination Against Indigenous People

_____ A Their loss of natural resources as well as insufficient social and economic assistance have led to some troubling consequences for indigenous people.

_____ B What different groups of indigenous people have in common is the interruption of their lives by others who come to settle on native people's land.

_____ C One particular event in U.S. history shows how struggles over competing interests have hurt native people.

SECTION III: Discrimination Against Resident Minorities

_____ A There is much controversy, especially in France, about a particular article of clothing worn by many Muslim females.

_____ B In nations with predominantly white populations, blacks still experience discrimination and its socioeconomic consequences.

_____ C The lives of the Roma people have been improving in some ways; however, they are still victims of discrimination.

SECTION IV: Preferential Policies

_____ A The aim of preferential policies in the United States is to ensure that minority groups have equal opportunities as others in society.

_____ B People in the United States currently do not agree about the value of affirmative action.

_____ C India uses a special system to help the Dalit people.

SECTION V: Discrimination Against New Immigrants

_____ A Strict rules for immigrants hoping to go to the Netherlands reflect Dutch people's changing views.

_____ B Financial problems may lead to a decrease in immigration in some developed nations.

_____ C Governments do not always make it easy for people to move to another country.

A Closer Look

Look back at Reading 5 to answer the following questions.

1 According to the introduction, which two factors contribute to prejudice and discrimination in the world today?
   a People's misunderstanding of other cultures
   b People's lack of financial concerns
   c People's lack of a group to belong to
   d People judging others without knowing much about them

2 Why does the writer discuss the Native American experience during the California Gold Rush in paragraph 5?

   a To show how valuable gold was to the miners and the Native Americans

   b To show how indigenous people are connected to the land

   c To show how disappointing the Gold Rush was for miners and Native Americans

   d To give an example of the consequences of conflict on indigenous people

3 According to Figure 2.4, there were twice as many unemployed blacks as whites in the United States in 2011. **True or False?**

4 Which two statements best express two opposing views in the debate about the *hijab* in paragraph 11?

   a Private schools should not allow women to wear the *hijab*.

   b People should have the right to express themselves through their clothing.

   c Wearing the *hijab* will help women become part of French society.

   d People shouldn't be allowed to wear anything that indicates their religion in a non-religious society.

5 What is the writer's purpose in mentioning the Dalit in paragraph 13?

   a To show how the preferential policy in India works

   b To explain India's caste system

   c To criticize India's preferential policy

   d To evaluate India's preferential policy

6 Which two statements best express the ideas of supporters of affirmative action in the United States?

   a Affirmative action provides a good way to create multicultural environments.

   b Affirmative action programs ignore the skills and talents of individuals.

   c Affirmative action helps correct past injustices suffered by certain groups of people.

   d Affirmative action does not treat everybody equally.

7 Which statement is *not* true about Japan and the Netherlands?

   a They both have strict immigration policies.

   b Many people in both countries would like foreigners to assimilate quickly.

   c Many people in both countries would prefer an easing of immigration requirements.

   d Cultural identity is important to people in both countries.

8 According to the writer, what is the key to breaking the vicious cycle often begun by discrimination?

   a A widely shared realization of the value of cultural diversity

   b Additional laws against discrimination

   c An increase in the number and scope of preferential policies

   d A solution to global economic problems

Skill Review

In Skills and Strategies 6, you learned that writers often use reduced relative clauses to add variety to their writing and to avoid having too many clauses that begin with *who*, *which*, or *that*. Recognizing and understanding these clauses will help your reading of academic English.

In the following sentences from Reading 5, highlight the reduced relative clause, and underline the verb of the main clause of each sentence. Then rewrite the sentences on the blank lines by replacing each reduced relative clause with a full relative clause. Note that one sentence has two main clauses.

1 Sociologists generally define prejudice as a set of irrational judgments and biased views about a certain group of people based only on their membership in that group.

2 Although their pasts are markedly different, what all indigenous people share is a history characterized by disruption of their ways of life . . .

3 There are over half a million Native Americans living throughout the United States today, and about one-third live on reservations.

4 The preferential policies currently being used in India were established largely to benefit the Dalit.

5 Quota systems, such as the policies favoring the Dalit, are illegal in the United States . . .

Definitions

Find the words in Reading 5 that are similar to the definitions below.

1 having qualities that are the same (*adj*) Par. 1

2 showing an unreasonable dislike based on personal opinion (*n*) Par. 2

3 to kill large numbers of people, especially those who can't defend themselves (*v*) Par. 5

4 to slow something down (*v*) Par. 7

5 the process of mixing in and joining a society, often changing to suit their way of life, habits, and customs (*n*) Par. 7

6 the process of forcing someone to leave a place (*n*) Par. 9

7 fixed ideas, which are usually wrong, about someone (*n pl*) Par. 10

8 not having any connection with religion (*adj*) Par. 11

9 an arrangement of something in separated layers (*n*) Par. 13

10 the quality of being good and deserving praise or reward (*n*) Par. 15

11 extremely limiting or difficult (*adj*) Par. 17

12 a condition in which people are in close agreement; unity (*n*) Par. 17

13 a statement, made without giving proof that someone has done something wrong (*n*) Par. 19

14 to make something worse by increasing or adding to it (*v*) Par. 20

15 official orders (*n pl*) Par. 21

Synonyms

Complete the sentences with words from Reading 5 in the box below. These words replace the words or phrases in parentheses, which are similar in meaning.

banned	detrimental	impending	instituted	remedy
contradict	disruption	in favor of	irrational	resistant

1 Almost everyone was (in support of) _____ stricter airport security.

2 The new law (prohibited) _____ smoking in public parks.

3 The school (established) _____ a policy requiring students to wear uniforms.

4 Economists are warning people about the (approaching) _____ financial crisis.

5 Although he had never been on a ship, he had a/an (unreasonable) _____ fear of ocean travel.

6 The men were (opposed) _____ to having women on the team.

7 World leaders are working together to (correct) _____ the global economic problems.

8 One journalist predicted that immigration to Europe will decrease in the next decade; however, most population experts (say the opposite of) _____ this view.

9 The fire caused a huge (interruption) _____ in the family's life.

10 The stress of being out of work can have a / an (harmful) _____ effect on health.

Same or Different

The following pairs of sentences contain vocabulary from all the readings of this unit. Write *S* on the blank lines if the two sentences have the same meaning. Write *D* if the meanings are different.

_____ **1** Indigenous people have **endured countless hardships**.

Indigenous people have experienced a great many **disruptions** of their lives.

_____ **2** It may be difficult for some people in a **homogeneous** society to welcome people from other cultures.

Some people who value cultural **cohesion** may be **resistant** to the arrival of many people from other cultures.

_____ **3** Many people are worried about an **impending** economic crisis and the **profound** effect it is likely to have on the world.

Many people are concerned about the **colossal** challenges that global economic problems present.

_____ **4** **Opponents** of the immigration laws believe that the regulations are too **stringent**.

Regardless of the strictness of the immigration laws, most people are **in favor of** them.

_____ **5** In some **secular** countries, the wearing of religious symbols is **banned** in public schools.

In some nonreligious countries, there are **sanctions** against wearing religious symbols in public schools.

_____ **6** The families' **eviction** from their homes had a highly **detrimental** effect on their lives.

The families were **severely** affected by the experience of having been forced to leave their homes.

_____ **7** Their low **wages** and poor living conditions **fueled unrest** among the workers.

The workers were unhappy because they were **relegated** to low-wage jobs and **segregated** housing.

_____ **8** If a **destination** country **embraces** newcomers, it is more likely to have less strict immigration requirements.

Countries known for their **tolerance** of immigrants are less likely to **impede** the immigration process.

Academic Word List

The following are Academic Word List words from all the readings of this unit. Complete the sentences with these words. (For more on the Academic Word List, see page 256.)

authorities (n)	contradict (v)	diminish (v)	initially (adv)	persistent (adj)
bias (n)	core (n)	domestic (adj)	instituted (v)	secure (adj)
construction (n)	debating (v)	financial (adj)	integration (n)	stability (n)

1 In a global world, the economic problems of one country can cause a/an _____ crisis in the rest of the world.

2 When their country entered the war, many people left to find a more _____ place to live.

3 A preferential system for the Dalit was _____ shortly after Indian independence in 1947.

4 He had a/an _____ about urban life. Even though he had never lived in a city, he thought it would be unpleasant.

5 At the _____ of the Native American belief system is the idea that land is to be shared with one's tribe, not owned by individuals.

6 The _____ stopped him at the border and asked to see his passport.

7 Learning the language of the destination country can facilitate the _____ of a newcomer.

8 Because of its poor _____, the house constantly needed repairs.

9 Being unemployed for a long period of time can _____ a person's self-confidence.

10 His views on bilingual education have changed over the years; however, _____, he supported it.

11 She migrated to Canada because she viewed it as a country of economic and political _____.

12 Some people think it's boring to do _____ chores, such as cooking and cleaning.

13 Governors in the United States are still _____ the advantages and disadvantages of strict immigration laws.

14 Some people claim that affirmative action is not an effective way to diversify campuses; however, many university administrators _____ this view.

15 He finally got a reply from the immigration office because of his _____ phone calls.

Critical Thinking

In Reading 5, you learned about some of the controversies that have arisen in today's culturally diverse world.

A Read the controversial statements in the chart and think about your opinions. Are you in favor of or opposed to the idea expressed in each statement? Then check (✓) the boxes that reflect your opinions.

	IN FAVOR	OPPOSED
Students in public schools should be permitted to wear items that reflect their religions.		
Countries should establish preferential policies to help people who have been victims of past discrimination.		
All countries should have strict immigration requirements.		

B Compare your charts with a partner's. Then choose one issue to discuss, and share your opinions. Support your opinions with information from the reading as well as your own ideas.

Research

Research one kind of discrimination that is a problem in your country today. In addition to ethnic or racial discrimination, you may want to consider other forms, such as discrimination against women, older people, or people with disabilities. Find answers to the following questions:

- What kind of discrimination is a problem?
- Where does this kind of discrimination occur most often – at the workplace, in educational institutions, or in other environments?
- What is being done about the discrimination at the local, national, or international level?

Writing

Write two paragraphs about your research. The first paragraph will describe the discrimination, and the second will explain what is being done about it. Include your opinion about the effectiveness of the anti-discrimination efforts.

Exercise 1

Writers connect ideas between sentences in many different ways. The second sentence may:

  a contain a **correction** to a view that is reported in the first sentence
  b describe a **cause** of what is reported in the first sentence
  c add a **detail** or details to support the more general information in the first sentence

How does the second sentence in each pair of sentences below connect to the first sentence? Write *a*, *b*, or *c* on the line depending on whether it is a correction, a cause, or a detail.

_____ 1 One obvious quality possessed by most immigrants to the United States is their willingness to overcome challenges as they pursue the goal of a better life for themselves and their children. A significant proportion of them accept jobs that place them in a lower economic and social status than they had achieved at home.

_____ 2 Because immigrants continue using their native language, some native-born residents of the United States perceive them as not really committed to becoming fully integrated members of American society. Such a conclusion, however, assumes – erroneously – that immigrants who use both their native language and English cannot integrate into American society.

_____ 3 Between 1975 and 2012, the United States became a much more diverse society – ethnically and racially – than it had been in the previous 100 years. This development was the inevitable result of a shift from an immigration policy that was biased in favor of admitting Europeans to one that did not discriminate against people of other racial or ethnic backgrounds.

_____ 4 There is a widespread belief that all immigrant parents favor bilingual education for their children. Many of these parents, in fact, are opposed to bilingual education, especially when it aims to help children retain their native culture.

_____ 5 The Old Order Amish are often cited as an obvious example of an immigrant group that has successfully resisted assimilation into mainstream American society. For two centuries, they have retained their native language and preserved their religion and culture by selecting marriage partners from inside their communities and by limiting contact with the English-speaking world.

Exercise 2

Make a clear paragraph by putting sentences A, B, and C into the best order after the numbered sentence. Write the letters in the correct order on the blank lines.

1 In 1965, the U.S. Congress approved major changes to the Immigration and Naturalization Law. _____ _____ _____

| **A** In addition, it gave priority to admitting the immediate family of recent immigrants. | **B** These two features of the law have significantly increased the ethnic diversity of the United States. | **C** The new law eliminated the bias in favor of immigrants from Europe. |

2 Why do today's immigrants still follow the patterns established by earlier European immigrants and tend to settle disproportionately in a few urban areas of the United States? _____ _____ _____

A The primary reason is that immigrants perceive the ethnic communities in these areas as a source of support in the transition to a new life.

B These new immigrants inevitably tend to move to areas of the country in which they already have a network of family support.

C A second reason is that present immigration policy gives preference to admitting relatives of immigrants already in the United States.

3 There is a belief among some Americans that today's immigrants are not as committed to becoming fully integrated Americans as earlier immigrants were. _____ _____ _____

A In this process, the clear pattern is that the first generation acquires only some English, but their children and grandchildren will be native speakers of English.

B As evidence for this conclusion, they cite the tendency of first generation immigrants to retain their native languages for use in private and in public.

C Their claim, however, is unwarranted because it does not recognize what research has demonstrated about the process of adopting a second language as one's primary language.

4 Results of public opinion polls show that a large majority of Americans believe that immigration should be reduced or maintained at the existing level. _____ _____ _____

A This misperception suggests a more likely explanation for the poll results: The public is opposed to illegal immigration, not immigration in general.

B This claim, however, is questionable because other poll results have revealed the mistaken belief among many Americans that most immigrants arrive illegally.

C According to people seeking a change in immigration policy, these results reflect strong public opposition to immigration in general.

5 One possible cause of bias against a minority group is that the majority community does not have correct information about the minority group. _____ _____ _____

A The assumption, however, ignores considerable evidence that supplying such objective information is not enough to reduce the prejudice directed against the minority group.

B This causal connection might lead us to assume that we can remedy the bias by simply providing the majority group with correct information that contradicts their prejudices.

C In fact, these biases are likely to persist until members of the groups actually get to know each other by working and socializing with each other.

pronunciation

words   vocabulary

aspects of language acquisition

tones multilingualism

grammar

rhythm

rules

patterns

learning

sounds

use

ASPECTS OF LANGUAGE

SKILLS AND STRATEGIES

- Identifying the Thesis of a Reading
- Definition and Classification
- Passive Sentences

Identifying the Thesis of a Reading

In Skills and Strategies 1, you learned that each paragraph has one main idea, which consists of the topic and the writer's claim about the topic. Like paragraphs, a whole reading (an academic text, article, essay, etc.) usually has one *central* main idea – the thesis. Usually writers clearly state the thesis at the end of the introductory paragraph or paragraphs of a reading, and the main ideas of all of the paragraphs in the reading generally contribute to the thesis. It may be repeated in a new way in the final paragraph. In addition, each paragraph has a function and a specific relationship to the thesis. Understanding the thesis of a reading is an important academic skill.

Examples & Explanations

These are the main ideas from the six paragraphs of a whole reading:

① With 1.5 billion speakers, English is now a global language, but the numbers are not the most important issue.

② Languages become global when they gain official status in many countries.

③ Languages become global when they gain favored foreign-language status in many countries.

④ English is an official language in many countries that have no native speakers of English, and it is the most widely studied language in the world.

⑤ A large number of native speakers does not necessarily cause a language to become global.

⑥ The economic, military, and political power of the nations promotes their languages to global status.

The **topic** that connects the main ideas of all of these paragraphs is *global languages*. As you read, you should form a hypothesis about the writer's thesis: What does the writer want to say about global languages?

The main idea of paragraph 1 introduces the **thesis** with the topic and a **claim**, with English as an example.

The main ideas of paragraphs 2 and 3 are the ways in which a language may reach global status.

The main idea of paragraph 4 is that English is an example of the claims made in paragraphs 2 and 3.

The main idea of paragraph 5 is the common view: a factor that readers might think is important but the author claims is not.

Paragraph 6 provides the most fundamental reason for the global status of a language.

Together, the paragraphs support the writer's primary **claim**: *A language attains global status, not because of the number of its speakers, but because of the power of the nations in which its native speakers live.*

The main idea in paragraph 6 restates the central main idea – the thesis – that the writer wants to express in this reading.

Strategies

These strategies will help you identify the thesis of a whole reading.

- As you begin to read, ask yourself: *What is the topic?* The title often can help you decide.

- What claim do you think the writer will make about that topic? In other words, what do you think the thesis will be?

- Think about the main ideas of each paragraph that you read. Are they all related to this topic and the thesis?

- Pay attention to the first, second, and last paragraphs in the reading. Writers often state or restate the thesis of the reading in one of these places.

Skill Practice 1

Read the following lists of main ideas of each paragraph of a reading. Highlight the topic of the reading for each list. Then read the four possible claims below. Circle the claim you think best expresses the thesis of the reading.

1   Language and Machines

① Machine translation uses software to translate sentences from one language to another.

② Machine translation has a long history.

③ Early machine translation programs translated word for word.

④ Word-for-word translations are not satisfactory because they do not produce very natural texts.

⑤ New methods of machine translation are different because they rely on huge databases of real language samples.

⑥ Machine translation has improved a lot in the last few decades.

⑦ Humans often still have to clean up machine-translated texts.

    a The crucial difference between machine translation of the past and machine translation today is the use of massive databases.

    b There have been tremendous improvements in machine translation in recent years.

    c Machine translation has improved a lot, but it still usually requires human involvement.

    d It is still better to use human translators than machine translators because machines cannot really understand language.

2   Signed Languages

① Signed languages use facial expressions, as well as hand and body positions and movements, rather than sounds to express meaning.

② Signed languages are equivalent to spoken languages in their ability to express a wide range of meaning.

③ Signed languages have their own grammars.

④ Signed languages are not spelled-out spoken languages.

⑤ Signed languages are not related to the spoken languages of the communities in which they are used.

⑥ Signed languages have arisen in deaf communities for centuries.

    a Signed languages are fully expressive, independent, natural languages.

    b Signed languages are just like spoken languages.

    c All deaf people learn signed languages.

    d Signed language is the easiest way for deaf people to communication with one another so it is important for deaf children to learn it.

Skill Practice 2

Ⓐ **Read the following lists of main ideas of each paragraph of a reading. Highlight the topic of the reading for each list. Then write the claim that the writer is making about the topic on the blank line.**

1   **Extraordinary Language Learners**

① A polyglot is a person who can speak many languages.

② One of history's most famous polyglots, Emil Krebs, knew more than 100 languages.

③ Scientists believe that polyglots' brains are different than the brains of people who speak just one or two languages.

④ Some polyglots, called *language savants*, also have cognitive or mental disabilities.

⑤ One famous language savant, "Christopher," can read, write, and speak more than 15 languages, but he has trouble with life skills like shaving.

⑥ In 2004, the British language savant, Daniel Tammet, surprised the world by learning Icelandic after one week of study.

⑦ The abilities of language savants remain a scientific mystery.

Claim: _____

2   **"He said, she said"**

① Deborah Tannen, a language researcher, has studied communication between men and women.

② She claims that men's and women's communications styles differ in basic ways.

③ When men communicate with each other, they compete; when women communicate, they are more likely to offer each other support.

④ Men are more likely to offer advice; women are more likely to offer understanding.

⑤ Women stress compromise and avoid conflict; men do not try to avoid conflict.

⑥ These differences in style can often lead to misunderstandings.

⑦ Tannen admits these are generalizations but believes they reflect real differences.

Claim: _____

B Reread the paragraph main ideas. If one of them is like your claim statement, highlight it.

Skill Practice 3

A Read the following short text. As you read the first paragraph, think about what you think the thesis of the text will be. As you continue reading, decide if the rest of the text confirms this.

The Secret Language of Twins

Many children make up secret communication codes, but few of them can match cryptophasic twins. Cryptophasia is the secret language of twins. Parents of twins have often observed that their children seem to share a private language, but recently cryptophasia has been the focus of scientific research. Scientists say that it is a fascinating topic but that the secret language can create problems for the children who use them.

Scientists claim that cryptophasia emerges because twins spend so much time together. Compared to non-twins, twins spend more time with each other and less time with adults or other children. Twins imitate each other's speech and reinforce each other's invented words. Most children are motivated to learn the language around them so they can communicate with others and so they can get what they want, but for twins, there is less motivation to learn the language that the people around them are speaking.

Researchers who have studied twin language say it is usually very simple and also variable. For example, verbs, nouns, and adjectives may not appear in a consistent order; the twins just put the most important word first. The structure of twin languages may not resemble the structure of the adult language around them, but most of the words are based on the words the twins hear. The language is adequate for the twins to communicate about their child world, but it would probably not be sufficient for all the communication needs of an adult world.

There is concern that cryptophasia prevents twins from learning the language they will need as adults. Researchers also worry that the isolation created by their secret language means that twins don't make friends with other children, and they don't learn how to interact and behave appropriately. Scientists who have studied cryptophasia advise parents with twins who create their own language to encourage them to communicate in the language of the community and to get help from an expert if the twins do not make progress.

B With a partner, discuss what you think the thesis of the text is and how the main ideas in later paragraphs support this thesis.

C Review the first paragraph. Do any of the sentences include the thesis you discussed with your partner in Step B? If so, highlight the sentence.

Connecting to the Topic

Discuss the following questions with a partner.

1 Do you think babies can understand language before they can speak? Why or why not?

2 At what age do you think language learning begins?

3 Think about how you began to learn your *second* language. Do you think babies begin the process in the same way? Explain your answer.

4 How do people become bilingual (able to speak two languages well)?

Previewing and Predicting

Reading the title and first sentence of each paragraph is a quick way to predict what a reading will be about.

A **Read the title and the first sentence of each paragraph in Reading 1. What do you think this reading will be about? Put a check (✓) next to the topic or topics that you think will be included in the reading.**

_____ A Research methods in the study of child language learning

_____ B A baby's first sentences

_____ C Bilingual education

_____ D Early bilingual language learning

_____ E Language learning before birth

_____ F How infants begin to understand the sounds of language

B **Compare your answers with a partner's.**

While You Read

As you read, stop at the end of each sentence that contains words in bold. Then follow the instructions in the box in the margin.

When Does Language Learning Begin?

1   By the time children have reached the age of about five, they have accomplished something that few of us give much thought to but is actually quite extraordinary: They have learned how to speak their native language. They have perfect pronunciation, and they have learned most of the grammar necessary to speak and understand their language. Language acquisition takes place regardless of whether the children are born into educated, prosperous families in a society that uses advanced technology or into uneducated, even illiterate, poor families in a developing country. It occurs regardless of the disparities in individual children's intellectual abilities or their motivation. It also begins far earlier than scientists once thought.

2   This remarkable achievement, which takes place without formal teaching, has fascinated scientists for centuries. Once children begin to verbalize, with words or simply with sounds, scientists can study the language acquisition process fairly easily. However, the more mysterious part of the process takes place before that time, when a baby begins to perceive the sounds of language and understand their connection to meaning. How do babies begin this language acquisition **process**?

3   Recent research indicates that this process begins before babies are even born. From inside the uterus, fetuses cannot hear individual sounds, but they can perceive the rhythm patterns and tones of the language that they hear. Once they are born, babies use this fetal auditory experience to accomplish three crucial tasks. First, they recognize their mother's voice; second, they distinguish between language sounds and non-language sounds; and third, they differentiate between basic contours of their own language – the rhythm and tone patterns – and those of other languages. They can do all of these things within days of birth.

(within days of birth)

WHILE YOU READ 1

What do you think the topic of this reading is?
a) How babies learn language
b) The earliest stages of language learning
c) The most important factors in language learning

Children recognize their mothers' voices very early.

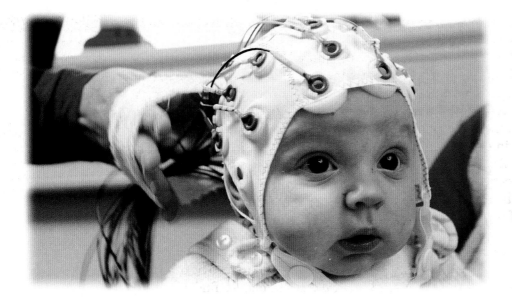

Scientists use brain imaging to analyze child-language development.

4   We know they can do **these things** because over the last 20 years, researchers have developed several techniques to assess these abilities in infants who are only a few months old or even younger, The two most widely used measures have been heart rate and sucking. For example, when babies recognize the voice of their mothers, their heart rate increases. When they hear a novel sound, they become more alert, and their sucking action gets stronger. Recently, researchers have also utilized brain-imaging techniques, which show how and where blood is flowing through the brain, indicating the focus of a baby's attention.

5   The results of this research make it clear that babies perceive and recognize the rhythm and tones of their own language from the moment of birth, and perhaps even more surprising, they reproduce these patterns in their cries. A study that compared the cries of newborn German and French babies found that their cries matched the contours of the language they heard around them.

6   In the acquisition process, infants first perceive these basic sound contours, and then they decipher the differences among specific sounds. For example, infants in English environments must learn that *t* and *d* are different sounds. By about six months, they can perceive these differences, but they can also perceive differences between sounds that are not part of their own language. For example, other languages, such as Korean, Hindi, and Thai have two kinds of *t* sounds. One is similar to the English *t*, and the other one is slightly different, but the difference is meaningful in those languages. At six months, babies raised in an English-speaking environment can perceive this difference without effort. For this reason, one researcher has referred to infants as "citizens of the world." At this age, they have the potential to learn any language. Adult English speakers, on the other hand, no longer have this universal potential. As a result, they have difficulty distinguishing between these two sounds; they hear them

WHILE YOU READ 2

Look back in paragraph 3 to find what *these things* refers to. Highlight the earlier idea that this continuing idea marker refers to.

all simply **as *t***. They may eventually be able to learn this distinction, but it will take considerable effort.

7   By their first birthday, babies become more like adults. Most of them will only be able to distinguish among the sounds that are important for their own language. Language researchers explain these changes in terms of brain development. When babies learn something new, connections between neurons, or nerve cells, are **formed**. The more often the babies use this new information, the stronger these connections become. So, as babies in an English environment hear the language around them, the English connections grow stronger.

8   Bilingual babies are a special case in that they can distinguish among the sounds of two different languages at the same time. In order to achieve this, babies have to be exposed to the sounds of the two languages when they are young. Some child language researchers wanted to find out how much of a second language babies would need to hear in order to establish and maintain the necessary neural connections. To find out, they exposed babies who were growing up in an English-speaking environment to Mandarin Chinese when they were 9 months old. A native speaker of Chinese talked with them for just an hour a week for 12 weeks. Even though the babies were exposed to Mandarin for just a short time, they could distinguish among the sounds of Mandarin, an ability they retained when they were tested again at 14 months.

9   There was one more remarkable finding in this study. The researchers had divided the babies into three groups. One group had Chinese-language sessions with a live person, one group watched the sessions on a television screen, and a third group heard the sessions on an audio recording. Only the babies who interacted with a human being learned to distinguish the sounds of Chinese. These findings suggest that learning a language is not just about making connections between neurons; it is also about making connections between human **beings**.

WHILE YOU READ 3

Look back through the last two sentences to find a cause-and-effect relationship. Highlight the effect.

WHILE YOU READ 4

Look back and highlight the words and phrases that can help you figure out the meaning of *neurons*.

WHILE YOU READ 5

Think about the topic of the reading again. Was your first guess correct? If not, circle a new choice.
a) How babies learn language
b) The earliest stages of language learning
c) The most important factors in language learning

Research shows babies learn language by interacting with people, not by watching TV.

Main Idea Check

Match the main ideas below to five of the paragraphs in Reading 1. Write the number of the paragraph on the blank line.

_____ A Brain development can explain the decline of babies' ability to distinguish between sounds that are not in their own language.

_____ B Scientists have used several different techniques to study infant perception of language sounds.

_____ C Language learning begins before birth.

_____ D Human interaction is necessary for language acquisition.

_____ E At the age of six months, infants are able to distinguish among sounds in any language.

A Closer Look

Look back at Reading 1 to answer the following questions.

1 Which of the following factors are important in child language acquisition?
   a Level of education of the family
   b Motivation
   c Intelligence
   d All of the above
   e None of the above

2 Babies can understand words even before they are born. **True or False?**

3 Which of the following specific abilities do researchers believe infants have soon after birth? Circle all that apply.
   a They can imitate the sound patterns of their language when they cry.
   b They can distinguish between language and non-language sounds.
   c They can distinguish between different sounds in any language.
   d They can recognize their mothers' voices.

4 How do researchers know that infants can perceive differences among sounds? Circle all that apply.
   a An increased heart rate indicates the infant has noticed something new.
   b Scientists can follow the connections between neurons.
   c Special sensors in an infant's ears can detect what he or she hears.
   d Images of blood flow can show the infant's brain activity.

5 Why are infants sometimes called "citizens of the world"?
   a Their cries can match any language that they hear.
   b Many infants grow up to be bilingual.
   c They can pronounce the sounds of many different languages.
   d They have the potential to learn any language.

6 Babies need a lot of exposure to a language in order to establish and maintain neural connections for that language. **True or False?**

Skill Review

In Skills and Strategies 7, you learned that most readings have a central main idea – the thesis – that the writer wants to express. Identifying the thesis of a reading is an important academic skill.

A **Review Reading 1, and then answer the questions below.**

1 What is the topic of the reading?

_____

2 What claim is the writer making about this topic?

_____

3 State the thesis of the reading.

_____

B **Compare your answers with a partner's. Discuss any differences you find.**

C **Do any of the sentences in the first paragraph include the thesis of the reading? If so, highlight the sentence.**

D **Look back at your answers in the Main Idea Check. Then, with your partner, decide whether the main ideas in each of the paragraphs in the Main Idea Check support the thesis you discussed in Step B.**

Definitions

Find the words in Reading 1 that are similar to the definitions below.

1 remarkable *(adj)* Par. 1
2 financially successful *(adj)* Par. 1
3 babies before they are born *(n pl)* Par. 3
4 related to hearing *(adj)* Par. 3
5 new and different *(adj)* Par. 4
6 used something effectively *(v)* Par. 4
7 to copy *(v)* Par. 5
8 to figure out the hidden meaning of something *(v)* Par. 6
9 a difference between things that are similar *(n)* Par. 6
10 periods of time for a particular activity *(n pl)* Par. 9

Word Families

A The words in **bold** in the chart are from Reading 1. The words next to them are from the same word family. Study and learn these new words.

B Choose the correct form of the words from the chart to complete the following sentences. Use the correct verb tenses and subject-verb agreement. Use the correct singular and plural noun forms.

NOUN	VERB
accomplishment	**accomplish**
acquisition	acquire
exposure	**expose**
perception	**perceive**
retention	**retain**

1 As people reach their seventies and eighties, they often find it difficult to _____ new information.

2 When he lived in the Middle East, he _____ knowledge of both Arabic and Farsi.

3 Some people with special talents can learn a language after just a few weeks of _____ .

4 The two sounds were so similar that I could not _____ any difference.

5 She stayed home from work because she did not want to _____ others to her cold.

6 Teachers often worry about their students' _____ of skills during summer vacations. They think the students may forget what they have learned.

7 _____ of a second language is usually much easier for children than adults.

8 His proudest _____ was winning a 10-kilometer race when he was 40.

9 New techniques have allowed scientists to study infant auditory _____ .

10 Recently, scientists have _____ the goal of mapping human genes.

Critical Thinking

In Reading 1, you learned that neural connections are an important part of the learning process.

A Briefly define the term *neural connection*. Then, with a partner, discuss the following questions.

1. What are neural connections?
2. How are they formed?
3. How do they become stronger?
4. How might neural connections become weaker?

CLARIFYING CONCEPTS

Critical thinking includes exploring a concept in a text by restating it and applying it to a different context.

B You have learned about neural connections in language learning. With a partner, think of other areas of learning that might occur in the same way. What exposure would be necessary to establish these connections? Use your ideas to complete the chart. One example has been done for you.

AREA OF LEARNING	NECESSARY EXPOSURE
reading	print material

Research

You have learned that babies can distinguish between different sounds by the age of six months. Research some other milestones in child language development. Find answers to the following questions.

- When do most children begin to say their first words?
- When do most children begin to make sentences?
- When do most children begin to read?

Writing

Write two paragraphs about your research. Choose two milestones and write one paragraph about each.

Connecting to the Topic

Discuss the following questions with a partner.

1 Do you know more than one language? How well do you know it (or them)?

2 Choose one additional language that you know. How did you learn it? In school? At home?

3 When did you begin learning this additional language?

4 Have you found learning an additional language difficult? What aspects are the easiest? The hardest?

Previewing and Predicting

Looking at illustrations and graphic material (pictures, photos, charts, tables, or graphs) can help you predict what a reading will be about.

A **Read the title of Reading 2, and look at Figures 3.1 and 3.2. What do you think this reading will be about? Put a check (✓) next to the topic or topics that you think will be included in the reading.**

_____ A The difference between first and second language learning

_____ B The location of five senses in the brain

_____ C Right-handed people and left-handed people

__✓__ D The relationship between age and language learning

__✓__ E Language centers in the brain

_____ F Why language learning is critical for education

B **Compare your answers with a partner's.**

While You Read

As you read, stop at the end of each sentence that contains words in **bold**. Then follow the instructions in the box in the margin.

Learning a Language as an Adult

1   The question of how people learn an additional, or second language (L2), has received a great deal of attention from scholars. Their research has offered evidence for a number of conflicting claims about L2 learning. However, there is no dispute about one fundamental observation. It is possible, and quite common, for adults to achieve a high degree of success in learning L2 vocabulary, and even grammar. In their vocabulary and sometimes their grammar, they may become very much like a native speaker. The same degree of success is relatively rare in L2 pronunciation, however. Second language speakers' pronunciation is related to the age at which they are first exposed to the L2. This is the single best predictor of how closely their pronunciation will approximate the accent of native speakers. Speakers who were very young when they were first exposed to their L2 almost always have better pronunciation that those who were exposed at an older age. (See Figure 3.1.)

2   Results from a number of research studies offer evidence for the existence of this phenomenon. They support the basic rule that "younger is better in the long run." Older learners may begin with an advantage, presumably because they have superior cognitive abilities. However, eventually, younger learners always catch up and overtake older learners, especially in pronunciation. It is important to stress that this has been shown in *second* language contexts, that is, where learners are living in the L2 community and receiving constant exposure to the L2. The same

Figure 3.1 Critical Period for Language Learning

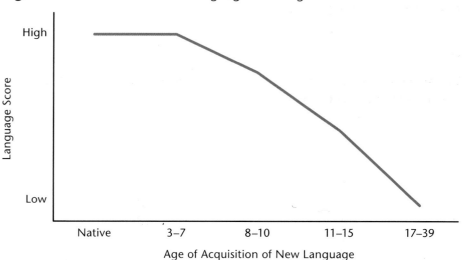

Source: TED Talks 2010: The linguistic genius of babies

results have not been demonstrated in situations in *foreign* language learning, where learners live in the first language community and their primary exposure to the L2 is in the **classroom**.

3   How have scientists accounted for the fact that adult learners rarely attain nativelike pronunciation in the L2? One explanation is the *critical period hypothesis.* This idea has a much broader application than L2 learning and extends to other animals and other kinds of learning. The hypothesis states that if an animal or human does not receive the necessary stimulation during a critical period of development, it will not develop a specific ability. For example, baby cats that do not receive visual stimulation during a particular period will grow up blind, although there is nothing wrong with their eyes. Baby birds that are not exposed to the song of their species will not develop normal songs. Their songs will sound different.

4   **These ideas** have important implications for language learning. Proponents of the critical period for language learning argue that complete acquisition of language is only possible before *cerebral lateralization* ends – about the age of twelve. Cerebral lateralization occurs when two hemispheres of the brain increasingly specialize in particular functions. (See Figure 3.2.) At the end of this process, control of most, although not all, language function is permanently located in the left hemisphere. The right hemisphere is responsible, among other things, for visual and spatial perception. When lateralization is complete, according to the theory, the critical period closes. This is the period during which most humans

WHILE YOU READ ❶

What do you think the topic of the reading is?
a) Second language learning
b) Comparison of second and foreign learning
c) Age and language learning

WHILE YOU READ ❷

Look back in paragraph 3 to find what *These ideas* refers to. Highlight the earlier ideas that this continuing idea marker refers to.

Figure 3.2 Functions of the Left and Right Hemispheres of the Human Brain

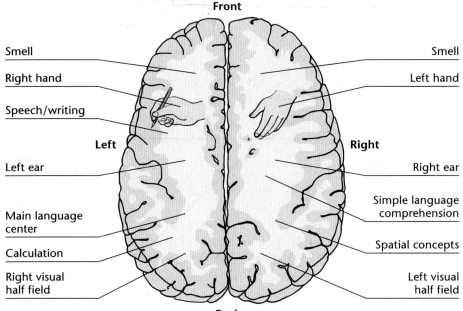

can achieve nativelike mastery of a language, particularly in the area of pronunciation.

5   There is not a lot of evidence for the critical period for first language learning because there are not many situations in which children have no exposure to language until they are 12 years old. There have been just a few cases of modern *feral children,* or children who have grown up away from adults and civilization. There is also one famous case of Genie, a child abused by her parents locking her in a room and never speaking to her. The authorities found her when she was 13 years old. Both in her case and in the case of feral children, the critical period hypothesis was supported: These individuals never fully mastered language. They acquired an extensive vocabulary, but their grammar and pronunciation were not **nativelike**.

6   There is more evidence for the critical period hypothesis for L2 learning than for first language learning. It seems to apply most strongly to pronunciation. It suggests that learners who wish to acquire a nativelike accent need to begin learning when they are children and that adult learners are

WHILE YOU READ 3

Look back and highlight the words and phrases that can help you figure out the meaning of *feral children.*

When a family immigrates to a new country, the children are far more likely than their parents to develop native-like pronunciation.

unlikely ever to attain that goal. Nevertheless, there are counterexamples. There are adult L2 learners who can pass as native speakers, and there are learners who, with extensive exposure to the L2 as children, are not nativelike in their L2 as adults. However, both of these are relatively rare. In addition, there does not seem to be a precise age at which complete mastery is no longer possible. The ability to pronounce the L2 like a native speaker does not disappear suddenly; instead, it declines gradually. For this reason, many L2 researchers prefer the term *sensitive period* to critical period.

7   It should be emphasized that these ideas do not justify an end to the teaching of L2 pronunciation. It is possible for learners to achieve very good pronunciation in the L2 through instruction, hard work, and practice. Second language learners can develop speech that is grammatical, expressive, and perfectly comprehensible. They do not need to sound like native **speakers**.

WHILE YOU READ 4

Think about the topic of the reading again. Was your first guess correct? If not, circle a new choice.
a) Second language learning
b) Comparison of second and foreign learning
c) Age and language learning

Main Idea Check

Match the main ideas below to five of the paragraphs in Reading 2. Write the number of the paragraph on the blank line.

_____ A Brain lateralization provides a possible explanation for the critical period of language acquisition.

_____ B The critical period is not limited to language; it applies to other skills and abilities as well.

_____ C Several cases of feral and abused children provide support for the critical period hypothesis.

_____ D The ability to pronounce a second language like a native speaker is related to the age at which learning begins.

_____ E Although adult second language learners may retain an accent, they can still develop comprehensible pronunciation.

A Closer Look

Look back at Reading 2 to answer the following questions.

1 Which of these statements does *not* accurately reflect the information in paragraph 2?
   a Adults have a cognitive advantage over children.
   b Children learn their second language faster than adults.
   c Second language learning success differs depending on learning context.
   d Children are more successful language learners than adults in the long run.

2 What does the *critical period hypothesis* propose?
   a Cognitive and perceptual abilities develop at specific times and in a specific order.
   b Animals need visual and auditory stimulus in order to survive.
   c Adults cannot learn languages as well as children.
   d There is a limited period during which the brain must receive stimulus in order to develop certain abilities.

3 All language functions are located in the left hemisphere. **True or False?**

4 What two facts about the experience of Genie and feral children provide support for the *critical period hypothesis*?
   a They did not have exposure to language during the critical period.
   b They lived without contact with adults during the critical period.
   c The never fully acquired their first language.
   d They acquired a normal vocabulary.

5 There are some adult second language learners who develop nativelike pronunciation. **True or False?**

6 Why do some scientists prefer the term *sensitive period* rather than *critical period*?

   a They are not really sure if the critical period applies to everyone.

   b People are especially sensitive to any exposure to a second language when they are children.

   c The loss of language learning ability is gradual rather than sudden.

   d Animals as well as human beings share this important developmental period.

Skill Review

In Skills and Strategies 7, you learned that most readings have a central thesis that the writer wants to express. Identifying the thesis of a reading is an important academic skill.

A **Review Reading 2, and then answer the questions below.**

1 What is the topic of the reading?

_____

2 What claim is the writer making about this topic?

_____

3 Is there a sentence that contains the thesis? If so highlight it.

_____

B **With a partner, match the function of each paragraph in the reading in the right hand column with the correct paragraph. Write the paragraph number in the left hand column.**

PARAGRAPH NUMBER	FUNCTION OF PARAGRAPH
6	Shows more specific application to *second* language learning
4	Provides scientific explanation for thesis
3	Shows broad application of thesis
1	Presents thesis
7	Discusses importance of main idea for teaching
2	Provides evidence for thesis
5	Shows specific application to language learning

Vocabulary Development

Definitions

Find the words in Reading 2 that are similar to the definitions below.

1 opposing (*adj*) Par. 1

2 argument (*n*) Par. 1

3 to be almost the same as (*v*) Par. 1

4 something that exists and can be seen and often is unusual (*adj*) Par. 2

5 most likely; most probably (*adv*) Par. 2

6 to reach the same place or standard as someone else (*phrasal v*) Par. 2

7 to go past someone or something (*v*) Par. 2

8 to reach; to stretch (*v*) Par. 3

9 something that causes another thing or person to become more active (*n*) Par. 3

10 related to seeing (*adj*) Par. 3

11 a group of animals or plants that have similar characteristics (*n*) Par. 3

12 complete control or understanding of something (*n*) Par. 4

13 wild (*adj*) Par. 5

14 to treat someone very badly (*v*) Par. 5

15 exact (*adj*) Par. 6

Words in Context

Complete the passages with words or phrases from Reading 2 in the box below.

attain	fundamental	implications	observation	scholars
counterexamples	hypothesis	in the long run	proponents	superior

1   U.S. students do not have a very good record in learning foreign languages.

_____ who study language learning claim that the _____
        a   b

problem with foreign language education in the United States is that children do not

begin learning when they are young. As a result, it is unlikely that many of them will

ever _____ advanced proficiency. _____ of foreign language
                    c   d

education argue that this lack of proficiency has negative _____ for the
                                                                                                        e

nation, especially in international business and government relations.

2   Educators often discuss the contributions of ability and hard work to school

performance. One _____ is that hard work is important, but
                                        f

_____ intelligence is even more important. These educators argue that
            g

people with _____ abilities usually perform better in school than people
                            h

who work hard but have average abilities. They admit, however, that this is simply a generalization and that it is always possible to find _____ to this
i
general _____.
j

Academic Word List

The following are Academic Word List words from Readings 1 and 2 of this unit. Use these words to complete the sentences. (For more on the Academic Word List, see page 256.)

acquisition (*n*)	attain (*v*)	distinctions (*n*)	fundamental (*adj*)	utilize (*v*)
approximate (*v*)	conflicting (*adj*)	exposure (*n*)	perceive (*v*)	visual (*adj*)

1 She listened to the teacher and tried to _____ his pronunciation.

2 _____ information is processed in both hemispheres of the brain.

3 There are _____ arguments about the best way to learn an additional language.

4 It is a common belief that language _____ becomes easier with the third and fourth language, but scientists are not sure that this is true.

5 Research has demonstrated that it is easier to _____ sounds in women's speech than in men's speech.

6 Language learning scholars _____ advanced technology in their research.

7 _____ to print material in the home, such as books and newspapers, is an important predictor of a child's reading performance.

8 Some people with extraordinary abilities can _____ a high level of proficiency in a new language after a very short period of study.

9 Speakers of English have difficulty hearing the _____ between tones in languages such as Chinese and Vietnamese.

10 Reading is a skill that is _____ to success in modern life.

Critical Thinking

Reading 1 discusses the earliest stages of language learning and the importance of early exposure. Reading 2 suggests some limitations on language learning, especially in learning the sounds of language.

APPLYING
INFORMATION

You use critical thinking skills when you apply information you have just learned to new situations.

Work with a partner. Based on what you have learned in Reading 1 and 2, what advice would you give the following people about what to expect from language learning experiences.

1 A married couple – he speaks English, she speaks Korean: They have a six-month-old baby, and they want her to become bilingual. They want your advice on what to do.

2 An Arabic-speaking high school student who will study at a university in Australia next year: He wants to know the best way to spend his time in his study of English.

3 The director of a school district's foreign language program: She wants to know when children should begin foreign language instruction.

4 The director of a government agency that prepares military and intelligence officers to work in other countries: The officers must be able to work in these countries as if they are native speakers. He wants your advice on language education for these officers.

Research

Research a case of a child who was raised in isolation, such as Genie. Find answers to the following questions.

- What were the circumstances of his or her childhood?
- What have researchers learned about language acquisition from this case?

Writing

Write two paragraphs about your research. The first paragraph will describe the person's childhood, and the second will describe the importance of this case to language learning research.

Improving Your Reading Speed

Good readers read quickly and still understand most of what they read.

A Read the instructions and strategies for Improving Your Reading Speed in Appendix 3 on page 273.

B Choose either Reading 1 or Reading 2 in this unit. Read it without stopping. Time how long it takes you to finish the text in minutes and seconds. Enter the time in the chart on page 274. Then calculate your reading speed in number of words per minute.

Definition and Classification

As you read academic textbooks, you will meet unfamiliar technical words and their definitions. You will also find that writers use classification to divide general concepts into a number of different types. Identifying and understanding texts that contain definitions and classifications will help your academic reading.

Examples & Explanations

Phonetics is the study of speech sounds made in human language.

Here the writer uses the verb *to be* to introduce the definition of the term *phonetics*.

Matter is defined as anything that occupies space and weight.

In this example, the verb phrase *is defined as* introduces the definition of *matter*.

National fertility rates and mortality rates (i.e., the number of births and deaths in a country per year) are used to predict future population growth.

Here two technical terms are defined by words that follow the marker *i.e.,* which means *that is,* and are enclosed in parentheses.

Research shows that there is a relationship between a healthy lifestyle and **cognitive ability, the ability** to think and to reason.

The writer explains the term *cognitive ability* by providing the definition in a noun phrase that follows the term. The noun phrase is always set off by a comma.

A hypothesis refers to an idea or explanation for something that is based on known facts but has not yet been proven.

The definition marker *refers to* introduces the meaning of the term *hypothesis*.

The Language of Definition and Classification

Here are some common definition and classification markers.

DEFINTION MARKERS		CLASSIFICATION MARKERS		
Verbs	Others	Verbs	Nouns	
to be	i.e.	to categorize	category	kind
to be called	in other words	to classify	class	part
to be known as	+ a comma between a technical term and its defining noun or noun phrase: ____, ____	to distinguish	component	section
to define		to divide	division	sort
to refer to		to group	group	type

Strategies

These strategies will help you recognize and understand texts that contain technical terms, definitions, and classification.

- Expect writers to use technical terms and to define them in a text.
- Look for definition markers. They will help you to identify the technical terms and their meanings.
- When you meet a technical term, highlight it and its definition. This will help you remember and understand the term.
- Look for classification markers. This will help you to identify the general term and its types.
- When you meet classifications, make notes in the margins to show the general term and its types.

Skill Practice 1

Read the following sentences. Highlight the technical terms and the definition markers. Underline the definitions. The first one has been done for you.

1 Cognates refer to words in two or more languages that share the same origin and have similar spellings and meanings.

2 Primary school teachers often find that although their students have good decoding skills (i.e., they use their understanding of letter-sound relationships to correctly pronounce written words), this does not necessarily mean they understand the text.

3 An ethnic group can be defined as a group of people who share the same ancestry and culture and who often live as a minority in a larger society.

4 The family is the most important influence in teaching children how to interact with one another and to become members of society, a process known as socialization.

5 Geographers often use toponyms, in other words, place names, as important clues about the social, historical, and physical geography of a place.

6 Acquiring linguistic competence (i.e. the rules that govern grammar, vocabulary, and pronunciation of a language) is, of course, an important part of second language learning, but it is also important to know how to adapt your speech to different social situations.

7 In the English language, intonation (i.e. changes in the tone or frequency of language) usually falls at the end of a sentence but rises at the end of a question.

8 Supporters of the whole language approach to teaching claim that students learn better by this approach than by phonics instruction, an approach that emphasizes teaching students how to sound out words.

Skill Practice 2

Read the following paragraphs. Highlight the general term and underline the classification markers. Then draw a diagram showing the classification. The first one has been done for you.

1   Nutritionists have determined that there are two main types of fats in food: saturated fats and unsaturated fats. Within unsaturated fats, we can distinguish between monounsaturated fats and polyunsaturated fats.

```
fats ─┬─ saturated
      └─ unsaturated ─┬─ monounsaturated
                      └─ polyunsaturated
```

2   Linguists who study phonetics distinguish between two approaches to speech sounds. One approach is to focus on the way speech sounds are produced by the speaker. This is known as articulatory phonetics. A second approach is to study the way in which speech creates waves of pressure that move through the air. This field of research is called acoustic phonetics.

3   Status is usually defined by sociologists as the position of an individual in relation to other members of a group. Scientists distinguish two kinds of statuses. An individual has ascribed status, regardless of his or her abilities and wishes. This refers to being born male or female and being born into a social class or racial or ethnic group. Achieved status, the other category, refers to the social position an individual reaches through choice, ability, and competition.

4   Psychologists studying motivation and its effects on achievement have identified two types of motivation. One kind is intrinsic motivation, the desire to perform a task successfully for its own sake. For example, answer these questions: Are you working hard in this class because you enjoy learning? If you had time, would you take more classes like this? If you answer "Yes" to these questions, then you are intrinsically motivated. The other type, extrinsic motivation, is the desire that results from outside incentives – the rewards or punishment that individuals may receive for doing or failing to do something. Are you working hard in this class to get a good grade or to be admitted to university so that you can get a good job later? If your answer to these questions is "Yes," then you are extrinsically motivated.

Skill Practice 3

Reread paragraphs 2–4 in Skill Practice 2, and highlight the definitions of the following terms.

1 articulatory phonetics   3 ascribed status   5 intrinsic motivation
2 acoustic phonetics   4 achieved status   6 extrinsic motivation

Connecting to the Topic

Discuss the following questions with a partner.

1 How would you make a polite request to borrow something, for example, a book, in English? In your native language?

2 Would your answers to question 1 be the same for a friend and a teacher?

3 Have you ever heard a second language learner making a request in your language that sounded strange or perhaps impolite? Explain your answer.

4 Do you think there are rules for doing things like making requests or saying *thank you*? Explain your answer.

Previewing and Predicting

> Reading the title and first sentence of each paragraph is a quick way to predict what a reading will be about.

A Read the first sentence of paragraphs 2–7 in Reading 3, and think of a question that you expect each paragraph to answer. Then choose the question below that is most like your question. Write the number of the paragraph next to that question.

PARAGRAPH	QUESTION
4	What is a *speech act*?
2	What is one explanation for miscommunication?
6	What knowledge is required for speaking appropriately?
7	What is the research evidence for cross-cultural differences in rules of speaking?
5	How do rules of speaking differ across cultures?
3	What are *rules of speaking*?

B Compare your answers with a partner's.

While You Read

As you read, stop at the end of each sentence that contains words in **bold**. Then follow the instructions in the box in the margin.

Rules of Speaking

1   Acquiring a second language involves learning many rules, including the rules that govern the grammar, vocabulary, and pronunciation of a language. However, mastering these rules is not sufficient to make a speaker an effective communicator in the second language. For effective communication, it is crucial to be able to understand and produce socially appropriate speech in the second language, and appropriate speech requires cultural knowledge.

2   The following conversation and its outcome illustrate the importance of cultural knowledge and how miscommunication may result when such knowledge is lacking. This conversation between a U.S. host and an international student is hypothetical, but the same type of situation has been documented by language researchers.

> *U.S. Host:* Would you like some more dessert? Do have some!
> *Student:* No. Thank you very much.
>
> The host changes the topic of conversation and doesn't mention dessert again. The student really did want more dessert but was trying to appear polite by refusing. He remains hungry and might even feel offended because the host has not repeated the offer.

Clearly, the speech of each participant is linguistically correct – there are no errors in grammar or vocabulary choice. What is also clear, however, is that a breakdown of communication has occurred in the situation. The student has given the host a false impression of his wishes. She thinks he does not want more dessert, but this is not true. She has interpreted the refusal as sincere. She is following her culture's rules for politeness, which are based on the idea that hosts should not impose on their guests

There may be different rules of speaking across cultures, such as the rules for table talk.

by continuing to offer food after they have refused. Unfortunately, the host might be giving the student the impression that she is impolite by not encouraging him to take more food. Furthermore, neither participant in the conversation realizes that there has been a misunderstanding.

3   Such misunderstandings offer evidence for the existence of *rules of speaking*. These are rules that enable us to interact in socially and culturally appropriate ways. They are learned and used, usually unconsciously, by members of a *speech community*. A speech community is defined as a group of people who share both a language and rules of speaking. In the example, the host is following a rule in her culture, which states that offers of more food are made once, or at most, twice. The student, on the other hand, applies a rule from his own culture, which states that you should never accept the first offer of food or even the second. In his culture, it is polite to wait until the third or fourth offer, which he knows will come. In other words, in the same way that second language learners may transfer pronunciation and grammatical structures from their first language to their second language, they may also transfer rules of speaking.

A speech community

How is the differences between other cultures

4   Understanding **such differences** is particularly important for performing successful *speech acts*. Speech acts are actions that are performed by speaking. There are many types of speech acts, including making and refusing requests; making and accepting apologies, compliments, and offers; expressing gratitude; and making complaints, among others, and are used in every culture. Knowing how to perform these speech acts appropriately is essential for maintaining good relations among members of a community. In general, all members of a community have this knowledge and use it when they perform these speech acts. Some scholars have described them as the lubrication that keeps interactions among community members smooth and successful.

WHILE YOU READ 1

What is the continuing idea that *such differences* refers to? Highlight it.

speech acts

5   Although these speech acts are probably universal, the rules for when and how to perform them may differ considerably from one culture to another. To perform them successfully, learners need two kinds of knowledge. First, they must know |when| to perform them, and second, they must know |how| to perform them. For the first kind of knowledge, they must know the situations in which it is appropriate to perform these speech acts. For example, under what circumstances is it necessary to apologize? If you are 5 minutes late for an appointment? Or 30 minutes late? If you walk into class after it has already begun? If you bump into someone on the street? If you push ahead in line? Do the answers to these questions change depending on the person you are speaking to – your sister, your friend, your teacher, or a stranger? Cultures differ about which situations require an apology. In some cultures, being late does not call for an apology or explanation; in others, it may cause offense. The answers to these questions require considerable cultural knowledge.

what are the two kinds of knowledge to perform the speech acts successfully?

6 + 7 explination

6   Once learners understand that a certain speech act is appropriate or even necessary, they must figure out how to perform it. For example, if a situation requires an apology, what form should it take? Is a simple "I'm

WHILE YOU READ 2

Look back in paragraph 5 for an example of classification. Highlight the sentence with the classification marker.

In many cultures, being late requires an apology.

sorry" sufficient, or is something more elaborate necessary? Should it include a reason or excuse? "I'm sorry I'm late. Traffic was terrible." Should it include a promise about the future? "I'm sorry I'm late. It won't happen again." Should it include some self-criticism? "I'm sorry I'm late. I am a very bad student." Cultures differ as to how speech acts such as apologies should be performed. In some cultures, offering an excuse is not really an apology at all. If you want an apology to sound sincere, you must accept blame. In addition, interacting with different people might call for different apologies: "I'm terribly sorry that I made that mistake" for your boss, and "Sorry about that" for your **roommate**.

7   There is extensive empirical data supporting both the claim that these rules of speaking exist and that they often differ across cultures. For example, one study showed that Japanese speakers are generally less willing than North American speakers to directly refuse a request. Another study suggests that South Asians, unlike North Americans and Europeans, often do not thank shopkeepers, close friends, or family members. Cross-cultural research has demonstrated that successful speech acts can be quite complex. For example, North Americans tend to minimize rather than accept compliments. If a woman receives a compliment such as, "What a beautiful sweater," the appropriate response is first to offer brief acceptance, "Thank you," but then to minimize the compliment. Examples of such responses include "Oh, it's my sister's" or "I got it on sale," or "This? It has been hanging in my closet for years!" Acceptance of the compliment with a response, such as "Thanks, it is very nice. I think so, too," would be considered impolite and inappropriate. A simple "thank you" and no more would be considered adequate but too brief to be truly **polite**.

8   Learners of a second language, especially those who live in the second language culture, need to be aware that the rules of polite interaction are not universal. Learners should be able to identify situations in which the rules of the cultures are different, and they must also be ready to modify their speech to conform to the conventions of the society in which they live. It may be difficult for learners to accomplish these two tasks, but without an understanding of rules of speaking, there may be serious misunderstandings.

WHILE YOU READ ❸
What is the main idea of paragraph 6? Highlight it.

examples

WHILE YOU READ ❹
Look back in paragraph 7 for an example of a reduced relative clause. Highlight it.

Main Idea Check

Match the main ideas below to five of the paragraphs in Reading 3. Write the number of the paragraph on the blank line.

_____ **A** Learners need to understand when to perform a particular speech act.

_____ **B** Research suggests that rules of speaking vary across cultures.

_____ **C** Second language learning entails acquisition of rules for social interaction as well as language rules.

_____ **D** Learners must acquire *rules of speaking* – the rules that govern social interaction.

_____ **E** It is important to learn how to perform speech acts appropriately.

A Closer Look

Look back at Reading 3 to answer the following questions.

1 What principle does the conversation in Reading 3 demonstrate?
 a Second language learning is a very complex and difficult process.
 b When people visit another country, they should try hard to learn how to be polite.
 c People from different cultures often have communication problems when they interact.
 d Learning a second language involves more than learning grammar and vocabulary.

2 Most native speakers would be able to describe the rules of speaking that they use. **True or False?**

3 Which of the following would *not* be an example of a speech act.
 a Promising to meet someone
 b Reading a poem aloud
 c Thanking someone for help
 d Complimenting someone on a new haircut
 e Asking someone to lend you money

4 Why does the writer refer to *rules of speaking* as "lubrication"?
 a The writer wants to demonstrate that society is like a car that needs gas and oil.
 b The writer wants to show that like oil that keeps a machine running well, appropriate speech helps interactions operate smoothly.
 c The writer wants to illustrate the idea that human relationships can sometimes break down like a car or other kinds of machines.
 d The writer wants to convince readers that rules of speaking are very important for society.

5 According to paragraphs 5 and 6, what two factors would speakers from a different culture need to consider when deciding when to thank a person for a favor?
 a They would need to think about cross-cultural misunderstanding.
 b They would need to think about how to say *thank you*.
 c They would need to consider their relationship to that person.
 d They would need to consider the circumstances: How big was the favor?

6 In acquiring rules of speaking, what two things must second language learners do, according to paragraphs 5 and 6?

   a They must discover the contexts in which particular speech acts are considered appropriate or necessary.
   b They must learn vocabulary, grammar rules, and pronunciation.
   c They must acquire cultural differences.
   d They must learn which words and phrases they need to perform speech acts.

Skill Review

In Skills and Strategies 8, you learned that academic writers often define technical terms and divide important concepts into categories. Identifying definitions and classification is important in academic reading.

A Reread paragraphs 3 and 4 in Reading 3. Highlight the definitions for the following terms:

- Rules of speaking
- Speech community
- Speech act

B Work with a partner. Write definitions for the following speech acts from Reading 3. Use a variety of definition markers from the Language of Definition and Classification chart on page 147.

1 apology

_____

2 promise

_____

3 complaint

_____

4 refusal

_____

oblivious: not notice
Incentive: stimulation, reward
Etiquette: good manners
refrain: refuse from something
uncivil: ttaex in
conduct: behaving well

Definitions

Find the words in Reading 3 that are similar to the definitions below.

1 an idea of what something is like (*n*) Par. 2

2 to decide on the meaning of something (*v*) Par. 2

3 honest; genuine (*adj*) Par. 2

4 to force someone to accept something (*v*) Par. 2

5 to move something from one place to another (*v*) Par. 3

6 remarks that show approval or admiration (*n pl*) Par. 4

7 to need or require (*v 2 words*) Par. 5

8 having a lot of detail (*adj*) Par. 6

9 a reason that you give when you have done something wrong (*n*) Par. 6

10 to make something seem less important than it really is (*v*) Par. 7

Synonyms

Complete the sentences with words from Reading 3 in the box below. These words replace the words in parentheses, which are similar in meaning.

breakdown	conventions	empirical	gratitude	modify
conform	document (*v*)	govern	hypothetical	unconsciously

1 Because immigrants want to succeed in their new country, they often encourage their children to (fit in) _conform_ to their new culture.

2 There was a (failure) _break down_ in the discussions between the workers and the company managers.

3 Researchers presented a/an (data-based) _empirical_ report that showed the role of age in second language learning.

4 Immigrant children do not always understand the language of their new country so their teachers often have to (change) _modify_ their lesson plans for them.

5 It is important to (record) _document_ any changes in your health so you can inform your doctor.

6 Every culture has its own (customs) _conventions_ regarding social interaction.

7 The students showed their (thanks; appreciation) _gratitude_ by giving their teacher a gift.

8 Children learn their first language (without thinking) _unconsciously_.

9 The speaker asked what we would do in a/an (imagined) _hypothetical_ situation.

10 Many health professionals believe that patients' attitudes (control) _govern_ how quickly they recover from surgery.

Critical Thinking

Reading 3 emphasizes the importance of cultural knowledge in successful communication.

A Chose one of the speech acts in the chart below, and think about how you would perform it in your own language when speaking to (1) a close friend and (2) to someone whom you respect or is older, perhaps a teacher, a doctor, or your boss. Fill in the chart with an English translation of your response.

SPEECH ACT	A FRIEND	A TEACHER, DOCTOR, ETC.
Apology		
Request		
Invitation		
Refusal of an invitation		

B Share your chart with your classmates, and discuss any similarities or differences you find.

Research

Do some research by interviewing classmates or people in your community. Find some examples for the following.

- Speech acts that nonnative speakers have trouble performing correctly in the native languages of your classmates
- Speech acts that your classmates have had trouble performing in English. In other words, speech acts that have ended in miscommunication.

Writing

Write two paragraphs about your research. The first paragraph will describe one speech act and how it should be performed. The second paragraph will be about the problems that second language speakers have in performing it. Use information from your interview.

Connecting to the Topic

Discuss the following questions with a partner.

1 Do any people in the community where you live speak more than one language?

2 Are there any services in your community for people who do not speak the dominant language?

3 Are there advantages to having more than one language in a community? Are there disadvantages? Explain your answers.

Previewing and Predicting

Reading section headings and the first one or two sentences of each section can help you predict what a reading will be about.

A Read the section headings of Reading 4 and the first two sentences of each section. Then decide what content will be in each section. Write the number of the section (*II–IV*) next to the topics that best describe it. Each section has two topics.

SECTION	TOPIC
	How multilingual communities are established
	Why some languages disappear
	The role of the government in language use
	Communities that use more than one language
	Suppression of minority languages
	Economic factors in language use

B Compare your answers with a partner's.

While You Read

As you read, stop at the end of each sentence that contains words in **bold**. Follow the instructions in the box in the margin.

Languages in Contact

I. Introduction

1   In Sri Lanka, 2012 was the "Year of Trilingualism." In India, multi-lingualism is so common that government forms ask people to list their first, second, and third languages. In 2010, the city of New York listed 176 different languages used in the public schools there; Los Angeles schools had more than 90. Multilingualism is common all over the world; in fact, it is far more common than monolingualism. Throughout history, contact between people who speak different languages has had a wide range of outcomes. The outcomes depend on a variety of factors, including the type of contact; the economic, political, and cultural status of the communities where the languages are spoken; and government policies.

II. Multilingual Communities

2   In some cases, different language communities coexist for a long time; that is, they exhibit what is known as *stable bilingualism*. In stable bi-lingual communities, residents speak two languages with varying levels of proficiency. Switzerland is a good example of this kind of *language contact* situation, where several languages have equal status. A Swiss person may have German, French, Italian, or Romansch as a native language, but can probably also speak at least one of the others. This has been the case in Switzerland for centuries.

3   In other cases, the language contact is relatively sudden. There are two main categories of rapid language contact. The first type occurs when a

> **WHILE YOU READ ①**
>
> Look back for a definition marker. Highlight it.

Languages Spoken in Switzerland

■ German, 64%   ■ French, 19%   ■ Italian, 8%   ■ Romansh, <1%

conquering group moves into a new language community, bringing its language with it. The British colonial empire is a good example of this. The British brought English to North America and later to South Asia and a large part of the African continent. Conquest introduces status differences between the two language communities. English had a higher status in relation to the local languages in the colonies.

← first type

4   A second kind of rapid language contact occurs with migration, which often creates communities with *transitional* **bilingualism**. A group of people moves to a new community, bringing their home language with them. For example, when large numbers of Chinese immigrated to Canada and the United States in the nineteenth and twentieth centuries, they established Chinese-speaking communities in their new countries. In cases like these, often bilingualism does not persist. After a while, one language loses ground to the other in a process known as *language shift*. There is a complex set of factors that determine the outcome.

← second type

← language shifts

5   In most cases of language contact, the most powerful factor is economics. In colonial contexts, learning the dominant language could be a path to advancement. Under British colonial power, for example, in present-day India, Kenya, and Malaysia, many residents were eager to learn English in order to improve their economic situation. For the British, this was also advantageous because the literate, bilingual population in these countries

what is a very important factor?

helped them administer their colonial empire. When there is considerable disparity in the number of speakers of each language, there is unlikely to be language shift. In the British colonies, for example, there were far more local residents than native speakers of English. In these circumstances, the more likely outcome is bilingualism among a relatively small, higher-status sector of the population. In the British colonial empire, the use of English persisted, but English remained a minority language.

6   The economics of the immigrant language situation is similar in some respects. Adopting the language of their new country is generally a path to greater prosperity. Immigrants know they have a better chance of finding a job in a new country if they learn the language. They also encourage their children to acquire the new language quickly. These decisions generally accelerate the process of language shift. However, in contrast to the colonial situation, there are fewer people in the immigrant community than the host community so language

WHILE YOU READ ❷

Look back for a cause-and-effect marker. Highlight it.

WHILE YOU READ ❸

What is the continuing idea that *this* refers to? Highlight it.

Immigrants learning
the language of their
new country

shift may eventually lead to the gradual disappearance of the immigrant
language. This has occurred with most early immigrant languages in the
United States and Canada, such as Italian, German, and Swedish. For communities in which there is continuing immigration, however, it is easier to
maintain the immigrant language. This is one reason why Spanish remains
a vibrant language in the United States. Immigrants, and especially their
children, learn English, but the flow of new immigrants maintains the
status of Spanish and the need for community bilingualism.

III. Endangered Languages and Language Death

7   Economic utility is paramount in the future of any **language**. Even in
areas with stable bilingualism, languages that are spoken in rural areas
often lose ground to dominant languages of the city, as young people leave
farms and villages in pursuit of better jobs. This can begin a process of
shift to the dominant language that may take several generations. This
happened in Scotland and Ireland, where fewer and fewer people chose
to speak the Gaelic languages of their communities, and more and more
people shifted to English. English was, quite simply, more useful to them.
The same thing has happened to the Maori language in New Zealand as
young people shifted to English. These have become *endangered languages.*

8   People in a community may choose to speak the dominant language,
but when children cease learning the community language and learn
only the dominant language, the result is called *language death.* In North,
Central, and South America, the dominance of English, Spanish, and
Portuguese has led to the death of many native American languages. When
European explorers came to the Americas, there were thousands of local
languages. Scholars believe that today there are between 150 and 175 of

> **WHILE YOU READ 4**
>
> Look ahead in this
> paragraph for a
> supporting detail for this
> main idea. Highlight it.

them; almost half of them will probably die when the current native speakers die. There are no new native speakers. Around the world, 60 percent of all languages have fewer than 10,000 speakers. For many of them, the future is **uncertain**.

WHILE YOU READ 5

What is the main idea of paragraph 8? Highlight it.

IV. Language Policy

9   Government policy can also have considerable influence in language contact situations, including the future of endangered languages. A government may ban the use of minority or local languages in order to encourage the use of the language of those in power. It can restrict services, for example, health care, and only provide them in the dominant language. Perhaps most important, if education is provided only in the dominant language, children will be forced to learn and use it. In the eighteenth century, Russia banned the use of local languages, such as Polish and Lithuanian, in their empire. Only Russian was used in the schools. In the twentieth century, under the Spanish dictator Franco, the use of local languages, such as Basque and Catalan, was prohibited in schools and public places. Only Spanish was permitted. Even giving a child a minority-language name was forbidden.

the government part

10   This kind of suppression of local or minority language can hasten language shift and even language death. However, other outcomes are also possible. For many minority communities, language is a powerful and emotional symbol of their religion, culture, and identity. Native speakers keep their language alive by using it at home and making sure that the next generation learns it. Although in the past, Polish, Lithuanian, Basque, and Catalan were all suppressed by governments that promoted the dominant language; today they are all vigorous and healthy languages. The governments no longer prohibit the use of these languages. Active leaders have fought to save them, and members of the communities have also worked to keep their languages alive.

11   The outcome of language contact situations depends of a variety of factors. Economic utility is generally the most important factor in the health and longevity of any language. However, if the language is an important part of the community's cultural identity and there are speakers who are willing to take an active part in maintaining its vitality, people will continue to use it.

Main Idea Check

Match the main ideas below to five of the paragraphs in Reading 4. Write the number of the paragraph on the blank line.

_____ A Language death occurs when the children no longer learn the community language.

_____ B Economics has an important influence on language choice.

_____ C Conquest and colonization bring languages into rapid contact.

_____ D Governments sometimes suppress minority languages.

_____ E Immigrant languages often disappear in language shift.

A Closer Look

Look back at Reading 4 to answer the following questions.

1 Most people in the world speak more than one language. True or False?

2 In which of the following circumstances is transitional bilingualism most likely to occur?
   a Two communities, where languages of equal status are spoken, exist side by side.
   b A western country has established a colony in a distant place.
   c Immigrants have come to a new country where they have established a small community.
   d A city with speakers of different languages grows and spreads into the countryside.

3 What factors are important in determining the outcome of language contact according to the reading? Circle all that apply.
   a Government policies
   b Literacy rates
   c Longevity of the community
   d Economic necessity
   e Cultural identity

4 At what point is a language dead?
   a When children no longer learn it
   b When the last native speaker dies
   c When governments suppress it
   d When it is no longer taught in schools

5 Which of these circumstance is *most* likely to lead to stable bilingualism in an immigrant community?
   a Parents speak the immigrant language to their children.
   b The government does not suppress the immigrant language.
   c There are cultural programs in the immigrant language.
   d New immigrants continue to join the community.

Skill Review

In Skills and Strategies 8, you learned that academic writers often use words and phrases to mark definitions and classification. Identifying definitions and classification is important in academic reading.

A Review Reading 4 to find the sentences that contain the terms *language shift* or *language death*. Write the sentences on the blank lines below. Then highlight the definition markers, and underline the definitions for each term.

1 _____

2 _____

B Reread paragraph 3 and 4 in Reading 4.

1 Find classification markers to help you understand the term *rapid language contact*. Highlight the markers.

2 Find the categories for *rapid language contact*, which are identified in the reading. Write them on the blank lines below.

a _____

b _____

C Write a classification statement for the two types of bilingual communities described in Reading 4. Review the Language of Classification box for markers of classification. Then write a definition of each type of bilingual community.

Classification statement: There are two _____

Definition 1: _____

Definition 2: _____

Definitions

Find the words in Reading 4 that are similar to the definitions below.

1 sets of plans or rules followed by a government, business, or other group (*n pl*) Par. 1

2 people who live in a place (*n pl*) Par. 2

3 helpful; beneficial (*adj*) Par. 5

4 able to read and write (*adj*) Par. 5

5 to control the operation or management (*v*) Par. 5

6 a specific part of society (*n*) Par. 5

7 to make something go faster (*v*) Par. 6

8 changing or developing slowly (*adj*) Par. 6

9 to keep up; continue (*v*) Par. 6

10 energetic; lively (*adj*) Par. 6

11 usefulness (*n*) Par. 7

12 most important (*adj*) Par. 7

13 to stop an action (*v*) Par. 8

14 a leader with complete power (*n*) Par. 9

15 a long life (*n*) Par. 11

Words in Context

Complete the sentences with words from Reading 4 in the box below.

coexisted	eventually	hastened	path	vigorous
contact	exhibited	lost ground to	suppressed	vitality

1 The patient _____ strange symptoms that the doctors had never seen before.

2 When immigrants first arrive in a new country, they often choose to live in close _____ with other immigrants from the same country.

3 Minority languages have fewer speakers today than 100 years ago because they have _____ the world's 10 most widely spoken languages.

4 The French- and English-speaking communities have _____ in Canada for more than 200 years.

5 When languages lose most of their native speakers, they lose their _____ and often disappear.

6 For many immigrants, education is the _____ to success in their new countries.

7 Indigenous languages and culture were often _____ by colonial governments.

8 European diseases _____ the decline of many Native American groups in the seventeenth and eighteenth centuries.

9 There has been a/an _____ ongoing debate on immigration policy in many western countries.

10 Experts believe that half of today's languages will _____ disappear.

Academic Word List

The following are Academic Word List words from Readings 3 and 4 of this unit. Use these words to complete the sentences. (For more on the Academic Word List, see page 256.)

ceased (*v*)	impose (*v*)	maintain (*v*)	policy (*n*)	sector (*n*)
hypothetical (*adj*)	interpret (*v*)	modify (*v*)	residents (*n*)	utility (*n*)

1 Scientists have learned how to _____ defective genes by using viruses.

2 Only a small _____ of society will benefit from the new law.

3 Colonial leaders often tried to _____ their religion and culture on indigenous people.

4 After several defects were found in their products, the medical equipment company _____ production.

5 The Dutch government established a new immigration _____ at the beginning of the twenty-first century.

6 Unfortunately, some students do not recognize the _____ of a second language.

7 Miscommunication may result if you cannot _____ the meaning of another person's comments.

8 The _____ of the city voted against an increase in taxes.

9 As part of their training, medical students must decide what to do in _____ emergencies.

10 Some scholars believe that it is important to _____ language diversity in the world, so they are working to save endangered languages.

Critical Thinking

Reading 4 discusses language death, which decreases language diversity around the world.

A Read the following two arguments about language diversity and language death. Which one do you agree with and why?

1 Linguistic and cultural diversity are an important source of knowledge. When languages and cultures die, we often lose knowledge of these cultures as well as knowledge about the natural world. We should not allow languages to die.

2 People make intelligent choices about the language they want to speak. Languages have emerged and died throughout history. We should not interfere with this natural process. We should not force people to learn endangered languages.

B Find a partner who has the opposite opinion, and discuss your reasons for your opinions.

Research

Research a dying language. Find answers to the following questions.

- What is the history of this language?
- Are there many native speakers left? About how many?
- Are any children learning the language?
- Have there been any efforts to save the language? Explain your answer.

Writing

Write two paragraphs about your research. The first paragraph will describe the history of the language, and the second will describe its current status and efforts to save it.

Improving Your Reading Speed

Good readers read quickly and still understand most of what they read.

A Read the instructions and strategies for Improving Your Reading Speed in Appendix 3 on page 273.

B Choose either Reading 3 or Reading 4 in this unit. Read it without stopping. Time how long it takes you to finish the text in minutes and seconds. Enter the time in the chart on page 274. Then calculate your reading speed in number of words per minute.

Passive Sentences

Writers frequently use passive sentences in academic writing. Using the passive allows writers to focus on the action rather than the performer, or agent, of the action. Recognizing passive sentences and understanding why writers choose to use passive sentences will help you better understand academic texts.

Examples & Explanations

Forensic linguists analyze written and spoken language in order to provide help in legal and criminal cases.

In active sentences, the writer focuses on who performed the action (the agent). In this sentence, the agent is *forensic linguists*.

In the last two decades, considerable progress **has been made** in the field of forensic linguistics.

In passive sentences, the writer focuses on what happened, that is, the action, rather than the agent.

The threatening letter **was analyzed by** an experienced forensic linguist who later gave evidence in court.

In this sentence, the writer emphasizes the action – *the analysis of the letter*. The writer has added a *by* phrase, believing that including information about the agent is an important detail.

The letter **must have been written by** two different people, one of whom most likely was raised in the north of the country.

Note that a modal is often used in passive sentences.

A phone call **had been made** just before the attack. Police were using voice analysis to identify the caller.

In this sentence, the writer uses the passive because the agent – *the caller* – is unknown.

The Language of the Passive

The passive has two parts: any form of the verb *to be* and a past participle verb. If it is important to identify the agent, writers will add a *by* + noun phrase.

At least one form of the verb to be:	A past participle verb, for example:
be	argued
am / is / are	considered
was / were	made
being	thought
been	written

Strategies

These strategies will help you identify and understand passive sentences as you read.

- If you see one of the eight forms of the verb *to be*, scan ahead and look for a past participle.
- If you see a past participle, scan back to look for one of the eight forms of the verb *to be*.
- If you see a *by* + noun phrase, scan back for a passive verb.
- Remember that a reduced relative clause drops the "to be" part of the passive verb; for example: *Today's government follows rules ~~that were~~ established by previous governments.*
- Use the general context of the reading to understand why the writer has chosen to use the passive.

Skill Practice 1

Read the following short texts and highlight all examples of the passive verb.

1   Sociolinguists are interested in how languages vary. This variation is found in each of the three main components of language. It is visible in the lexicon (i.e., the vocabulary of a language); in its grammar (i.e., the rules which are used to form phrases and sentences); and in its phonology (i.e., the sounds of language and the rules that govern their pronunciation).

2   Research has also confirmed the existence of gender varieties, the English that is used by men and women. For example, in both British and American English, men tend to use the nonstandard pronunciation of *-in* of the *-ing* ending. They say "I'm eatin'" more often than women do, for example. Men also tend to use nonstandard grammar more often than women. The following is more likely to be spoken by a male: "I didn't see nothing."

3   In one final exam, students were shown exam questions the day before. University administrators admitted that mistakes were made and that security needed to be improved. They claimed, however, that the identity of the person or persons responsible for the cheating was unknown. They promised this would not happen again as all examination papers would be locked up until distributed at the time of the exam.

4   The language that is used by parents with two-year-olds has qualities that distinguish it from the speech used with older children and adults. Research has found, for example, that adults pronounce words more clearly when they are talking with children of around two. It has also been established that adults often repeat nouns rather than use pronouns.

5   How children acquire language has been a focus of study for many years. One theory was that children imitate, or copy, what they hear. Parents then praise children when they use correct vocabulary and grammatical structures and correct them when they make mistakes. This theory of language learning is known as the behaviorist theory. However, this theory has been disproven. Research has shown that children are not good imitators, and when their language is corrected by caregivers, children are often reluctant to repeat the model they are given.

Skill Practice 2

Decide which form of the verb, the active or the passive, correctly completes each sentence.

1 In recent years, several dictionaries of teenage slang _____ in part to help adults understand the language of their adolescent children.
  a have been published   b have published

2 In court, the attorney claimed that his client was innocent. He argued that a key part of the evidence – the recorded phone call – _____.
  a had not been adequately analyzed   b had not adequately analyzed

3 In languages that have two forms of the pronoun "you," the familiar form _____ with close friends and family.
  a uses   b is used

4 The expert concluded that the suspect _____ the threatening e-mail, but he could not be absolutely sure.
  a may have written   b may have been written

5 After a few months in a new country, behavior, values, and identity _____ to adapt to the new culture.
  a will shift   b will have been shifted

Skill Practice 3

In each of the following short texts, identify a clause in the second sentence that would benefit if the writer used the passive instead of the active. Rewrite that sentence in the passive. Add a *by* clause if necessary. The first one has been done for you.

1 Within every country, accents vary from one geographical region to another. In addition, people associate some accents with the speaker's gender, social class, or ethnic origin.

   In addition, some accents are associated with the speaker's gender, social class, or ethnic origin.

2 Personal questions are often considered rude in some cultures. For example, people often consider it impolite to ask about such things as salary or how much a house costs.

   _____

3 The university officials admitted that they had made mistakes in their application process. In some cases, the university accepted students but a month later, rejected them.

   _____

4 Research has shown that many people suffer from a "sleep debt." People build up this sleep debt from weeks, even months, of lack of sleep.

   _____

5 The government announced that a small amount of taxpayers' money had been lost. Someone illegally transferred the money to an unknown account, and it is likely that the government will be unable to recover the money.

   _____

6 Clinical trials of new medical treatments should not begin until the risks and benefits to patients have been adequately assessed. Experts who are not working on these research projects and who have no financial interest in their success or failure should make such assessments.

   _____

7 Extremely high death rates, like those that are associated with HIV/AIDS, are not new in history. Bubonic plague, a disease that fleas transmit from rats to people, killed 35 percent of Europe's population in the fourteenth century.

   _____

Connecting to the Topic

Discuss the following questions with a partner.

1 What are some advantages to knowing more than one language?

2 Do you use or plan to use your additional language in your career? Explain your answer.

3 How do you feel about raising children in a bilingual environment? Do you think it helps them or hurts them?

Previewing and Predicting

> Reading the section headings and looking at the graphs and photographs can help you predict what a reading will be about.

A **Read the title and section headings in Reading 5. Look at the graphs and photographs. Then decide what content will be in each section. Write the number of the section (II–VI) next to the topics that best describe it.**

SECTION	TOPIC
	Employment opportunities for people who know more than one language
	The growing importance of Chinese on the Internet
	Going to school in more than one language
	Economic benefits of knowing an additional language
	Multilingualism and the brain
	How multilingualism improves thinking
	How language is connected to culture
	The importance of languages other than English

B **Compare your answers with a partner's.**

While You Read

As you read, stop at the end of each sentence that contains words in bold. Then follow the instructions in the box in the margin.

The Advantages of Multilingualism

I. Introduction

1   A U.S. soldier who speaks Arabic receives $1,000 more every month than his fellow soldiers who speak only English. A multinational company promotes a Belgian manager to vice president because she can speak English, French, and German in addition to her own language. A report shows that the test scores of French-English bilingual Canadian children are consistently higher than the scores of the children who speak only French. A five-year-old girl in Manchester, England, listens to her grandmother tell stories in Urdu. All of these people are enjoying the wide range of advantages of knowing more than one language.

II. Practical Advantages

2   The world grows more interconnected every day. Recent economic problems throughout the world have shown that it is no longer possible to think of countries in economic isolation; what happens to one country's economy is likely to have an impact on many other economies. Businesses are interconnected, as well. Whereas the public once thought of Apple as a U.S. company, Siemens as German, and Ericsson as Swedish, in fact, they are all multinational, with manufacturing operations and distribution networks all over the world. Thanks to technology, smaller companies can also reach across the globe. Billions of people are connected through the Internet and cell phones. The global markets are no longer limited by

Multinational companies and their products connect the world.

Multilingual skills are important for business success.

space, time, or international borders; language may be the final remaining barrier to global communication.

They get Pay more

3   A global world demands global skills. Both employees and customers are international and mobile. This means that businesses need to operate in multiple languages, and employees who can help them do that may have advantages over their colleagues who cannot. A 2010 survey of British businesses revealed that knowledge of other languages was second on a list of the most desirable skills for job candidates, just after knowledge of information technology. Employers are also willing to pay more for employees with **these skills**. The same survey found that the average salary of employees 3 years after graduating from college was higher for students who had studied languages than students who had studied math, physics, and chemistry. In Canada, a 2008 study reported that fluent bilinguals earn an average of 10 percent more than English monolinguals and 40 percent more than French monolinguals. In short, there is ample evidence showing that advanced proficiency in an additional language can boost earnings. At the same time, however, it is important to note that these studies compare workers who are equal in other respects, for example, in socioeconomic status and educational level. Simply knowing an additional language cannot always compensate for disparities in these areas.

WHILE YOU READ ❶

What are the continuing ideas that *these skills* refers to? Highlight them.

4   Companies are willing to pay more for employees who know more than one language because there is a shortage of people with these crucial skills. In a recent study by the European Commission, more than 10 percent of the 2,000 companies in the study reported that they had lost business because of the lack of language and culture skills in their workforce. Many described incidents of miscommunication with their business and trade partners as a result of language deficits. To increase productivity in

European countries, the Commission says the ideal employee should be proficient in two languages beyond his or her native **language**.

III. Not Just English

5   Although English is the language most widely used in business and in the greatest demand, many companies are looking for expertise in other languages, as well. Business executives say that in order to remain competitive, it will be necessary to go beyond English. One U.S. business survey named Mandarin Chinese as the most important language of business after English, followed by French, Arabic, and Spanish.

6   One measure that reflects both the global use of and demand for different languages is Internet content. English is more widely used than any other language on the Internet; however, its dominance has dropped to just over 27 percent of all Internet content. (See Figure 3.3.) In 2000, English was the language of more than half the Internet content and Chinese just over 2 percent. The number of Chinese Internet users increased by more than 1,000 percent between 2000 and 2010. Experts say the percentage of Chinese language content on the Internet is likely to overtake English. The demand for bilinguals with Chinese language proficiency is likely to grow, as **well**.

7   It is not only in business that knowledge of an additional language beyond English is of practical value, however. The U.S government has made a significant investment in language training for its military forces, which have traditionally relied heavily on translators. Military personnel are learning languages that are of strategic importance to the American government. One commander maintains that skill in local languages is as valuable to a soldier as skill with a rifle. The U.S. Secretary of Defense went even further, saying, "Languages are the key to understanding that world."

WHILE YOU READ ②

Look back at this sentence. Find a cause-and-effect relationship. Highlight the cause-and-effect marker. Then highlight the cause.

WHILE YOU READ ③

Look back over paragraph 6, and highlight the sentence with a passive verb form.

Figure 3.3 Language of Internet Content – 2010

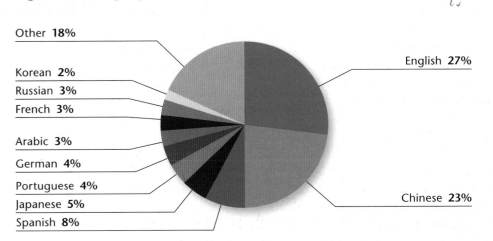

Other **18%**
Korean **2%**
Russian **3%**
French **3%**
Arabic **3%**
German **4%**
Portuguese **4%**
Japanese **5%**
Spanish **8%**
English **27%**
Chinese **23%**

Source: Internet World Stats, 2010

IV. Multilingual Education

8   Parents today understand the economic advantages that proficiency in an additional language can bring their children, and their decisions about their children's education are often informed by this understanding. Even when their children are very young, parents seek out opportunities for them to be exposed to an additional language. Wealthy parents can provide this opportunity for their children by hiring a caregiver who speaks more than one language. Bilingual babysitters and nannies are in high demand. Parents hire them to speak to their children in the hope that the exposure and interaction will help their children become bilingual. Many of these children develop some ability in the second language, particularly in understanding it. However, experts say that unless the exposure and interaction extend beyond the child's early years, the experience is unlikely to lead to proficiency.

9   The potential benefits of bilingualism are also behind the rise of dual language immersion programs, particularly in North America and Europe. Dual immersion is not remedial education for immigrant children that people often associate with bilingual education; instead, these programs mix children who are native speakers of two languages, say, Spanish and English, and attempt to build language proficiency and literacy in both languages. These programs recognize the increasing demand for bilingual and bi-literate workers and the positive effects of having students who are learning English and students already fluent in English, but are learning another language, in the same classroom. The popularity of these programs has risen steadily in the United States, where there were more than 2,000 in 2011. Spanish is the most frequent second language, but the popularity of Mandarin is not far behind. In 2000, there were only 10 Chinese dual immersion programs; 10 years later, there were 75.

Many parents choose bilingual education for their children.

10   Sometimes the quest for proficiency in a second language, particularly English, can divide families. Some Asian families, mostly from Korea, Taiwan, and Hong Kong, have decided their children can get a better education outside of their home countries. They want their children to get a western education and develop advanced proficiency in English, so the mother and children go to live in Australia, Canada, New Zealand, or the United States while the father remains home and works to support the family. In other cases, the young students go alone and live with relatives or friends. These students are sometimes referred to as "parachute kids" or "wild **geese**." The number of Korean "wild geese" reached a peak of about

WHILE YOU READ ④

Look back to find a definition marker. Highlight it.

40,000 in 2006 and has since declined. These families believe that the sacrifice of separation and loneliness is worthwhile because the children will have an advantage when they apply for college and enter the workforce.

V. Cognitive Advantages

11   The practical and economic advantages of advanced second language proficiency seem clear. However, research in psychology over the past 20 years indicates that there are additional advantages of bilingualism. They show that bilingualism actually changes neural connections in the brain and improves cognitive performance outside of the domain of language. This is an enormous shift from past perspectives on bilingualism. For much of the twentieth century, experts thought that bilingualism was a barrier to academic success. Scientists and educators believed that knowledge of an additional language delayed language development and academic progress in the language used in schools. This belief was supported by data from tests of the cognitive abilities of bilingual and monolingual children, which revealed consistently superior performance by the monolinguals.

12   Subsequently, however, more sophisticated tests contradicted these results and showed that bilinguals reach the milestones of language development at about the same time as monolingual children. Analysis of the earlier tests showed that that these tests were flawed because they were really a kind of language **test**. This put the bilingual children at a disadvantage because the test was in their weaker language. The scientists needed to develop a test of the children's cognitive abilities that was not also a language test. When they began to use nonverbal tests, such as asking the children to sort shapes and colors, the results were very different.

13   In the nonverbal tests, the superior cognitive abilities of the bilingual children became **evident**. They were better than the monolingual children at focusing their attention and ignoring distractions. In addition, they were better at paying attention to changes in their environment and using this information to solve complex problems. Furthermore, they were able to remember information about one task while they were working on another task. Bilinguals have to do this all the time when they switch back and forth between languages so it makes sense that they are able to do this well in other cognitive domains. These studies also examined brain images of the two groups, which showed that the bilinguals were able to perform these tasks with less mental effort than the monolinguals. In other words, their brains worked more efficiently.

14   This bilingual advantage begins early and lasts through life, if speakers continue using both languages. In a scientific study, seven-month-old babies from a bilingual environment showed more cognitive flexibility than babies from a monolingual environment. Scientists played a sound for both groups of babies; the sound was a cue that a dancing puppet would appear on one side of a screen. After the babies listened and watched this a

WHILE YOU READ 5

Look back in this paragraph, and find a contrast and an assessment marker. Highlight them.

WHILE YOU READ 6

Scan ahead and highlight three details that support the main idea expressed in this sentence.

few times, they began to turn their heads to that side in anticipation of the puppet's appearance on the screen. Then the scientists moved the puppet to the other side of the screen. The bilingual babies quickly absorbed this new information and changed the direction of their gaze, whereas the monolingual babies continued to look in the original direction. The scientists interpreted this behavior as the superior ability of bilingual babies to pay attention to cues in their environment and to modify their behavior in response to those cues.

Bilingual children have been shown to have some advantages over monolingual children.

الاولاد
الهنار

15   Studies of older children have shown that bilingualism can also have a positive impact on school performance. A series of studies comparing the academic performance of monolingual and bilingual children have shown that the bilingual children do better on problem-solving tasks and especially on reading tasks. In other words, bilingualism seems to give a cognitive advantage. One psychologist was interested in whether this bilingual advantage could help children of lower socioeconomic status, who generally have lower test results than students of higher socioeconomic status. In 2009, she and her colleagues conducted a study with particularly exciting results: They indicated that socioeconomic status was less significant in predicting the test scores of the bilingual children. In other words, even the poor children in the study showed the bilingual advantage in reading and language tests. The authors of the study suggest it is possible that early and sustained bilingualism could compensate for other educational deficits.

16   At the other end of life, scientists have also detected a bilingual advantage. As they reach old age, many adults experience **dementia**, a gradual loss of their memory and mental abilities. Several studies have shown that lifelong bilingualism can delay these symptoms of dementia by as long as 6 years. The more proficient bilinguals showed the longest delay in the onset of dementia. Many studies have shown that keeping the brain active can help postpone dementia; it seems bilingualism is one way to do this. Switching from one language to another is a form of mental exercise.

WHILE YOU READ 7

Look back at this sentence, and find clues in the context to help you understand the meaning of *dementia*. Highlight the clues.

VI. Cultural Advantages

17   The practical and cognitive advantages of knowing more than one language can be measured, but there are other advantages that may be harder to calculate. The cognitive flexibility that comes with knowledge of an additional language may also lead to greater flexibility in social choices

and greater tolerance of social and cultural differences. Studies of babies as young as 10 months raised in monolingual and bilingual homes show that monolinguals have a preference for interaction with people who sound familiar, whereas bilinguals are more willing to accept people who sound different. By the age of five, monolingual children tend to select playmates that sound like they do and reject those who do not. They have begun to form a group identity. For the bilingual children, group identity is more flexible and fluid. The researchers claim that these findings have implications for adults as well. They believe that children who grow up with more than one language may become more tolerant adults.

18   Many children who grow up with two languages also develop a connection to and an understanding of two cultures. Their language creates a bond to their family across generations and a connection to their heritage.

Bilingual children are connected to two cultures.

Because they understand two cultures, they can act as a bridge between them, in their families, their communities, and in the wider world. For these reasons, and also for practical reasons, there has been increased interest in *heritage languages*. The idea behind heritage language education is that children from second language communities begin their language education with an advantage. For example, Chinese children in Canada might be encouraged to develop their knowledge of Mandarin rather than learn a new, additional language. This practice builds cultural bonds and strengthens communities at the same time that it improves potential resources for the nation.

19   Multilingualism is a resource for individuals, communities, businesses, and governments. Although English is the dominant world language and is likely to remain so for the immediate future, experts stress that languages, like empires, rise and fall. Knowledge of more than one language will almost certainly be a requirement for the global citizens of the **future**.

WHILE YOU READ 8

Look back in paragraph 19 to find a main idea that expresses the thesis of the whole reading. Highlight it.

Reading Skill Development

Main Idea Check

For sections II–VI of Reading 5, match the main ideas to two of the paragraphs in each section. Write the number of the paragraph on the blank line.

SECTION II: Practical Advantages

_____ A There are not enough multilingual employees to meet the demand for them.

_____ B Employees who know more than one language often earn more than employees who don't.

SECTION III: Not Just English

_____ A One indication of the demand for a specific language is the amount of Internet content in that language.

_____ B Military leaders understand the benefits of a multilingual force.

SECTION IV: Multilingual Education

_____ A Some children from Asian countries come to study in western countries without their parents.

_____ B Some parents hire bilingual caregivers in order to expose their young children to a second language.

SECTION V: Cognitive Advantages

_____ A Studies suggest that bilingualism can delay the symptoms of dementia.

_____ B The bilingual advantage has been demonstrated in small babies.

SECTION VI: Cultural Advantages

_____ A Studies suggest that bilingual children are more tolerant than monolingual children of people who are different than they are.

_____ B Knowledge of a second language can strengthen cultural connections.

A Closer Look

Look back at Reading 5 to answer the following questions.

1 According to a survey in Great Britain, what skills do employers want the most from their employees?
   a Business skills
   b Multilingualism
   c Information technology knowledge
   d Communication and writing ability

2 In paragraph 3, the writer cautions that knowledge of an additional language may not always result in higher salaries. Which situation is the best illustration of this possibility?

a An American teacher in Japan speaks English and Japanese.

b An immigrant from El Salvador cleans hotel rooms in New York. She has no high school degree but has learned English.

c A college student from Mexico is hired to take care of a doctor's two small children in Los Angeles. She is bilingual.

d A Bulgarian manager has just been hired by a German company to open an office in Sofia, the capital of her country. She speaks German, English, and Bulgarian.

3 Why do you think U.S. military leaders are providing language training for their personnel instead of using translators? Circle all possible answers.

a Translators are not always available when they are needed.

b They think that local people are more likely to trust soldiers who speak their language.

c They believe that knowing a second language will help soldiers to think better.

d It is cheaper to train soldiers than to hire translators.

4 Bilingualism was once considered a barrier to academic development. **True or False?**

5 Which of these abilities are the result of the "bilingual advantage" over monolinguals? Circle all that apply.

a Greater ability to concentrate on a task

b Faster reading speed

c Ability to change behavior more quickly in response to new information

d Greater ability to process information from many different sources in sequence

6 What can explain the delay of symptoms of dementia among bilinguals?

a The cognitive benefits of bilingualism can be saved for old age.

b Using and responding to two different languages keeps the brain more active than using and responding to one language.

c Scientist believe that connections in the brains of bilinguals last longer than those of monolinguals.

d Scientists are not sure of the reason.

7 Match the skills and qualities below to the type of advantage it represents.

Skills and Qualities	Types of Advantages
_____ 1 higher reading test scores	a practical
_____ 2 greater tolerance for others	b cognitive
_____ 3 faster processing of new information	c cultural
_____ 4 higher pay	
_____ 5 closer ties to home community	
_____ 6 more job options	

Skill Review

In Skills and Strategies 9, you learned that passive sentences are frequent in academic writing. Writers use the passive to focus on the action rather than the performer, or agent, of the action. Recognizing passive sentences and understanding why writers choose to use passive sentences will help you better understand academic texts.

A Read the following sentences and parts of sentences from Reading 5. Find the passive verbs, and highlight them.

1 Thanks to technology, smaller companies can also reach across the globe. Billions of people are connected through the Internet and cell phones. The global markets . . . (Par. 2)

2 The global markets are no longer limited by space, time, or international borders; language may be the final remaining barrier to global communication. (Par. 2)

3 One measure that reflects both the global use of and demand for different languages is Internet content. English is more widely used than any other language on the Internet; however, its dominance . . . (Par. 6)

4 Parents today understand the economic advantages that proficiency in an additional language can bring their children, and their decisions about their children's education are often informed by this understanding. Even when their children are very young . . . (Par. 8)

5 These students are sometimes referred to as "parachute kids" or "wild geese." The number of Korean "wild geese" reached a peak . . . (Par. 10)

6 Scientists and educators believed that knowledge of an additional language delayed language development and academic progress in the language used in schools. This belief was supported by data from tests of the cognitive abilities of bilingual and monolingual children, which revealed consistently superior performance by the monolinguals. (Par. 11)

7 The practical and cognitive advantages of knowing more than one language can be measured, but there are other advantages that may be harder to calculate. (Par. 17)

8 The idea behind heritage language education is that children from second language communities begin their language education with an advantage. For example, Chinese children in Canada might be encouraged to develop their knowledge of Mandarin rather than learn a new, additional language. This practice builds cultural bonds . . . (Par. 18)

B With a partner, discuss why the passive was used in each of sentences in Step A.

Definitions

Find the words in Reading 5 that are similar to the definitions below.

1 to raise someone to a higher or more important position (*v*) Par. 1
2 always happening in the same way (*adv*) Par. 1
3 the state of being alone or not connected to anything else (*n*) Par. 2
4 people who are applying for jobs (*n pl*) Par. 3
5 to improve or increase something (*v*) Par. 3
6 events that are unusual or unpleasant (*n pl*) Par. 4
7 an insufficiency in or lack of something (*n*) Par. 4
8 perfect; best possible (*adj*) Par. 4
9 people who are paid to care for children (*n pl*) Par. 8
10 area; field (*n*) Par. 11
11 to pay no attention to something (*v*) Par. 13
12 things that take your attention away from what you should be doing (*n pl*) Par. 13
13 a usually positive feeling about what will happen next (*n*) Par. 14
14 the beginning of something (*n*) Par. 16
15 cultural history (*n*) Par. 18

Words in Context

A **Use context clues to match the first part of each sentence to its correct second part and to understand the meaning of the words in bold.**

_____ 1 The tests we use to measure language proficiency are

_____ 2 If you want to learn a second language, you should

_____ 3 The actor listened for

_____ 4 The restaurant staff were very nice but

_____ 5 Young children often

_____ 6 The teacher gave the paper a poor grade because she said it contained

_____ 7 The company requires all

_____ 8 Some students are required to take

_____ 9 One important personality factor in a successful study-abroad experience is

_____ 10 Many people claim they can guess speakers'

a **personnel** to take a drug test before beginning employment.

b his **cue** before he made his speech.

c a **flawed** argument.

d **socioeconomic status** based on how they speak.

e more **sophisticated** than in the past.

f **remedial** courses in math when they enter college.

g **seek out** opportunities for practice.

h this could not **compensate for** the poor quality of the food.

i develop strong **bonds** with their grandparents.

j **flexibility**. You must be ready to do things differently than in your own country.

B Compare your answers with a partner's. Discuss what clues helped you match the parts of the sentences and helped you understand what the words in **bold** mean.

Same or Different

The following pairs of sentences contain vocabulary from all the readings of this unit. Write *S* on the blank lines if the two sentences have the same meaning. Write *D* if the meanings are different.

_____ 1 Learners who **seek out** native speakers as friends can **acquire** a second language quickly.

Exposure to native speakers can **boost** second language learning.

_____ 2 It is possible to **attain** a high level of language proficiency quickly, but it is more difficult to **maintain** it.

Learners can achieve **mastery** of a second language but they cannot **catch up** with native speakers.

_____ 3 **Remedial** math classes can sometimes make up for **deficits** in academic preparation.

Classes that give extra help in math can often **compensate for fundamental** problems in past education.

_____ 4 **In the long run**, the dominance of English will probably **hasten** the decline of some minority languages.

It is likely that English will **eventually accelerate** the decrease in minority language use.

_____ 5 The survey reported on the **implications** of the company's **personnel policy**.

The reported described the **ideal** characteristics for the company's employees.

_____ 6 Her **elaborate excuses** for why she did not come to work sounded false.

She gave some complicated reasons for her absence, but she did not seem **sincere**.

_____ 7 The town's **residents** were proud of their **accomplishments** during the disaster.

The people in the town **exhibited extraordinary** behavior during the storm.

_____ 8 The **incident** showed the new manager's **flexibility**.

The new manager **documented** the incident and was able to resolve the **dispute**.

Academic Word List

The following are Academic Word List words from all the readings of this unit. Complete the sentences with these words. (For more on the Academic Word List, see page 256.)

anticipation (*n*)	conventions (*n*)	eventually (*adj*)	ignore (*v*)	promote (*v*)
conform (*v*)	documented (*v*)	exhibited (*v*)	implication (*n*)	retain (*v*)
consistently (*adv*)	empirical (*adj*)	flexibility (*n*)	isolation (*n*)	transfer (*v*)

1 The doctors kept the patient in _____ so no one would be exposed to her infection.

2 It is important not to _____ the early signs of heart disease.

3 _____ studies support the idea of a sensitive period of language acquisition.

4 When community activists _____ the use of endangered languages, they can sometimes revitalize it.

5 The _____ of the study are clear; an early start in second language acquisition is the best.

6 One of the requirements of the position is _____ because the business is always changing.

7 Doctors _____ all of the patient's symptoms and responses to medication for the report.

8 When you are living in a new country or community, it is important to learn about its cultural _____.

9 Studies have _____ demonstrated that language use and cultural identity are closely connected.

10 The patient _____ strange symptoms that the doctors could not explain.

11 We could see the _____ on the children's faces as they waited for the music to begin.

12 It took a long time, but _____ they were able to find a translator who speaks Estonian.

13 Because they are in high demand, it is sometimes difficult for companies to recruit and _____ multilingual employees.

14 Independent people often prefer not to _____ to the social rules of groups and organizations.

15 The army _____ the soldier to a new position because of his knowledge of Korean.

Critical Thinking

In Reading 5, the writer suggests there may be exceptions to the bilingual advantage.

A With a partner, review the figures on the graph below. It shows the median income of white Americans, Asian Americans, and Hispanics Americans in the United States in 2011. Many, though not all, of the Asian and Hispanics in the workforce are bilingual.

ANALYZING INFORMATION

Critical thinking involves thinking carefully about important topics that the writer has not completely explained.

B Now discuss these questions with your partner.

1 What do you think might account for these disparities in income among the three groups?
2 What role do you think bilingualism might play in income disparities?

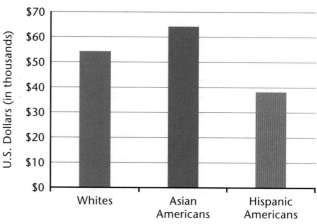

Figure 3.4 Median Annual Income 2011

Source: U.S. Census Bureau

Research

Many parents want to raise their children to be bilingual. They get lots of advice on how to this. Do some research on what experts and parents say are the best methods for raising bilingual children. Find answers to the following questions.

- When should exposure begin?
- How should parents behave?
- What worries do parents have?
- What should parents do if their children resist?

Writing

Write two paragraphs. The first paragraph will describe the ideas that you read about raising bilingual children. The second paragraph will give your own ideas of what methods you think will work best.

Exercise 1

Writers may connect ideas between sentences in many different ways. The second sentence may:

    a describe a **result** of what is reported in the first sentence

    b provide a **contrast** to what is described in the first sentence

    c add a **detail** or details to support the more general information in the first sentence

How does the second sentence in each pair of sentences below connect to the first sentence? Write *a*, *b*, or *c* on the line depending on whether it is a result, a contrast, or a detail.

_____ 1 Early critical period studies of language acquisition contained a number of flaws in their research design and methods. Later studies avoided some of these fundamental weaknesses by using real language samples and powerful statistical analysis.

_____ 2 Researchers analyzed overgeneralization errors that children make, such as "I eated everything," and "My mommy brang me a cookie," which have been documented extensively in the child language literature. This helped them to understand some of the most basic principles of language acquisition.

_____ 3 We can define linguistic competence, or knowledge, as the ability of the native speaker to comprehend and produce novel utterances. One of the components is phonological competence, that is, knowledge of the sounds of the language and the rules for combining those sounds in appropriate ways.

_____ 4 As children, we all attain a uniform level of competence in our first language, apparently with little effort, just by interacting with native speakers in our environment. For most adults, however, learning a second language seems to be a fundamentally different process, which involves considerable effort and produces widely varying outcomes.

_____ 5 When immigrants come to a new country, it is usually their children that acquire the language of the host country most rapidly. Because their knowledge of the new language is superior to their parents, the children often have to translate for them at stores, hospitals, and government offices.

Exercise 2

Make a clear paragraph by putting sentences A, B, and C into the best order after the numbered sentence. Write the letters in the correct order on the blank lines.

1 Bilingualism has clear practical advantages, but recent research indicates that it also has significant cognitive benefits. _____ _____ _____

A They also found that learning and maintaining a second language can delay some of the effects of aging on the brain.	B Since that time, researchers have shown that bilinguals are often better at focusing their attention and performing complex tasks.	C This view is in contrast to the perspective of 50 years ago, which characterized bilingualism as a barrier to cognitive development and academic progress.

2 People often assume that the rules and conventions for polite interaction are universal. _____ _____ _____

| **A** These research results document a tendency for Americans to say thank you in situations where such an expression would be inappropriate, or even offensive, in some South Asian cultures. | **B** However, data collected in investigations of one instance of interaction – thanking – in different cultures are inconsistent with this popular notion. | **C** Such evidence reinforces the position of researchers who argue that the rules for appropriate speech often vary from culture to culture. |

3 A fundamental challenge for psycholinguists has been to account for children's remarkable capacity to acquire their native language. _____ _____ _____

| **A** Empirical evidence has emerged from research on language development that children know things about language that they have not been taught or heard. | **B** This evidence supports the conclusion that some aspects of language development are part of our human genetic code. | **C** This conclusion has led linguists to compare the emergence of language to other genetically determined stages of development, like the first appearance of teeth. |

4 Ironically, it is often the language errors made by children that provide evidence for how children acquire their native language. _____ _____ _____

| **A** Such overgeneralization errors, which are extremely rare in adult English but are typical of children's speech, reveal that children do not simply imitate the English they hear. | **B** For example, we consistently find utterances such as, "I seed Santa Claus," "I holded the rabbit," and "We readed a story." | **C** They also suggest that children have the natural capacity to construct grammatical rules for the language they are exposed to and to apply these rules as they create novel utterances. |

5 Military conquest can often lead to enduring changes in language use but also in language structure and vocabulary. _____ _____ _____

| **A** Examples of common present-day English words of French origin include *beef, table, fruit*, and *people*. | **B** An example of such enduring changes is found in the influence of Norman French, the language of the forces that conquered England in the eleventh century. | **C** Over the hundreds of years of Norman French rule, English absorbed many words from French, with some experts claiming that as much as 30 percent of the English lexicon is of French origin. |

SUSTAINING PLANET EARTH

SKILLS AND STRATEGIES

- Problem-Solution Texts
- Graphic Material
- Nominalization in Subjects

Problem-Solution Texts

> Writers sometimes use problem-solution organization for paragraphs, for sections, and for entire readings. They may use specific words to signal problems and their solutions. Becoming familiar with this type of organization and the language that signals it will help you understand academic texts.

Examples & Explanations

①In both cities and rural areas, food deserts are a source of growing **concern**. ②Food deserts exist where there are no supermarkets or food stores, so residents have **difficulty** finding healthy food, especially fresh fruit, vegetables, and meat, in their communities. ③There are two basic options for **alleviating** food deserts: (i) attract new shops to the areas or (ii) convince existing shops to include fresh food among their products. ④The city of New York has **responded** with an idea for the first option. ⑤The city has issued permits for small food carts to sell fresh fruits and vegetables in food deserts around the city. ⑥Not only has this program **relieved** the fresh produce **shortage**, it has also **eased** the **problem** of unemployment among New York residents who have had consistent **trouble** finding a job. ⑦Most food cart owners are new immigrants or people who have lost their jobs.

In sentence 1, the writer clearly identifies a problem (food deserts).

Sentence 2 defines the problem and explains it in more detail.

In sentence 3, the writer offers two basic categories of solutions to the problem.

Sentences 4 and 5 provide a specific example of one of these solutions.

In sentences 6 and 7, the writer names a second problem (unemployment among a specific population) and how the solution to the problem of food deserts has also helped ease this second problem.

The Language of Problem-Solution

Here is a list of problem-solution markers that are often used in academic texts.

PROBLEM MARKERS			
Nouns			
burden	damage	excess	puzzle
challenge	danger	hardship	risk
complication	deficiency	issue	setback
concern	difficulty	lack	shortage
conflict	dilemma	obstacle	threat
crisis	dispute	problem	trouble

SOLUTION MARKERS			
Verbs			**Nouns**
to address	to ease	to resolve	relief
to alleviate	to improve	to respond	remedy
to answer	to overcome	to settle	resolution
to cope with	to relieve	to solve	response
to deal with	to remedy	to tackle	solution

Strategies

These strategies will help you recognize and understand texts that have problem-solution organization.

- Look for problem markers and solution markers while you preview or read an article.
- When you see a problem marker, scan forward through the text to identify if and where the writer starts discussing solutions.
- After identifying a problem or a solution marker, read closely to determine the specific problem or solution.
- Expect some cause-and-effect analysis of problems. Then look for the logical connection between the cause of a problem and the suggested solution.

Skill Practice 1

In the following sentences, highlight the problem markers and underline the problem. The first one has been done for you.

1 Most countries face the dilemma of how to strengthen their economies and at the same time protect the environment.

2 When people move to another country, one obstacle they may face is their inability to speak and understand the language of their new home.

3 Cholera and other communicable diseases are a threat to the economies of many developing countries.

4 People who take multiple medications for several different conditions often experience complications when these medications interact.

5 Toxic materials, such as chemicals, old computers, batteries, and waste from hospitals present a danger to the communities where they are stored.

6 Many experts argue that our excessive dependence on nonrenewable energy sources is likely to lead to a new energy crisis in the near future.

7 Human activity continues to be a threat to biodiversity in some of the most fragile ecosystems in the world.

8 Government regulations can be an obstacle to the development of alternative energy sources and other emerging technology.

Skill Practice 2

In the following sentences, highlight the solution markers, and underline any solutions.

marker

1 One way to alleviate the burden of having large numbers of immigrants settle in one *Problem* area of the country is to offer them incentives to live elsewhere. → *Solution*

2 Increased support from the government for climate research would improve our chances of stopping global warming.

3 Ethnic communities have been a source of support for new immigrants as they learn to cope with the challenges and hardships of life in the United States.

4 The United Nations is attempting to persuade the two countries to begin tackling a resolution of the environmental conflict between them.

5 Many countries in Sub-Saharan Africa are anticipating a severe water shortage in the coming decades, so government agencies are making preparations to address this issue.

Skill Practice 3

In the following paragraphs, circle the problem markers and the solution markers. Then highlight each problem, and underline each solution.

1   In most cities, roofs on buildings are covered with thick, black tar. Tar is inexpensive and effective in keeping out water, but it creates environmental challenges: It absorbs an enormous amount of heat so that buildings with tar on their roofs become very hot in the summer. This leads to a need for constant air-conditioning, which uses a great deal of energy. One practical remedy is a roof garden. Recently, government buildings have been replacing their black tar roofs with roof gardens, which keep the buildings cooler and reduce energy costs.

2   The *tragedy of the commons* is a dilemma that results when competing interests continue to use a shared resource until that resource has been exhausted. Overfishing is an example of a tragedy of the commons. Overfishing has led to the collapse of several species of fish, such as cod, and the extinction of several others. In an attempt to overcome this problem, several governments and international organizations have imposed limits on the amount of fish that can be taken from the ocean every year.

3   Many people think that the energy crisis is about oil and gas. However, in sub-Saharan Africa, there is another energy crisis. People don't have oil or gas for cooking, so 70 percent of the people burn wood for cooking. Every day they cut down trees for cooking fuel. This practice has led to widespread deforestation. As the trees disappear, the soil dries up and blows away, and crops fail. This leads to a constant threat of famine. One solution to this destructive cycle is bamboo. Bamboo is not a tree; it is a grass that grows quickly, sometimes as fast as a meter a day. In addition, it is renewable, unlike trees, which die when you cut off their branches. When bamboo is cut, it grows back and can be used again.

4   Acid rain refers to rain (or snow) that has high levels of nitric and sulfuric acid. Acid rain causes many problems when it falls. It burns the leaves of the plants it touches; it sinks into the soil and makes it more difficult for plants to grow. It poisons lakes and rivers, resulting in the death of many fish. The damage to the forests causes hardships for the animals that depend on the plants for food and shelter, and the shortage of fish leads to problems for the animals that eat them. The primary cause of acid rain is the burning of fossil fuel by factories and cars. The only way to deal with this problem is to cut back on fossil fuel use. Alternative energy sources and hybrid cars can also help reduce the effects of acid rain.

Connecting to the Topic

Discuss the following questions with a partner.

1 How would you describe the world's population growth right now? Is it growing quickly or slowly?

2 Do you think the population is growing at the same rate in all regions of the world?

3 What effect does rapid population growth have on a country's economy? What happens to an economy when the population rate slows down?

4 In what way is the environment affected as countries expand their economies?

Previewing and Predicting

> Reading the first and last paragraph and looking at any illustrations can help you predict what a reading will be about.

A **Read the first paragraph and last paragraph of Reading 1, and look at the photos. Then put a check (✓) next to the topics you think will be included in the reading.**

_____ A The effect of population on the environment in the nineteenth century

_____ B World population trends today

_____ C Positive effects of population on the environment

_____ D Economic policies used by developed nations in the past

_____ E Examples of economic practices that do not harm the environment

_____ F Positive environmental policies of developed nations

B **Compare your answers with a partner's.**

While You Read

As you read, stop at the end of each sentence that contains words in **bold**. Then follow the instructions in the box in the margin.

Ecology, Overpopulation, and Economic Development

1   Approximately 10,000 years ago, when the first permanent human settlements emerged after about 2 million years of hunter-gatherer society, the total population of the earth was only about 5 million people. By the beginning of the nineteenth century, it had increased to 1 billion. During this time, the human species had a negligible influence on the ecology of the planet as a whole.

2   By the beginning of the twentieth century, however, the population stood at 2 billion. By 1950 it was 2.5 billion, and in the next 50 years it more than doubled to 6.1 billion, reaching 7 billion by October 2011. By 2050, the population is projected to reach 10.6 billion. The majority of this growth will be in less developed countries, which will be home to more than 86 percent of the world's people in 2050. Today, as a direct result of population growth, the impact of human activities on the world's ecology *nature and earth* is considerable. In the future, the damage may be catastrophic.

3   **Studies** have consistently shown that rapid population growth represents a massive threat to the environment at local, national, and global levels. In areas of Nepal, for example, the pressure of overpopulation and poverty has forced farmers into the hills. There they cut down vegetation to provide wood for heating and construction and food for their animals. Then they begin to raise crops on the cleared land. However, within a short time, the fertile topsoil is eroded by rain because it is now without the protection that had been offered by the natural vegetation of the area. Soon the hillside fields become unproductive, incapable of supporting the people who have settled there. The farmers then move on and begin the same destructive process again. The result can be devastating: In 2011, 16 percent of Nepal's population of 30 million did not have enough to eat;

Deforestation begins a destructive cycle.

Burning forests release large amounts of CO₂.

children are particularly affected, accounting for 39 percent of this undernourished population.

4   Elsewhere, in the world's tropical zones, nations like Indonesia, Malaysia, Thailand, and Brazil have been cutting down or burning their hardwood forests faster than they can be replaced. These hardwood forests are a valuable resource that provides much-needed employment and earns money from exports. In the 15 years between 1990 and 2005, Indonesia cut down almost 25 percent of its forests; Malaysia cut down 6.5 percent. By 2010, Brazil, in an attempt to relieve poverty and create economic growth, had destroyed, often by burning, at least 141,046 square miles (365,307 square kilometers), or 9 percent, of the Amazon rain forest. This was mainly to support cattle ranching, subsistence farming – that is, growing only enough food to feed the farmer's family – and some commercial woodcutting. Figures for 2011 were not encouraging. Deforestation in Brazil during March and April totaled 228 square miles (593 square kilometers) and represented a 473 percent increase over the same two months in 2010. As in the case of Nepal, while deforestation provides short-term economic gains, the land quickly becomes unsuitable for traditional farming as deforestation interrupts the recycling of natural nutrients to the land.

5   The destruction of these forests has global consequences. The burning of the forests releases large amounts of carbon dioxide (CO_2) into the atmosphere, emissions that are contributing to potentially disastrous changes in global climate patterns. Next, as the forests vanish, so too does their diverse plant and animal life. Thus an enormous source of scientific knowledge and an equally vast source of natural material, with potential for economic benefit to the world, are lost.

6   Ecological damage caused by overpopulation, deforestation, and unwise development is a global problem requiring immediate action. However, there is no single solution. One remedy to this crisis is to control population growth, and many countries have already taken steps to do **this**. China introduced its One-Child Policy in 1979, a policy that has brought the fertility rate down to 1.8 children per woman. India began an intensive

WHILE YOU READ ❷

Reread the previous two sentences. Highlight the solution markers.

family planning program in 1994, which has reduced the average birthrate from six to fewer than three children per woman. Significant reductions in the birthrate have also been experienced by other countries, which have similar family planning programs, including South Korea, Thailand, Mexico, and Tunisia.

7   Reducing birthrates helps relieve pressure on overpopulated areas. However, it is only part of the solution for two critical **reasons**. First, a large proportion of the populations of developing countries consists of children. As a result, the world's population will inevitably increase when these children reach adulthood and start their own families. Even if birth control becomes universally accessible and acceptable, the world's population will still increase to 10.6 billion people by 2050. Second, sharply decreasing birthrates can have a negative economic effect on a nation. The Chinese government, for example, is currently considering allowing some families to have two children because its population is now unbalanced. As a result of its strict One-Child Policy, there are not enough adults of working age to support their elders. Therefore, controlling population growth is, by itself, not enough to counter the ecological damage brought on by overpopulation.

WHILE YOU READ ❸

As you read, highlight the two reasons.

8   According to most experts, the second essential component of a solution to the overpopulation-environment problem is sustainable and environmentally friendly social and economic development. The history of the industrial world clearly shows that birthrates fall and stabilize at lower levels when the standard of living increases. Prosperity, educational and career opportunities, adequate health care, and relative financial security for people in their old age are all factors that have contributed to the low, stable birthrates of the relatively affluent nations. For this reason, most experts believe that the birthrates of the less developed nations will decline as their populations experience the benefits of economic development. Therefore, experts argue, more emphasis should be placed on helping developing countries become economically stronger.

Family planning programs can reduce birth rates.

9   The situation today, however, is more complex than this apparently simple solution would suggest. A major complication is that one essential component of the solution, namely economic development, is also one cause of the problem. Birthrates will not fall without economic development. However, most of the danger to the world's ecological systems comes

directly from the attempts by nations to pursue economic development. Emerging economies, for example, are typically reliant on fossil fuels, particularly coal. Coal emits CO_2, which is widely seen as a major factor responsible for an increase in global temperatures. China, for instance, has fueled much of its rapid economic growth by the use of coal and now is responsible for 25 percent of global emissions. In 2010, CO_2 emissions worldwide grew at the fastest rate in four **decades**.

10   In order to limit ecological and environmental damage caused by such practices as deforestation and coal burning, developing nations have to forgo the same strategy for economic development that brought today's developed world its prosperity, that is, the exploitation of natural resources with little thought for the future. The pursuit of economic development has led to the loss of 80 percent of European forests and 75 percent of the forests covering North America. Today North Americans and Europeans are asking the people of developing nations to cease doing what they themselves did for centuries.

11   This seems like an unfair burden on developing countries. All nations have the right to pursue the goal of economic development for their people. Nevertheless, developing countries are currently pursuing traditional development policies that are exhausting their own ecological resources and are causing serious, sometimes irreversible, damage to the world's ecology. The developed world, which includes the planet's most prosperous nations, has an obligation to respond to this crisis. They must provide leadership by establishing a new paradigm of economic development. They can do this by modifying many of their own unsustainable policies and practices and by offering economic and technical assistance to those less developed countries that are willing to do the same. In this way, both developed and less developed countries will be supporting, and not undermining, global efforts to encourage sustainable, environmentally friendly development.

WHILE YOU READ 4

Which sentence contains the main idea of this paragraph?
a) The first
b) The second
c) The last

WHILE YOU READ 5

What continuing idea does *This* refer to? Highlight it.

what develoRed nation must do

how to make it happen

Economic development can cause damage to the environment.

Main Idea Check

Match the main ideas below to five of the paragraphs in Reading 1. Write the number of the paragraph on the blank line.

_____ A Developed nations are asking developing nations to avoid using the same strategies that brought them economic strength and prosperity.

_____ B Nations can only reduce and stabilize population growth with sustainable social and economic development.

_____ C Limiting population growth is one solution to ecological damage.

_____ D Economic development is both part of the problem and the solution to ecological damage.

_____ E Tropical countries are destroying forests for short-term economic gains.

A Closer Look

Look back at Reading 1 to answer the following questions.

1 Which statement is correct according to the reading?

    a During the nineteenth century, population growth had little effect on the environment.

    b In the last 10,000 years, the population has doubled.

    c Most of the population growth is occurring in developing rather than developed countries.

    d Experts predict global population will double again from 2011 to 2050.

2 Which of the following statements contains evidence that deforestation is only a short-term solution to poverty and unemployment?

    a The process of cutting down forests increases employment opportunities and local economic activity.

    b By 2010, Brazil had cut down 9 percent of the Amazon rain forest in order to provide jobs.

    c Farmers took up the practice of cattle and subsistence farming in areas where the forest had been cleared.

    d Since deforestation breaks the natural nutrient cycle, newly cleared land becomes increasingly hard to farm.

3 The following diagram represents the process of environmental destruction occurring in Nepal. Reread paragraph 3 about the environmental destruction occurring in Nepal. Then complete the diagram with sentences A–D. Write the correct letter in each box.

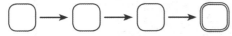

    A The fertile topsoil is eroded by rain.

    B The hill areas can no longer support the new settlers.

    C The soil's natural protection is removed.

    D For a better life, farmers move into the hill country where they cut down the natural vegetation.

4 What reason does the writer give for the claim that limiting population growth is only a partial solution to the problem of overpopulation?

    a It is unrealistic to expect that governments will be able to control population growth in all societies and all cultures.

    b The high percentage of children in the world's population guarantees a huge increase in population in the future.

    c Governments approach this challenge differently, by applying different rules and incentives for different countries.

    d Developing nations are becoming more prosperous and therefore parents can afford to have larger families.

5 What factor(s) does the writer identify as contributing to a decline in a nation's birthrate? Circle all that apply.

    a Increasing prosperity   d Financial security for the elderly

    b Poverty   e Economic development

    c Adequate health care

6 Emerging economies, such as China's, are both part of the solution and part of the cause to the overpopulation-environment problem. **True or False.**

Skill Review

In Skills and Strategies 10, you learned that problem-solution organization is common in academic writing. You also learned to look for problem and solution markers. Understanding this pattern of organization will help you improve your academic reading.

Reread paragraphs 6 and 7 about ecological damage. As you read, highlight problem and solution markers. Then determine what the problems and the solution are, and fill in the boxes below.

Ecological Damage

Problem	Problem

Solution

Vocabulary Development

Definitions

Find the words in Reading 1 that are similar to the definitions below.

1 the connection between living things and the environment (*n*) Par. 1

2 able to produce a large number of high-quality crops (*adj*) Par. 3

3 not eating and not having enough food to maintain good health (*adj*) Par. 3

4 the substances that any living thing needs to live and grow (*n*) Par. 4

5 the production and releasing of light, heat, or gas (*n*) Par. 5

6 having a lot of money; wealthy (*adj*) Par. 8

7 according to what seems to be true or likely (*adv*) Par. 9

8 the use of someone or something for personal gain (*n*) Par. 10

9 cannot be changed back to original condition (*adj*) Par. 11

10 a very clear example, which is used as a model (*n*) Par. 11

Words in Context

Complete the sentences with words from Reading 1 in the box below.

catastrophic	deforestation	interrupts	obligation	sustainable
counter	emerging	negligible	reliant	vanished

1 In some tropical countries, complete forests have _____, leaving bare and unproductive land.

2 Experts argue that the present fast economic growth is not _____ because of its dependence on rapidly shrinking resources.

3 The _____ economies of Brazil, Russia, India, and China are providing some much-needed employment opportunities within these nations.

4 _____ is a clear example of a short-term solution to poverty that also leads to environmental destruction.

5 The damage from the 2011 earthquake and tsunami in Japan was _____.

6 People who care very much for the environment believe that humans have a / an _____ to protect it and to keep it healthy.

7 The city planned to develop a park in the new industrial area, but this was not enough to _____ the loss of farmland.

8 Families who make their living from subsistence farming are _____ on the weather: periods of drought, for example, can be life-threatening.

9 The company claimed that the effects of the oil spill were _____, but the local government argued that the spill caused many people to lose their jobs.

10 Falling leaves provide essential nutrients to the earth. Therefore, cutting down trees _____ this process, thereby requiring farmers to use artificial fertilizers.

Critical Thinking

Reading 1 discusses ecological problems brought on by overpopulation and economic development. The writer suggests that an important part of the solution to these problems is for developed countries to support sustainable, environmentally friendly policies in developing countries.

CLARIFYING CONCEPTS

Critical thinking includes exploring a concept in a text by restating it and applying it to a different context.

A Discuss the following questions with a partner.

1 What does the writer mean by sustainable, environmentally friendly development? Give a definition in your own words.

2 Read the following examples of different types of development projects. Put a check (✓) next to the examples you think are sustainable and environmentally friendly.

DEVELOPMENT	SUSTAINABLE / ENVIRONMENTALLY FRIENDLY
Manufacturing solar panels	
Coal mining	
Manufacturing electric motorcycles	
Developing wave energy technology	
Drilling for oil in deep sea areas	
Planting fast-growing trees for wood harvest	
Developing suburbs far from cities	

B Share your answers and discuss your reasons with a partner.

Research

Research two examples of sustainable, environmentally friendly development from the list above. Find answers to the following question.

● Why is the development sustainable and environmentally friendly?

Writing

Write two paragraphs. The first paragraph will describe the importance of encouraging sustainable and environmentally friendly development. The second paragraph will describe specific examples from your research.

Connecting to the Topic

Discuss the following questions with a partner.

1 How would you define the term "environmental crisis"?

2 Can you think of a recent example of an environmental crisis?

3 What caused this crisis? A human activity? A natural event?

4 What were some of the effects of this crisis?

Previewing and Predicting

> Reading the first sentence in each paragraph can help you predict what a reading will be about.

A Quickly read the first sentence of paragraphs 2–7 in Reading 2. Decide what the topic of the paragraph will be. Then read the following topics. Write the number of the paragraph (2–7) next to the topic that best describes it.

PARAGRAPH	TOPIC
	Solutions to the Aral Sea crisis
	The environmental damage caused by agricultural development
	The Soviet development of agriculture in this area
	The effects of the environmental crisis on residents
	Description of the Aral Sea in the 1960s
	Short-term benefits of agricultural development

B Compare your answers with a partner's.

While You Read

As you read, stop at the end of each sentence that contains words in **bold**. Then follow the instructions in the box in the margin.

The Aral Sea: An Environmental Crisis

1   For decades, environmental scientists have warned of the ecological damage that results from poorly planned economic development. As land clearing in many areas of the world has shown, apparently reasonable solutions to the need for more employment, housing, and food are often shortsighted. In the worst cases, these solutions have the potential to render an area unlivable. One of the world's most extreme cases of ecological disasters is the Aral Sea region, located between Kazakhstan and Uzbekistan. This region is a clear example of the damage that poorly planned human economic activity can have on the **environment**.

the main idea

2   In the 1960s, this inland sea was the world's fourth largest lake. Its basin extended into three other countries, and the sea covered 26,300 square miles (68,000 square kilometers), roughly the same size as Belgium and the Netherlands combined. It had a mean depth of 52 feet (16 meters), and its waters were fresh with a low salt content of about 1 percent. Two large rivers, the Amu Darya and the Syr Darya, flowed into the sea. The water from these rivers, combined with the annual rainfall, maintained the volume and level of the water. Although the land around the sea and the rivers was dry and desertlike, the region still supported a wide diversity of wildlife, including 500 species of birds, 200 species of mammals, and numerous species of fish.

WHILE YOU READ 1

Reread paragraph 1. Highlight the general problem and the specific example.

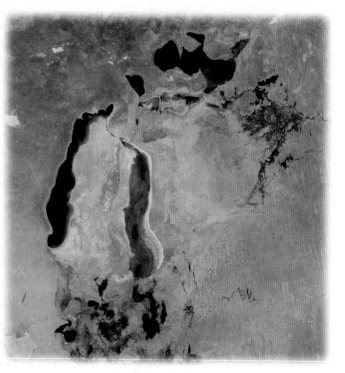

The Aral Sea in 2000 and 2012

3   In the late 1950s, the government of the Soviet Union decided to develop agriculture in this dry area by using water from the two rivers for irrigation. At that time, the Soviet Union was pushing agricultural development in the region as part of its national economic development plan. The government built huge farms, digging long canals to bring water from the rivers. By 1965, the Amu Darya was providing water across 7 million acres of wheat and cotton. These crops flourished with the help of huge amounts of chemical pesticides and **fertilizers**.

Rusting ships stand on land that was once under the Aral Sea.

4   In the short term, this plan was successful. In the early 1960s, the farms and the fishing industries saw marked economic benefits. Each year, more than 40,000 tons of fish were caught and transported by rail to Moscow. Thousands of people were employed in the boats, processing plants, and railroad yards. The irrigation system made the once dry desert fertile, encouraging more farms to be established. There were 19 villages and 2 cities on the lake. The population in the northern city of Aralsk grew to 80,000 while to the south, another 40,000 people lived in Muynak.

5   Within a few years, however, it was clear that this agricultural effort was not only unsustainable, but was, in fact, causing devastating damage to the **environment**. The Amu Darya river shrank drastically, to about half its original size by the early 1990s; its flow fell from 28,000 cubic feet (2,600 cubic meters) per second to just 5,000 cubic feet (465 cubic feet) per second. Eventually, as it receded, this river was cut off from the Aral Sea. Moreover, the reduction in volume and water flow led to increased salinity. Salt content climbed from 10 to 30 grams per liter, almost as high as the oceans. Native species of fish died out, and the commercial fishing industry collapsed. Today, huge and rusting Soviet ships remain on what was once water, a reminder of how quickly this industry fell.

6   For the residents of the region, it became increasingly hard to cope with living within this environmental crisis. To address the problem of high unemployment, the Soviet government transferred many of the fishermen to work in the Caspian and Baltic **seas**. However, thousands of families were left behind to struggle in the inhospitable Aral region. Their health quickly began to suffer. The land was now dry again, with salt flats stretching hundreds of miles. The pesticides and artificial fertilizers, which had been needed to support the wheat and cotton, saturated the earth. Every few weeks, dust storms kicked up hundreds of tons of salt, sand, and pesticides into the air and into people's lungs. Toxic chemicals contaminated local drinking water leading to an increase in respiratory diseases and throat cancer, and as is often the case with environmentally

WHILE YOU READ 2

Which sentence expresses the main idea?
a) The first
b) The second
c) The last

WHILE YOU READ 3

As you read, highlight the negative effects of this development on the environment.

WHILE YOU READ 4

Highlight the solution marker in this sentence.

linked illnesses, infants and children were the most vulnerable. Infant mortality rose to 60 in 1,000, which was the highest rate in the Soviet Union. Tuberculosis reappeared, and by 2002, was killing more than 2,000 of the region's people every year.

7   The first real scientific response to the Aral crisis came in 1990, when a conference of international scientists met and concluded that the region *the first response* was an ecological disaster area. Massive changes in agricultural practices were urgently needed to reverse the process of environmental destruction. If such measures were not taken, scientists warned that the region would become a wasteland, incapable of supporting human settlements.

8   Because of the enormous size and complexity of the crisis, practical responses were slow to appear. After the collapse of the Soviet Union, however, the World Bank stepped in, and together with the newly independent Kazakhstan, began to tackle the problem by funding extensive projects aimed at saving the northern part of the Aral Sea. By 2005, they had built a dam intended to raise the water level of the North Aral by about 13 feet.

The Kokoral Dam on the North Aral Sea

This would return the water to its previous salt level, and therefore, allow native fish to repopulate. The results were promising. The North Aral grew by 20 percent. The salinity fell to almost the 1960 level, and freshwater fish returned. The fishing industry slowly rebounded, with 1,500 tons caught in 2008. Today, fish-processing plants are operating again, providing badly needed employment. However, the cost for this improvement has been high. Furthermore, the condition of the South Aral Sea has continued to worsen, and scientists predict that it will be completely dry by **2020**.

9   Unfortunately, the case of the Aral Sea region is not unique. It is one of many examples of poorly planned economic development that has devastating ecological consequences. However, while the Aral Sea is a clear warning for the catastrophic dangers of this type of development, the continuing survival of the North Aral also offers hope for ecologically-damaged areas as well as for sustainable development worldwide.

WHILE YOU READ ⑤

Reread paragraph 8. Highlight the problem and solution markers.

Main Idea Check

Match the main ideas below to five of the paragraphs in Reading 2. Write the number of the paragraph on the blank line.

_____ A The first few years of development brought significant benefits to the region.

_____ B The Aral Sea illustrates that serious ecological damage can be caused by careless economic development of a region.

_____ C It soon became apparent that the agricultural development was severely damaging the environment.

_____ D Soviet agricultural development resulted in serious health effects on the residents of the Aral region.

_____ E Although huge projects have improved the northern Aral region, the South Aral Sea situation continues to worsen.

A Closer Look

Look back at Reading 2 to answer the following questions.

1 What changes did the Aral Sea undergo between the 1960s and the early 1990s? Check all that apply.

   a It became saltier.

   b It expanded because of irrigation.

   c A combination of rainfall and flow from the rivers maintained its levels.

   d It decreased in both area and volume.

2 What step did the Soviet government take in order to resolve the environmental problems in the Aral region?

   a It helped some of the unemployed fishermen by moving them to areas where there was work.

   b It organized a conference to discuss the crisis and to find solutions.

   c It funded projects to try to improve the situation in the northern Aral.

   d It built a dam to raise the sea level in the North Aral Sea.

3 Which statement best summarizes the conclusions reached by scientists attending the 1990 conference?

   a Although the situation was critical, scientists believed time was needed to carefully research solutions.

   b Unless steps were taken soon, the area would return to the condition it was in prior to Soviet agricultural development.

   c The process of environmental destruction could not be stopped.

   d Without immediate action, the area would no longer be fit for human habitation.

4 The World Bank worked with the Soviet Union and Kazakhstan to fund projects aimed at saving part of the Aral Sea. **True or False?**

5 By 2005, a dam had been built in the northern part of the Aral Sea. What were some of the results of this project? Check all that apply.

   a Salinity levels fell to pre-agricultural development levels.
   b Both the North and the South Aral seas grew by 20 percent.
   c The fishing industry immediately recovered to its 1960 production levels.
   d Freshwater fish returned, helping the fishing industry to slowly recover.

6 The following diagram represents the general process exemplified by the history of the Aral Sea. Complete the diagram with sentences A–E. Write the correct letter in each box.

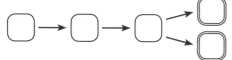

   A Humans may no longer be able to make a living, or even live, in the region.
   B The government of a region believes that economic development is a major priority.
   C The economic development policies cause great damage to the region's ecology.
   D The pressure for economic growth leads to poorly planned economic development.
   E Ecological damage will reverse the economic advances that the region may have made.

Skill Review

> In Skills and Strategies 10, you learned that writers use problem-solution organization in academic texts. Understanding this type of organization will improve your academic reading.

A Identify problems and solutions from Reading 2 in order to complete the following chart. The third item has two problems with one solution.

PROBLEM	SOLUTION
Land in the Aral region was too dry to support extensive crop-growing.	
	A conference of international scientists was organized in 1990.
a) b)	A dam was built in 2005.

B Compare your answers with a partner's.

Definitions

Find the words in Reading 2 that are similar to the definitions below.

1 to cause someone or something to be in a particular state (*v*) Par. 1

2 average (*adj*) Par. 2

3 the movement of liquid, gas, electricity, etc. (*n*) Par. 2

4 the amount of space with length, height, and width (*n*) Par. 2

5 clear; noticeable (*adj*) Par. 4

6 to move farther back (*v*) Par. 5

7 the amount of salt in something (*n*) Par. 5

8 to fall apart (*v*) Par. 5

9 to deal with problems or difficulties (*v*) Par. 6

10 unfriendly; unwelcoming (*adj*) Par. 6

11 completely full (*adj*) Par. 6

12 chemicals used to kill insects (*n*) Par. 6

13 a large meeting with talks on a specific topic (*n*) Par. 7

14 to reach a decision after careful thought (*v*) Par. 7

15 to return to an earlier and better condition (*v*) Par. 8

Word Families

Ⓐ The words in bold in the chart are from Reading 2. The words next to them are from the same word family. Study and learn these new words.

Ⓑ Choose the correct form of the words from the chart to complete the following sentences. Use the correct verb tenses and subject-verb agreement. Use the correct singular and plural noun forms.

NOUN	VERB
intention	*intend*
irrigation	irrigate
reminder	remind
reversal	*reverse*
transportation	*transport*

1 Thousands of Egyptian farmers depend on the Nile River to _____ their farmlands.

2 The city announced that they _____ to switch from gas-powered buses to electrical buses within the next 2 years.

3 One of the most important priorities for many developing countries is the improvement of their _____ systems, including roads, railways, and airports.

4 The photo of burning forests in the Amazon region is a/an _____ of how quickly a valuable resource can be destroyed.

5 The government _____ its previous policy of collecting all debts and agreed instead to swap land for the money owed.

6 Hurricanes _____ us of the immense force of nature.

7 The Colorado River in the United States provides _____ to seven states as well as parts of Mexico.

8 In Sub-Saharan Africa, military forces from several countries _____ food, water, and medical supplies to victims of the current drought.

9 With its emphasis on solar powered energy, China's _____ are clear: The country aims to become a worldwide leader in this type of energy production.

10 In a significant _____ of earlier trends, the average size of Russian families is beginning to increase.

Academic Word List

The following are Academic Word List words from Readings 1 and 2 of this unit. Use these words to complete the sentences. (For more on the Academic Word List, see page 256.)

collapsed (v)	conference (n)	paradigm (n)	reversed (v)	transport (v)
concluded (v)	exploitation (n)	reliant (adj)	sustainable (adj)	volume (n)

1 Efforts to reach an agreement _____ when the government refused to meet the environmental group's demands.

2 Experts warn that short-term _____ of natural resources inevitably leads to long-term environmental problems.

3 In spite of growing support for solar and wind energy, the world remains _____ on oil and coal.

4 An international _____ was organized to assess the progress in slowing down global deforestation.

5 The Aral Sea is a/an _____ of the terrible environmental consequences of short-term economic planning.

6 Experts warn that a decrease in _____ will result in increased salinity for Mono Lake, California.

7 Using cleared forestland for agricultural purposes is not _____ since without the trees, the land quickly becomes infertile.

8 A year after the massive oil spill, scientists reviewed the evidence and _____ that fishing was once again safe.

9 During the nineteenth century, railways were developed to _____ coal to England's industrial areas.

10 After new evidence emerged about long-term environmental problems, the city _____ its previous decision and refused the company's request to build a new factory.

Critical Thinking

Readings 1 and 2 are about the devastating effects economic development can have on the environment. Different human actions led to the cutting down of tropical forests and the crisis in the Aral region. Yet the root causes are very similar.

Work with a partner. Answer the following questions. Refer to the readings if necessary.

1 What was the general problem that caused both deforestation and the Aral region crisis?
2 This general problem led to a "short-term" or "quick fix" approach to developmental planning. What do we mean by these two terms?
3 What was the short-term solution in each case?
4 What happened in the early days of development in both of these cases?
5 How would you describe the long-term results of these two cases?
6 In order to avoid an environmental crisis like these in the future, we need more careful planning. What can businesses and governments do in order to plan more carefully?

SYNTHESIZING

Critical thinking includes connecting new information to information you learned in previous readings.

Research

The global economy depends on oil. Do some research to find out the short-term advantages of using oil as fuel. Then consider some of the long-term problems. Make a list of both the advantages and the problems associated with oil.

Writing

Write two paragraphs about your research. The first paragraph will be about the short-term benefits of using oil. The second paragraph will be about the negative issues surrounding the use of oil and will offer some solutions. Include specific examples in each paragraph.

Improving Your Reading Speed

Good readers read quickly and still understand most of what they read.

A Read the instructions and strategies for Improving Your Reading Speed in Appendix 3 on page 273.

B Choose either Reading 1 or Reading 2 in this unit. Read it without stopping. Time how long it takes you to finish the text in minutes and seconds. Enter the time in the chart on page 275. Then calculate your reading speed in number of words per minute.

Graphic Material

Academic textbooks often present information in the form of graphic materials, such as tables, pie charts, bar graphs, and line graphs. This is both an efficient and an effective way to provide the reader with more information than is in the text. Examining this material before and while you read will help you better understand academic texts.

Examples & Explanations

①The United Nations has just issued a report on the health of the world's forests. ②The report contains mixed news. ③Forest loss is slowing. ④In the 1990s, 16 million hectares (39.54 acres) of forestland was destroyed per year; by 2010, this had slowed to 13 million hectares. ⑤The rate of loss, however, continues to be alarming, particularly in Brazil, Indonesia, and Australia. ⑥These countries each lost more than 2.5 million hectares from 2005 to 2010. ⑦However, the rate of reforestation – the planting of new trees – is increasing. ⑧This is promising news.

If you look at the bar graphs in Figures 1 and 2 before you read the paragraph, you can predict that the reading will be about the world's forests.

Sentence 1 indicates that your prediction is correct.

Sentence 2 suggests that there is positive and negative news about forests. This is indicated in the graphs.

Note that in Figures 1 and 2, the vertical axis indicates the amount of land (in millions of hectares), and the horizontal axis indicates world regions. The bars indicate different time periods.

Figure 1 shows that in areas such as Africa and South America, forests continue to be cut down.

Figure 2 shows an increase in new forests.

Sentences 4–6 provide additional information that is not in the graphs.

Figure 1 Changes in Total Forest Area 1990–2010

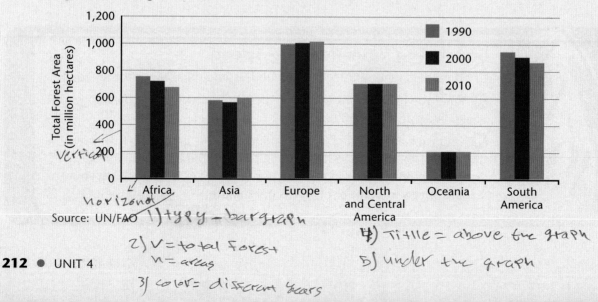

Source: UN/FAO

Figure 2 Increases in Newly Planted Forest 1990–2010

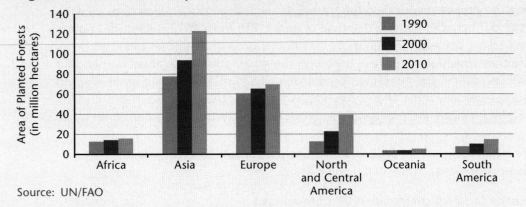

Source: UN/FAO

Strategies

These strategies will help you to connect information in graphs and charts to the text more effectively.

- Before you begin reading, look at any graphic material that might be included. Try to figure out the main idea of the graph or table.

- Make sure you understand the vertical and horizontal axes of any graphs.

- As you read the text, look for references to graphic material, such as "(See Figure 1)." When you find a reference, check the graph. This will help you connect its information with the text.

- When you take notes on a reading, include some information from the graphic material. This shows that you have understood both the written text and the graphics.

Skill Practice 1

Ⓐ **Study the line graph in Figure 3. Read the title and make sure you understand the vertical and horizontal axes. Then read the paragraph on the next page.**

Figure 3 Projected Annual World Oil Prices

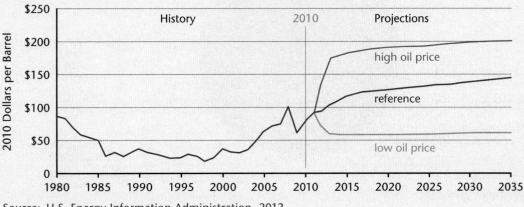

Source: U.S. Energy Information Administration, 2012

linegraen

The Annual Energy Outlook uses data on global oil production and economic growth to project oil prices in the future. At the low oil price prediction, oil will be $62 per barrel in 2036, a decrease of about $30 from 2012 prices. This figure is based on the assumption that global economic growth decreases over this period. In contrast, the high oil price is based on the assumption that global demand for oil will increase in the next few decades due to a high growth rate in developing nations, especially India and China. This will counter the decrease in demand from developed nations. According to this projection, oil will be $200 per barrel by 2035.

B **Use information from Figure 3 and the paragraph to complete the following sentences.**

1 The price of oil fell sharply in 2008 from about $_____ to around $_____ .

2 The high oil prediction assumes that demand from _____ increases while demand from _____ decreases.

3 If demand grows, the price of oil will be just under _____ by 2030.

4 _____ and _____ are predicted to have especially strong growth in the next few decades.

5 If demand does not increase, however, oil prices from _____ to _____ will remain approximately the same as they were in _____ .

Skill Practice 2

A **Study the pie chart in Figure 4. Read the title and make sure you understand the labels. Then read the paragraph on the next page.**

Figure 4 2008 Global Carbon Dioxide (CO_2) Emissions by Country

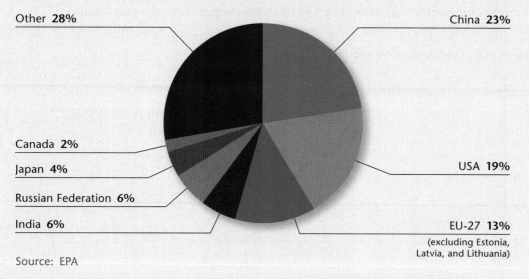

Other **28%**
China **23%**
Canada **2%**
Japan **4%**
USA **19%**
Russian Federation **6%**
India **6%**
EU-27 **13%**
(excluding Estonia, Latvia, and Lithuania)

Source: EPA

The news about global CO_2 emissions is mixed. The negative news is that global emissions have increased by over 16 times since the beginning of the twentieth century. There is general consensus now among the scientific community that this is a leading cause of global warming. The majority of these emissions are from heating and industry, but of real concern, 17 percent of CO_2 emissions come from forest fires and deforestation. On the other hand, it can be argued that increased emissions are also evidence of economic growth, especially in the developing world. With rapid economic growth fueled primarily by coal and oil, China is now the world's largest emitter. (See Figure 4.) Another promising trend is that while CO_2 emissions are increasing in developing nations, they are decreasing in developed nations such as the United States, Germany, and the United Kingdom.

B **Use information from Figure 4 and the paragraph to answer the following sentences. Write your answers on the blank lines.**

1 Why does the writer describe the state of global CO_2 emissions as "mixed"?

_____

2 Summarize the negative news about global CO_2 emissions.

_____

3 Why does the writer argue that a growth in emissions could be seen as positive? Use an example from Figure 4 to illustrate your answer.

_____

4 For what percentage of global CO_2 emissions are the United States and Japan currently responsible? What do you predict will happen to these percentages in the future?

_____

5 How do total CO_2 emissions from China compare to those from the United States and Canada?

_____

Connecting to the Topic

Read the following definition of *biodiversity*, and then discuss the following questions with a partner.

> **biodiversity** (*n*) the number and variety of living things found within a specified geographical location

1 Many scientists think that it is important to maintain biodiversity. What might be some reasons for this view?

2 How do you think human actions either encourage or reduce biodiversity?

Previewing and Predicting

> Reading a title and looking at any illustrations or graphic material can help you predict what a reading will be about.

A Read the title of Reading 3, and look at Figures 4.1 and 4.2. Then put a check (✓) next to the questions you think will be answered in the reading.

_____ A Is the total forest area increasing or decreasing worldwide?

_____ B What is the total global revenue from wood products?

_____ C To what extent do tropical forests contribute to biodiversity?

_____ D How does deforestation affect carbon dioxide emissions?

_____ E How does land become a conservation reserve?

B Compare your answers with a partner's.

While You Read

As you read, stop at the end of each sentence that contains words in bold. Then follow the instructions in the box in the margin.

Biodiversity and Tropical Rain Forests

1   By 2010, biologists had identified and named 1.9 million of the earth's natural species. With estimated numbers ranging from 5 million to 30 million, scientists' opinions are far from unanimous on the total number of species that may exist. However, there is a consensus among scientists that at least half of the world's species live in the rain forests of the earth's tropical zones.

2   For some years, however, tropical forests have been the scenes of massive destruction, as humans cut down or burn the trees to harvest hardwood or provide land for agriculture and settlements. (**See Figure 4.1.**) Between 1988 and 2010, for example, deforestation in Brazil's Amazon region totaled 148,637 square miles (384,968 square kilometers), the equivalent of an area almost as large as Sweden. Between 1990 and 2010, Malaysia lost 88,000 square miles (227,919 square kilometers), and during the same two decades, Indonesia lost more than 20 percent of its forest cover, equivalent to an area of more than 93,000 square miles (240,868 square kilometers).

WHILE YOU READ 1

Study Figure 4.1. Which country is increasing its forestland?
a) Canada
b) China

Figure 4.1 Annual Change in Forest Area by Country, 2005–2010

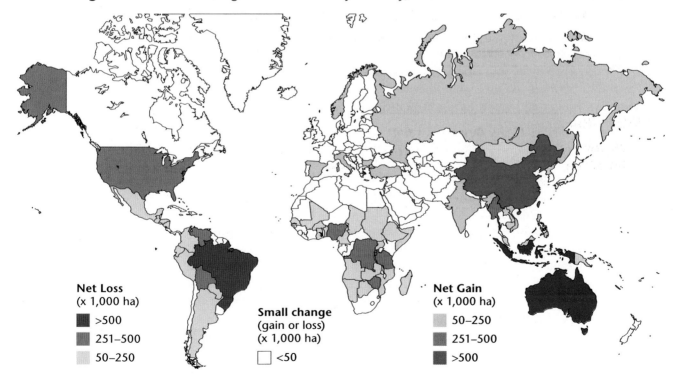

Net Loss
(x 1,000 ha)

■ >500

■ 251–500

■ 50–250

Small change
(gain or loss)
(x 1,000 ha)

□ <50

Net Gain
(x 1,000 ha)

■ 50–250

■ 251–500

■ >500

Source: http://www.fao.org/forestry/fra/62219/en/

3   One devastating impact of deforestation is that natural habitats are completely destroyed, resulting in species **extinction**. Extinction occurs naturally at a rate of one species per 10 years. In fact, from fossil evidence, scientists estimate that more than 99 percent of all species have become extinct over time. However, in the past few decades, human activity has accelerated this process, causing hundreds or perhaps thousands of extinctions per year. In 2010, botanists warned that, within 20 years, the extinction rate could reach around 10,000 per year, a rate that would be approximately 10,000 times greater than the extinction rate that existed prior to the appearance of humans on Earth. In 2011, even after mathematicians pointed out an error in previous estimates of extinction rates, there was little good news: the minimum extinction rate remained between 100 and 1,000 times higher than the rate that existed before the emergence of humans.

WHILE YOU READ 2

Reread this sentence. Highlight the phrase that helps you understand the term *extinction*.

4   **For a number of reasons**, the threatened species of the rain forests are an immense and irreplaceable resource. First, because of their genetic diversity, they are a source of information and material that can be utilized to strengthen domesticated varieties that become susceptible to pests or disease. For example, the wild American oil palm has a natural resistance to *spear rot*, a disease that is destroying the domesticated African oil palm. Researchers are using genes from the American plant to develop resistance to the disease in its African cousin.

WHILE YOU READ 3

Scan ahead for words that introduce these reasons. Highlight the words. Then reread paragraph 4.

5   Second, tropical species are a potentially vast source of tree and plant species that could be domesticated for human use. Twenty-four crop species have been domesticated in the Amazon region alone, and countless numbers remain. For example, *Caryocar villosum* is a tree that produces fruit valued highly by Amazonian peoples, and the *Copaifera lanfgsdorfii* tree species produces substances that can substitute for diesel fuel. In 2008, Australian farmers in Queensland began to plant *Copaiferas* as a renewable source of energy and wood for high-quality furniture. Species such as these could be of immense value to society.

6   Tropical species also have great potential as a source of medicinal drugs. Much of modern medicine is derived from wild species, and many of these come from tropical forests. The Madagascar periwinkle is a good example. This small native plant has amazing medicinal properties. It produces *vinblastine* and *vincristine*, which are extremely effective in the treatment of two forms of cancer: leukemia and Hodgkin's lymphoma. Vincristine alone has been responsible for raising the survival rate of childhood leukemia from lower than 10 percent to higher than 90 percent. This plant not only has considerable medical benefits, but economic ones, as well, generating an annual income of over $100 million a year for the pharmaceutical company that produces it.

7   What can be done to preserve the biological diversity of the tropical rain forests? It is unlikely that the extinctions can be completely halted. However, some authorities are cautiously optimistic that today's rate of

extinction can be slowed if both the immediate and the root causes of the crisis are **addressed**.

8   One way to preserve biological diversity is to designate land as forest reserves in which all economic exploitation of the forest is forbidden. This protects the habitats of tropical species, which in turn slows the pace of extinction. As Figure 4.2 shows, forest reserves are increasing in all global **regions**. One of the most successful methods of doing this has been the Debt for Nature Swap program. These are financial agreements that allow developing countries to reduce their foreign debt in exchange for preserving threatened forest habitat. It is estimated that banks and governments hold around $1 trillion in debt from developing countries, much of which will likely never be collected. In 2000 and again in 2008, the U.S. government, for example, forgave a debt of $40 million owed by Peru in exchange for that country's establishing a protected area of 27.5 million acres. This program is not without controversy, with some economists claiming that forgiving debt is poor economic policy. However, critics don't always take into account the immense value of tropical species.

9   The establishment of forest reserves is a positive development, but it is not enough. Experts argue that the pace of scientific research on tropical plant species needs to be accelerated. Not surprisingly, pharmaceutical companies are playing a major role in conducting this scientific research. For example, Merck, the world's largest biomedical company, paid $1 million dollars to a Costa Rican biology institute to locate and catalog all

WHILE YOU READ ④

Scan paragraphs 8–10 and find and highlight each solution.

WHILE YOU READ ⑤

Check Figure 4.2. Highlight the region that is increasing forest reserves the fastest.

Figure 4.2 Land Used for Forest Reserves, 1990–2010

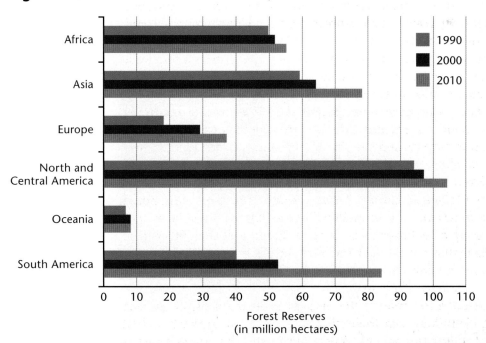

Source: http://www.fao.org/forestry/fra/62219/en/

native species. This is a promising partnership since it produces much needed research while also providing funding for the home country. Such research is the only means of identifying areas that should receive priority in **conservation decisions**. A further advantage is that it helps address another cause of the problem: human ignorance about the value of the natural world and about human dependence on it. This education is essential in convincing people that the biological resources of the rain forests are worth preserving.

WHILE YOU READ 6

Reread this sentence. Highlight the continuing idea. Use it to help you find and highlight the main idea of this paragraph.

10   A third essential step is to creatively address the root cause of biodiversity loss – the economic pressures that cause people to destroy the forests for short-term gain. Accomplishing this, however, is the greatest challenge facing the international community, because it involves tackling the complex and related problems of poverty, international debt, and overpopulation in the developing world. One part of this challenge is to allow countries a more equitable share of the revenue from pharmaceutical products originating in the tropical forests. The United Nations estimates this totals over $30 billion a year, but developing countries see little of this profit.

11   Tropical forests are incredibly rich ecosystems, which provide much of the world's biodiversity. However, even with increased understanding of the value of these areas, excessive destruction continues. There are a few promising signs, however. Deforestation in many regions is slowing as governments combat this practice with intensive tree planting. Asia, for example, has gained forest in the last decade, primarily due to China's large-scale planting initiatives. Moreover, the number of reserves designated for conservation of biodiversity is increasing worldwide with particularly strong gains in South America and Asia. Unfortunately, despite these gains, the capacity for humans to destroy forests continues to appear greater than their ability to protect them.

Tropical forests are biologically diverse.

Main Idea Check

Match the main ideas below to five of the paragraphs in Reading 3. Write the number of the paragraph on the blank line.

_____ A Different species of plants from tropical rain forests could be a source of important new medicinal drugs.

_____ B Human activity is speeding up the process of extinction.

_____ C Designating land as forest reserves is one part of a solution to prevent biodiversity loss.

_____ D Rain forest species are a valuable resource since their genes may enable scientists to strengthen domesticated species.

_____ E To provide information needed for both conservation and education, more emphasis is needed on tropical species research.

A Closer Look

Look back at Reading 3 to answer the following questions.

1 Which statement best describes changes in forest areas worldwide?

   a All regions of the world are experiencing a decrease in the percentage of land covered by forest.

   b Brazil, Malaysia, and Indonesia lost a combined total of over 280,000 square miles of forest.

   c The percentage of forestland is decreasing in developing countries, but it is increasing in developed countries.

   d Although some regions have increased the percentage of forestland, deforestation is still occurring at a devastating rate.

2 How fast are tropical species likely to become extinct within the next two decades?

   a At a rate similar to the rate that existed before the appearance of humans on the earth.

   b At a pace much faster than existed before the emergence of humans.

   c Faster now than at any other time since humans appeared on the earth.

   d At a rate 1,000 times higher than today.

3 What does the writer point out as justification for the claim that wild species in tropical forests are extremely valuable resources for humans? Circle all that apply.

   a Their potential as domesticated species

   b The high value of wood products

   c Their potential medicinal value

   d Their role in sustainable development

4 The country of Madagascar receives over $100 million from the use of its native plant, vincristine, being used as a cancer-fighting drug. **True or False?**

5 Which statements would the writer agree with according to paragraph 8? Circle all that apply.

a Developing countries probably lack the ability to repay all their debt.

b The Debt for Nature Swap is an example of shortsighted economic development.

c Swapping debt for the establishment of forest reserves is a fair exchange because of the value of species within these reserves.

d The creation of forest reserves is the only solution to the survival of biodiversity in tropical forests.

6 Which of the following is not offered as a solution to the problem of deforestation and the loss of tropical species?

a Governments should require pharmaceutical companies to pay a higher percentage of their profits to countries where native plants are used for medicinal drugs.

b The global problem of poverty in developing countries must be addressed.

c A percentage of international debt, particularly from developing nations, should be forgiven in exchange for conservation efforts.

d Governments need to restrict the size of families since overpopulation is clearly linked to deforestation and loss of biodiversity.

Skill Review

In Skills and Strategies 11, you learned that writers often use graphic material in a text in order to present additional information. Paying attention to and understanding graphic material will help you improve your academic reading.

Work with a partner. Use figures 4.1 and 4.2 to answer the following questions.

1 Although South America continues to lose tropical forests, it has increased the percentage of land designated for forest reserves. **True or False?**

2 Which developed country has the highest rate of forest loss?
   a The United States   c Canada
   b Russia   d Australia

3 Which world region saw the largest increase in conservation reserves between 1990 and 2010?
   a North and Central America c Europe
   b South America   d Asia

4 Which statement best describes the state of forestland in Africa?

a The situation in Africa is mixed, with both positive and negative developments.

b This region is countering deforestation with a rapid increase in the establishment of forest reserves.

c The situation in Africa is very similar to the situation in South and Central America.

d All African nations are experiencing deforestation to a certain degree.

Definitions

Find the words in Reading 3 that are similar to the definitions below.

1 in complete agreement (*adj*) Par. 1
2 the state of no longer existing (*n*) Par. 3
3 scientists who study plants (*n pl*) Par. 3
4 likely to be hurt or negatively affected by something (*adj*) Par. 4
5 the qualities something has (*n pl*) Par. 6
6 to create; to produce (*v*) Par. 6
7 to stop something from being damaged or lost (*v*) Par. 7
8 to choose something for a special purpose (*v*) Par. 8
9 an arrangement in which people work closely together (*n*) Par. 9
10 the protection of natural resources (*n*) Par. 9

Synonyms

Complete the sentences with words from Reading 3 in the box below. These words replace the words or phrases in parentheses, which are similar in meaning.

catalog	consensus	excessive	harvest	substitute
combat	debt	halted	renewable	tackle

1 With some adjustments to the engine, it is possible to (swap) _____ vegetable oil for gasoline in some vehicles.

2 With land burning throughout the western United States, more firefighters were brought in to (fight) _____ the huge wildfires.

3 These days, farmers use highly sophisticated machines to (pick) _____ their crops.

4 Before computers, librarians had to (organize, list) _____ all books by hand.

5 The heat was (too much) _____. People were warned to stay indoors.

6 There is general (agreement) _____ within the scientific community that global warming exists, but scientists hold different opinions about how to address it.

7 After he graduated from university, he managed to pay off all his (money owed) _____ within 3 years.

8 The city decided to (try to solve) _____ the housing problem by first holding public meetings in order to listen to the residents' ideas for improvement.

9 When a threatened species of bird was discovered in the forest, all tree cutting was (stopped) _____.

10 Wind and solar power are examples of (replaceable) _____ energy sources.

Critical Thinking

Reading 3 discusses the negative effects of deforestation on biodiversity within tropical forests. The writer then introduces several solutions to this problem.

A Read the following chart. Think about each of the following solutions to the problem of biodiversity loss. If necessary, look over Reading 3 again. Then indicate whether you think each solution is a very effective or not very effective way to solve this problem.

SOLUTION	VERY EFFECTIVE	NOT VERY EFFECTIVE
Debt for Nature Swap		
Establishment of forest reserves		
More education about the benefits of biodiversity in tropical forests		
Increasing research by pharmaceutical companies		
Tackling global problems of poverty		
Tackling global problems of overpopulation		

B Compare your answers with a partner's. Explain your opinions.

Research

Many countries are encouraging ecotourism, which is a holiday or travel to a threatened environment. It makes people aware of the need to protect the environment. Ecotourism is one way to both educate people about biodiversity and to provide much-needed funding to developing countries. Research ecotourism, and find answers to the following questions.

- What are some popular ecotourism destinations in the world?
- What kinds of activities can people participate in at these destinations?
- What type of ecotourism destination would you enjoy?

Writing

Write two paragraphs about your research. The first paragraph will describe some different ecotourism destinations, and the second will describe the destination you have identified as the most interesting and why.

Connecting to the Topic

Discuss the following questions with a partner.

1 What kind of activities do you use water for on a daily basis?
2 Where does the water come from where you live? Is there plenty of water available?
3 It is often said that many of us waste water. What steps could you take to reduce the amount of water you use each day?

Previewing and Predicting

> Reading the first sentence in each paragraph, and looking at graphic material can help you predict what a reading will be about.

A Read the first sentence of paragraphs 2–8 in Reading 4, and look at Figures 4.3 and 4.4. Think of a question that you expect each paragraph to answer. Then choose the question below that is most like your question. Write the number of the paragraph (*2–8*) next to that question.

PARAGRAPH	QUESTION
	Which regions in the world face serious water shortages?
	What do humans use water for?
	How does geography affect water supply?
	What is the financial effect of the water shortage?
	What is the definition of a low-impact solution?
	What are some general solutions to the water crisis?
	How does human behavior affect access to water?

B Compare your answers with a partner's.

While You Read

As you read, stop at the end of each sentence that contains words in bold. Then follow the instructions in the box in the margin.

The Water Crisis

factors = 2,3,4

Solutions = 7, 8

1   Clean, freshwater is essential to life, and the earth provides abundant supplies of such water. Even though 97 percent of the planet's water is in the ocean, there is still, in theory, enough freshwater for every person on the planet today. Each year, approximately 110,000 billion cubic meters of water falls to the land as rain or snow. Of this, humans use less than 10 percent for agriculture, industry, and personal use, and most of this water is eventually returned as part of the water cycle. Since this is the case, why is there insufficient water in areas of the world where billions of people live? Moreover, why do many experts believe the next wars may be about water, not oil? The answer lies not in the amount of freshwater, but in its unequal **availability**.

Three geographical factors determine water availability. First, global atmospheric conditions create areas of high pressure and low precipitation. Next, proximity to water also influences the amount of rain since prevailing winds bring moist air from large bodies of water to the land. The farther a country is from large bodies of water, the drier it is. Finally, topography has an important effect on rainfall. High mountains act as water catchers, trapping rainfall on one side of the mountains, but leaving

WHILE YOU READ ❶

Which is the main topic of this reading?
a) Water supply
b) Water cycle
c) Unequal availability of water

طبوغرافيا + القرب من المياه + الظروف الجوية

إعلان الطقس
جغرافية
facts

Figure 4.3 Freshwater Availability, Cubic Meters Per Person and Per Year, 2007

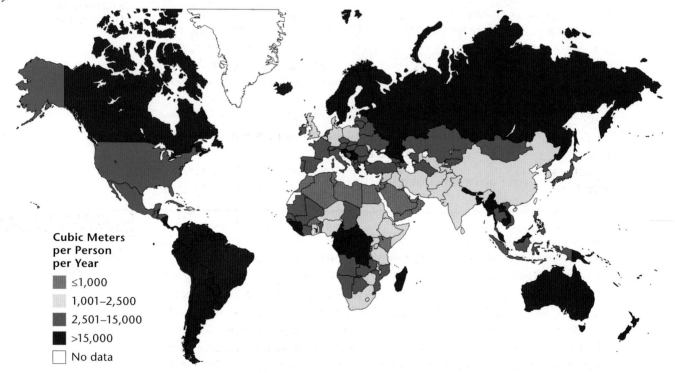

Cubic Meters per Person per Year
- ≤1,000
- 1,001–2,500
- 2,501–15,000
- >15,000
- No data

Source: http://www.un.org/waterforlifedecade/scarcity.shtml

Figure 4.4 Breakdown of Freshwater Use

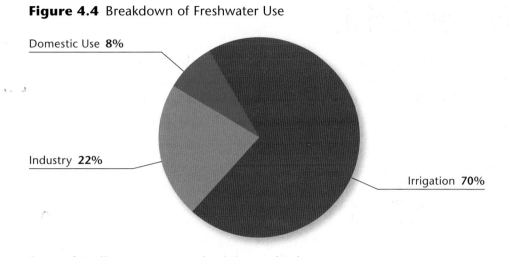

Domestic Use **8%**

Industry **22%**

Irrigation **70%**

Source: http://www.unwater.org/statistics_use.html

the other side dry in the rain shadow. In most parts of the world, all three factors influence rainfall. In addition to these factors, periodic droughts can also dramatically reduce the water supply within a specific region. These factors lead to some countries being water-rich while others are water-poor (See Figure 4.3.).

Human activity also plays an important role in freshwater availability. Population growth, urbanization, and farming can strain existing water supplies, reducing both the amount and quality of water available. Underlying the problem of water availability is the fact that most population growth occurs in developing countries, areas already short of water. Wells and piped water and sanitation systems are expensive to build and to maintain. As the population continues to grow in these less developed regions, and as more people move to urban areas, the World Bank estimates that the cost of supplying water will be triple today's costs. The United Nations warns that two thirds of the world's population will live in countries experiencing water shortages by 2025.

4   Water shortages have critical effects on individuals and nations because more than any other resource, water is essential for human activity. It is used in agriculture, industry, and domestic use, that is, for daily living. Of these uses, agriculture accounts for by far the biggest use of water. (See Figure 4.4.) Irrigation can quickly turn dry dirt into farmland, but it is costly in terms of water. It takes 634 gallons of water to produce a hamburger, 37 gallons for a cup of coffee, 650 gallons for a pound of rice, and 265 gallons for a glass of milk – statistics that highlight the hidden costs of food production. The environmental effect of agriculture is also significant. Farming depends on the use of fertilizers and pesticides. However, irrigation causes runoff of these chemicals, thereby contaminating local supplies of drinking water, and exacerbating water shortages. In the last 50 years, the use of fertilizers has more than tripled in the United States, and

WHILE YOU READ 2

Check the graphic illustration. Is Russia (a) Water-rich or (b) Water-poor?

WHILE YOU READ 3

Highlight the percentage of water used for agriculture.

as demand for food increases with population growth, the increased use of fertilizers is likely to continue.

5 With such reliance on water, it is not surprising that many regions worldwide face serious water shortages, including in both developed and developing nations. However, it is in developing nations where water shortage is critical. According to the United Nations, half of all people in developing countries have no access to clean water. In rural areas of these countries, women walk as many as 4 hours a day to collect water. In urban areas, water may be more easily available, but at a price. Because water is not piped into slum areas, people there have to buy water in containers. They often have to pay 5 to 10 times more per gallon than other people living in the same city because those people have access to piped **water**. This combination of poverty and lack of freshwater is deadly, causing high mortality rates, particularly for children. Each year, 5 times as many children die from water-borne illnesses than from HIV / AIDS.

WHILE YOU READ ④

Highlight the reduced relative clause in this sentence.

In some developing countries, women walk miles to get clean water.

6 This human crisis is also an economic crisis. The United Nations estimates that lack of access to clean water and sanitation costs developing nations a staggering 170 billion U.S. dollars a year. This estimate was determined by looking at the cost of health care from treating water-borne illnesses, and the time lost through walking long distances to collect water. For example, it is estimated that in Sub-Saharan Africa, women spend 40 billion hours per year collecting water. This is equivalent to the total of all the hours worked by the French workforce.

Solutions to the water crisis can be classified into two broad approaches: high impact and low **impact**. High-impact solutions include damming, altering the natural course of rivers for irrigation, and desalination – a process of converting seawater to freshwater. Countries across the

WHILE YOU READ ⑤

As you read, highlight the specific examples of each general solution.

A desalination plant converts seawater to fresh water.

globe are using these approaches, even though they come at an economic, human, and environmental cost. The Aswan High Dam in Egypt was built to irrigate thousands of acres of farmland. The Colorado River was dammed to provide water to California. China is investing $62 billion to pipe water from the Yangtze River to its dry cities and farmlands in the north. The desert-dry country of Saudi Arabia relies on the technology of desalination. More than 120 desalination plants in the Persian Gulf Region provide much of the water to North Africa and Middle Eastern countries.

8   Unlike high-impact solutions, low-impact solutions are usually on a local scale and are more ecologically sensitive. The emphasis tends to be on improving the efficiency of water use rather than seeking new supplies. For example, some cities in water-scarce areas in the United States subsidize the use of sanitation systems, which require less water and recycle more. Another important emphasis is the increased understanding of the role of wetlands in water management. These important ecological areas naturally filter and clean runoff water, allowing this water to return to rivers and reenter the water cycle. The Nakivubo Swamp in Uganda's Kampala district is a good example of this process. For years, this extensive wetland has received contaminated water from surrounding settlements, which lack proper sanitation. The wetland naturally purifies this water, returning it to Lake Victoria, where local people can use it more safely for their drinking water.

9   The solution to the global water crisis is the responsibility of all nations. In 2010, the United Nations passed a resolution that recognized clean drinking water and adequate sanitation as a basic human right. While this resolution has no enforcement power, it does clearly illustrate the fact that many countries understand water is not just a valuable resource; it is also essential to human life.

Main Idea Check

Match the main ideas below to five of the paragraphs in Reading 4. Write the number of the paragraph on the blank line.

_____ A Low-impact solutions both improve water efficiency and have minimal effect on the environment.

_____ B High population growth in water-poor areas is putting pressure on this resource.

_____ C The water crisis is also an economic crisis.

_____ D Dams, altered river courses, and desalination plants are examples of high-impact solutions.

_____ E Agriculture accounts for the largest use of water.

A Closer Look

Look back at Reading 4 to answer the following questions.

1 Which geographical factors does the writer identify as determining water availability? Circle all that apply.

a Distance from large bodies of water

b Heavy use of agriculture

c Diminishing water supply

d Periodic droughts

e Mountains

f Climate change

2 Why does the writer include statistics about how much water it takes to produce common food and drink items?

a These agricultural products illustrate the importance of agriculture.

b The examples illustrate that the production of everyday food and drink items requires an enormous amount of water.

c These products alone use over 70 percent of the freshwater supply.

d These food and drink items demonstrate the ability of water to transform arid land into productive farmland.

3 Which global regions generally have an adequate supply of water? Circle all that apply.

a Asia

b Southern Africa

c South America

d Australia

e Northern Africa

4 Which of the following is *not* given as an effect of lack of water in developing countries?

a Women need to spend hours each day collecting water.

b The population is growing faster there than in developed countries.

c The World Bank estimates that the cost of supplying water will triple in these areas.

d The poorest residents are forced to pay the most for water.

5 Although building dams is expensive, this ecologically sensitive practice increases the supply of freshwater to many people. **True or False?**

6 Why does the writer use the example of the Nakivubo Swamp in Uganda?

a It illustrates the important connection between the natural environment and water management.

b It demonstrates how water availability can be efficiently and inexpensively improved.

c The wetlands are an example of how easily humans can contaminate natural water supplies.

d It shows how humans can create new environments, which naturally purify water.

Skill Review

In Skills and Strategies 11, you learned that writers often use graphic material to present information additional to the text. Understanding graphs, charts, and maps will help you improve your academic reading.

A Read the following statements. Look over Figures 4.3 and 4.4 and the relevant text. Then put a check (✓) next to the statement if it is true or if it is false.

STATEMENT	TRUE	FALSE
1 Canada has greater freshwater availability than the United States.	✓	
2 On average, Russia has access to approximately the same amount of water per person as Australia.	✓	
3 Some countries in the Middle East have access to less than 1,000 cubic meters of freshwater per year, which explains why this region is constructing desalination plants.	✓	
4 The situation in India is more serious than northern Africa, even though both regions have extensive coastlines.		✗
5 The average person in South America has access to between 2,500 and 15,000 cubic meters of freshwater per year.		✗
6 Some African countries with no access to the oceans have a better freshwater supply than countries with coastal regions.	✓	
7 Developed countries throughout Europe are experiencing no water shortage.		✗
8 Taking steps to save domestic and industrial water use could have a significant impact on the water crisis since these activities account for almost one-third of all water use.	✓	

B Compare your answers with a partner's.

Definitions

Find the words in Reading 4 that are similar to the definitions below.

1 more than enough (*adj*) Par. 1

2 not enough (*adj*) Par. 1

3 relating to the mixture of gases surrounding Earth (*adj*) Par. 2

4 the natural features of land (*n*) Par. 2

5 happening repeatedly but not necessarily frequently (*adj*) Par. 2

6 to put pressure on something (*v*) Par. 3

7 real, but not immediately obvious (*adj*) Par. 3

8 expensive (*adj*) Par. 4

9 to draw attention to something (*v*) Par. 4

10 chemicals and animal waste that flow into rivers and lakes (*n*) Par. 4

11 because of this; as a result of this (*adv*) Par. 4

12 to pay part of the cost of something (*v*) Par. 8

13 to rid something of harmful substances (*v*) Par. 8

14 a formal statement of a decision or an opinion (*n*) Par. 9

15 the action of causing a law to be obeyed (*n*) Par. 9

Words in Context

Complete the passages with words or phrases from Reading 4 in the box below.

converting	filter	precipitation	proximity to	staggering
exacerbate	moist	prevailing winds	rain shadow	traps

1 Mount Waialeale, Hawaii, illustrates the effects of a / an _____.
   a
_____ from the east bring warm, _____ air from the ocean to
   b   c
the coast. As the air rises, it cools and falls as rain. The mountain _____
   d
most of the rainfall on the east side, leaving very little _____ on the west
   e
side. The difference is _____: almost 40 feet (12 meters) of rain on the
   f
east and 1.5 feet (46 centimeters) on the west.

2 Critics of desalination plants believe communities need to think carefully before they
embrace the idea of _____ seawater to freshwater. They argue that the
   g
process has hidden environmental costs. Huge amounts of energy are needed to
_____ the seawater. Emissions released by this process will
   h

_____ global warming. Another problem is that these plants must be in
close _____ the ocean, which limits fishing. For these reasons, critics
argue that communities should first explore low-impact solutions.

Academic Word List

**The following are Academic Word List words from Readings 3 and 4 of this unit. Use
these words to complete the sentences. (For more on the Academic Word List, see
page 256.)**

converted (v)	generated (v)	insufficient (adj)	subsidize (v)	thereby (adj)
enforcement (n)	highlights (v)	resolution (n)	substitute (v)	underlying (adj)

1 The government is beginning to focus on poverty, one of the most serious
_____ causes of deforestation.

2 In the second year of drought, the city government passed a/an _____
that called on people to limit their water use.

3 Hunting of threatened species is not allowed, but _____ of this law is
difficult because of the huge areas of land involved.

4 As the moist air rises, it cools, _____ causing precipitation in the form of
rain or snow.

5 The news story about local effects of global warming _____ a lot of
interest as people argued about how climate change would affect their daily lives.

6 In order to decrease emissions, the government decided to _____ the
production of electric cars.

7 Many people believe that the global effort to reduce deforestation is
_____. Much more needs to be done.

8 The Aral Sea _____ the devastating effects short-term planning can have
on the environment.

9 Unlike other countries, the United States has not fully _____ to the
metric system; it still uses miles, not kilometers, for example.

10 People are trying to _____ environmentally sensitive products for
everyday items such as soap, shampoo, and washing detergent.

Critical Thinking

Reading 4 suggests that the water crisis calls for careful water management by all nations.

CLARIFYING CONCEPTS

Critical thinking includes exploring a concept in a text by restating it and applying it to a different context.

A Work with a partner. Discuss the following questions.

1 What does the term *water management* mean?
2 What examples of water management can you find in Reading 4?

B Imagine you and your partner are government officials in charge of water management. Your city is experiencing a severe drought. You have been told to reduce the amount of water used per person. What steps would you take to (a) encourage or (b) force residents to reduce their daily use of this resource? Discuss your ideas.

Research

Find an example of either the building of dams or the altering of rivers. Using your example find answers to the following questions.

- What are the advantages and disadvantages of this approach to water shortage?
- What are the negative effects of this approach?

Writing

Write two paragraphs about your research. The first paragraph will describe the solution in general, and the second will describe its advantages and disadvantages.

Improving Your Reading Speed

Good readers read quickly and still understand most of what they read.

A Read the instructions and strategies for Improving Your Reading Speed in Appendix 3 on page 273.

B Choose either Reading 3 or Reading 4 in this unit. Read it without stopping. Time how long it takes you to finish the text in minutes and seconds. Enter the time in the chart on page 275. Then calculate your reading speed in number of words per minute.

Nominalization in Subjects

To concentrate a large amount of information in one sentence, academic writers often use a grammar technique called *nominalization*. For example, instead of a one- or two-word subject, they sometimes create complex noun phrases as subjects. These longer subjects make sentences more challenging to read. However, learning to recognize and understand nominalization will help you become a more efficient reader. Although nominalization can occur in other parts of a sentence, the focus here is on nominalization in subjects only.

Examples & Explanations

The emergence of drug-resistant bacteria is worrying health experts.

Noun + *of* + noun phrase + verb. To understand a nominalized subject with this pattern, follow the steps below to make two simpler sentences.
1 Change the first noun (*emergence*) into the verb from the same word-family (*are emerging*).
2 For the subject of the new verb from Step 1, use the noun phrase that follows the preposition of (*drug-resistant kinds of bacteria*).
3 Start a new, second sentence by inserting *This* before the verb of the original sentence (*is worrying*).

Drug-resistant kinds of bacteria are emerging. This is worrying health experts.

The company's decision to clean up its toxic waste site was welcomed by the town's residents.

Noun + *'s* + noun phrase + verb. To understand this pattern of nominalization, follow the steps below to make two simpler sentences.
1 Change the second noun (*decision*) into a verb (*decided*).
2 For the subject of the new verb from Step 1, use the first noun (*company* – without apostrophe *-s*).
3 For the second sentence, insert *This* before the verb of the original sentence.

The company decided to clean up its toxic waste site. This was welcomed by the town's residents.

The careless use of pesticides by farmers in the Aral Sea basin contaminated local supplies of drinking water.

Noun + *of* + noun phrase + *by* + noun phrase + verb. To understand this pattern of nominalized subject, follow the steps below to make two simpler sentences.
1 Change the first noun (*use*) into a verb (*used*). Change any adjectives with this noun (*careless*) into adverbs (*carelessly*).
2 For the subject of the new verb from Step 1, use the noun phrase after *by*.
3 For the object of the new verb, use the noun phrase after *of*.
4 Start the second sentence by inserting *This* before the verb of the original sentence (*contaminated*).

Farmers in the Aral Sea basin used pesticides carelessly. This contaminated local supplies of drinking water.

The Language of Nominalization

The noun markers in the chart will help you recognize many nouns that may be used to form nominalized subjects.

MARKERS OF NOMINALIZATION					
-ness	-ety	-ance	-ism	-ion	-ing
-ment	-ity	-ence	-asm	-tion	-th
-hood	-ty	-ency		-sion	

Note, however, that many nouns do not contain special noun markers (e.g., *attack, collapse, damage, increase, release, spread, use,* etc.).

Strategies

These strategies will help you understand nominalized English as you read.

- Look for a series of nouns that appear before the main verb.
- Identify the noun that shows an action or a state.
- Identify any phrases and noun clauses that belong with this noun.
- Change the original sentence into two simpler sentences by following the steps outlined under Examples & Explanations on page 235.

Skill Practice 1

In the following sentences, highlight the main verb and underline the entire nominalized subject. The first one has been done for you.

1 The researcher's claim that he had discovered a cure for the common cold was received with disbelief by the scientific community.

2 The government's decision to raise income taxes has angered a lot of people.

3 The allegation by some people that immigrants take more out of the economy than they contribute to it is rejected by most economists.

4 The destruction of large sections of the tropical rain forest by multinational companies has led to protests by environmental groups.

5 The tendency of new immigrants to settle in their ethnic communities is sometimes wrongly cited as evidence that they do not wish to become integrated into American society.

6 The current loss of biodiversity due to the extinction of species is a threat to the health of the planet that will last for hundreds of years.

Skill Practice 2

In the following sentences, highlight the main verb and underline the entire nominalized subject. Then rewrite the sentence as two simpler sentences. The first one has been done for you.

1 The research team's claim that they had discovered the gene responsible for some forms of breast cancer was received with enthusiasm by the scientific community.

   The research team claimed that they had discovered the gene responsible for some forms of breast cancer. This was received with enthusiasm by the scientific community.

2 The destruction of vast areas of the Amazon rain forest by wealthy cattle-farming businesses is driving large numbers of tropical species to extinction.

   _____

   _____

3 The government's decision to expand agriculture by using enormous amounts of water from the region's two main rivers for irrigation was the root cause of the environmental catastrophe in the Aral Sea basin.

   _____

   _____

4 The public's lack of appreciation of the ecological and scientific value of rain forest species is an obstacle to solving the problem of biodiversity loss.

   _____

   _____

5 The clearing of forests by early human settlers to provide fuel, wood for construction, and fields for farming probably caused the first major threats to the natural environment.

   _____

   _____

Connecting to the Topic

Read the definition of *global warming*, and then discuss the following questions with a partner.

> **global warming** (*n*) an increase in Earth's surface temperature over time, which can cause other long-lasting climate changes, such as different precipitation patterns or more intense storms

1 What is the climate like where you live? Has it changed in the past few years? Explain your answer.

2 What changes in climate would have the greatest impact on the people in your area? Explain your answer.

3 Do you think humans can have a positive or negative effect on climate? Explain your answer.

Previewing and Predicting

> Reading the title and section headings in a reading and looking at any illustrations and graphic material is a quick way to predict what a reading will be about.

A **Read the title and section headings in Reading 5 and look at the diagrams and graphs. Then decide what content will be in each section. Write the number of the section (*II–V*) next to the topic that best describes it. Some sections may have more than one topic.**

SECTION	TOPIC	/
	The need to alter our activities in order to cope with global warming	
	Possible consequences of global warming	
	Certain gases have a warming effect on Earth	
	What we know about global warming	
	The warming of Earth is causing polar ice to melt	
	Addressing the harm that global warming is likely to cause	

B **Compare your answers with a partner's.**

While You Read

As you read, stop at the end of each sentence that contains words in bold. Then follow the instructions in the box in the margin.

Managing Earth's Greenhouse

I. Introduction

1   Since the late twentieth century, climate scientists have been observing more and more evidence of global warming, that is, an increase in Earth's surface temperature over time. Although the causes of global warming remain a matter of contention, the existence of global warming is an unequivocal fact. In addition, widespread melting of snow and ice and the rising sea levels that result are a clear indication that global warming is not a myth.

2   Most climate scientists warn that the consequences could be dire if global warming continues at its present rate. Climate conditions around the world could change, bringing alterations in wind and precipitation patterns. In addition, we could experience a high frequency of extreme weather events, such as droughts, heat waves, and **floods.**

3   There is also broad agreement in the scientific community that global warming is primarily caused by human activity. Except for a small group of skeptics, scientists are generally convinced that we need to make some major behavioral changes in order to avoid widespread disruption of life on Earth. Fortunately, most experts believe that we can still curb the future effects of global warming if both governments and individuals make some changes now. The first logical step toward making informed decisions about what we can do in response to the situation is to identify the facts about global warming and its potential effects.

II. Facts About Global Warming

4   There is undeniable evidence that global warming results from rising concentrations of gases, such as carbon dioxide (CO_2), chlorofluorocarbons (CFCs), hydrofluorocarbons (HFCs), and methane (CH_4) in the atmosphere. These so-called greenhouse gases allow sunlight to pass through them and warm the earth. The earth then releases that heat in the form of energy called infrared radiation. The gases trap some of the outgoing heat and prevent it from escaping into space, similar to the way the glass sides and roof of a greenhouse work. The resultant rise in temperature on Earth is known as *the greenhouse effect*. (**See Figure 4.5.**)

5   Some degree of the greenhouse effect is essential for life on Earth. Without a blanket of gases around the planet, most of our heat would escape back into space, and life on Earth would be too cold for plants and animals to survive. However, in recent years, the concentration of greenhouse gases in the atmosphere has been increasing at an unprecedented rate. Analysis of the air contained in glacial ice shows that, over the last two centuries, there has been an increase of more than 30 percent in the

> **WHILE YOU READ ❶**
>
> Look back at paragraph 2. Highlight the cause and effect marker. Then highlight the effects.

> **WHILE YOU READ ❷**
>
> Study Figure 4.5. How much energy from the sun is absorbed by the earth?
> a) 100%
> b) 45%
> c) 88%

Figure 4.5 The Greenhouse Effect

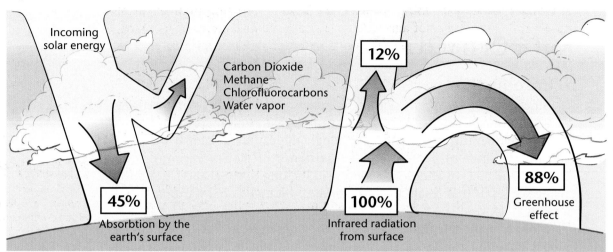

chief greenhouse gas, CO_2. Moreover, concentrations of this gas have been increasing rapidly from decade to decade since the late 1950s. Levels of atmospheric CO_2 have reached record highs, rising from the eighteenth-century high of 290 ppm (parts per million) to almost 396 ppm in 2012. Scientists generally agree that a safe level of CO_2 is 350 ppm.

6   The release of some CO_2 into the atmosphere happens naturally; however, human activity is responsible for most of the accumulation of this gas. The primary cause is the growth of industry, which began in Europe in the mid-nineteenth century and has continued around the world ever since. The process of industrialization in all countries has depended on the burning of coal, oil, and natural gas to produce energy, and the burning of these fossil fuels is considered to be the chief source of CO_2 **emissions**. The accumulation of CO_2 is also attributable to deforestation, particularly the burning of trees in the tropical rainforests of South America, Africa, and Asia. Furthermore, since trees absorb huge quantities of CO_2, the earth loses its natural capacity to absorb the gas when forests are destroyed.

WHILE YOU READ ❸

Look back at this sentence. Highlight the continuing idea. Then highlight the words it refers to.

7   Although CO_2 is the most prevalent greenhouse gas, there are others that are even more damaging to the atmosphere, such as HFCs. HFCs are gases that serve as coolants in refrigerators and air conditioners. The wide use of HFCs by manufacturers since the 1990s was motivated by the need to replace the CFCs that were formerly used in these appliances. CFCs began to be phased out because they harm the ozone layer, a layer of gas that protects Earth from harmful solar radiation. Although HFCs do not destroy the ozone layer, they are more dangerous than CO_2 because they trap even more heat. Atmospheric HFCs are of particular concern today because of the increasingly widespread use of air conditioners in the developing world, especially in India and **China**.

WHILE YOU READ ❹

Look back at this sentence. Highlight the problem marker. Then highlight the problem and the reason for the problem.

8   Just as industrialization and modern appliances have contributed to increased emissions of greenhouse gases, so too has agriculture. Since the

mid-twentieth century, there has been a tremendous expansion of rice growing and cattle farming in order to feed the growing population of the world. These types of agriculture are both major sources of methane, whose heat-retaining properties are approximately 20 times greater than those of CO_2.

9   In recent years, the accumulation of the heat-trapping greenhouse gases has caused average global temperatures to rise at a much more rapid rate than in the past. Data show that Earth's average global temperature increased by about 1.4 degrees Fahrenheit (0.8 degrees Celsius) over the past 100 years, with about 1.0°F (0.6°C) of this warming occurring over just the past three decades. **(See Figure 4.6.)** Scientists have also observed that 2011 was the ninth warmest year since the 1880s, when record keeping began. Since the 1970s, each decade has gotten progressively warmer, and 9 of the 10 warmest years have occurred in the twenty-first century.

10   Despite the abundance of well-established facts about global warming, there is still some uncertainty in predicting just how much temperatures will rise in the future. To make such predictions, scientists use computer models based on assumptions about the rate of increase of CO_2 in the atmosphere. Using such models, the National Resource Council in the United States recently predicted that average global temperatures are likely to increase between 3.6°F (2°C) and 11.5°F (6.4°C) by 2100. Many climate experts have stressed the importance of preventing a future rise of more than 3.6°F (2°C), and some believe that the threshold needs to be even lower in order to avoid dangerous climatic effects.

WHILE YOU READ 5

Study Figure 4.6. When was the average global temperature about 14.2°C?
a) 1920s
b) 1940s
c) 1980s

Figure 4.6 Average Global Temperature, 1880–2011

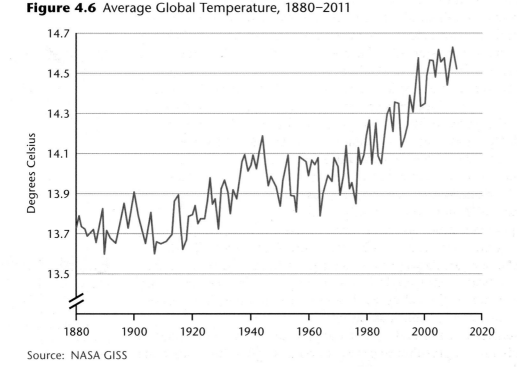

Source: NASA GISS

III. Potential Effects of Global Warming

11   It is likely that an increase at the lower end of the predicted temperature range would cause at least some disruption of human activity and Earth's ecosystems. On the other hand, a global temperature change at the higher end of the range would have a significantly disruptive effect. Consider, for instance, the potential effects of global warming on coral reefs, the world's most diverse marine ecosystem. Scientists have observed that Australia's Great Barrier Reef is just one of the reefs that is already showing signs of stress in response to a recent rise of about 1.3°F (0.74°C) and the increase of CO_2 in the ocean. Under these conditions, the ocean becomes more acidic, making it more difficult for coral to survive. Given the projected rise in CO_2 concentrations and a temperature increase in the range of 3.6°F (2°C) to 11.5°F (6.4°C) by the end of the century, it is likely that most coral reefs will not be able to adapt. They will probably die, bringing an end to all the plant and animal life they support. The decline of coral reefs would have a profound impact on people who rely on food and income from reef-based fisheries and tourism. Since most of the world's coral reefs are located in developing regions, people in those areas would suffer the most.

12   Sea levels are expected to rise as a result of global warming because ocean water expands as it heats up. The melting of glaciers, ice caps, and large sections of the Greenland and Antarctic ice sheets will also contribute to higher sea levels. In fact, this is already happening. Over the past century, the average global sea level has risen by nearly 7 inches (17.78 centimeters). Although estimates vary, some recent studies project that levels could rise as much as 2 feet (0.61 meters) by the end of this century. Such a change would pose an enormous threat to coastal areas, some of which are densely populated. These areas would undoubtedly experience more frequent flooding, and very low-lying areas, such as small island nations in the Pacific and the Caribbean and Bangladesh, could be completely submerged. Millions of people in highly vulnerable places would be forced to abandon their homes and endure social and economic upheaval on a massive scale.

13   Climate scientists also predict that if global warming continues unabated, the planet will experience a variety of weather extremes. In some areas, hurricanes and other tropical storms, which get their energy from warm ocean water, will become more intense as the ocean warms. Elsewhere, warming temperatures will cause heavier precipitation in the form of rain and snow. Global warming will also cause snow to melt earlier and rain to evaporate faster than normal, giving rise to parched land and drying vegetation. Dry trees and plants can then easily fuel fire during long periods of **drought**. In fact, recent studies show that the frequency of wildfires is already increasing in North America and Europe. Extreme weather events would adversely affect people's health as well. Severe and frequent heat waves would cause heat-related illness and death. Sustained heat would also decrease water resources and exacerbate air pollution.

WHILE YOU READ 6

Look back at the two previous sentences. Highlight the words and phrases that help you guess the meaning of *parched*.

Figure 4.7 The Shrinking Polar Ice Cap

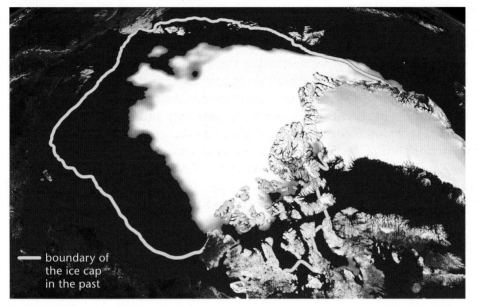

boundary of the ice cap in the past

Source: NASA

14   If global warming continues at present levels, agriculture will be seriously affected by climate changes. In regions that get more precipitation, it is likely that flooding will interfere with normal crop production. Areas that have a significant reduction in rainfall will experience a dramatic decline in crop yields. Experts predict that this will cause severe problems in large parts of Africa and Asia, where average temperatures are already near or above the maximum that crops can tolerate. One recent study predicts that India, for example, could experience a 30 to 40 percent reduction in agricultural productivity by 2080. Widespread reductions like this would inevitably lead to food shortages, higher prices, and growing world hunger.

15   It is clear that any potential effects of greenhouse gases will be both long-term and global. Although these gases remain in the atmosphere for different amounts of time, some of them, such as CO_2 and some CFCs, can affect the climate for thousands of years. It is also clear that greenhouse gases spread well beyond the areas in which they are originally released; thus their effects will be felt by future generations around the world.

IV. Responding to the Threat

16   In view of the potential damage that global warming could cause by the end of this century, most environmentalists and a growing number of political leaders believe that we should take immediate steps to reduce greenhouse gas emissions. There is also general agreement that increasing energy conservation, replacing fossil fuels with alternative sources of energy, and preserving the world's forests could accomplish such a **reduction**.

WHILE YOU READ 7

Look back at paragraph 16 to find the problem marker. Highlight it. Then highlight the solutions.

17   Environmentalists have identified several key energy-conserving strategies. One approach is to encourage reusing and recycling products. Both activities reduce methane emissions from landfills, cut down on the CO_2 released by incinerators, and avoid the use of fuel to transport waste. Reusing and recycling also save energy by decreasing the number of new products that need to be manufactured. Another energy-saving measure is for governments to create incentives, such as tax credits, which encourage manufacturers to develop more energy-efficient appliances and induce consumers to buy them. Substantial energy savings could also be achieved through energy-efficient building design and automobile manufacturing. Hybrid cars, for example, have been designed for better fuel economy and lower emissions than traditional **cars**.

18   The replacement of fossil fuels with clean, safe sources of renewable energy would also be a highly effective way to reduce greenhouse gas emissions. One of the biggest challenges is replacing coal, which many countries heavily depend on for heating and electricity. In fact, one-third of all global CO_2 emissions come from burning coal, which as the most polluting fuel, is also damaging people's health. Finding substitutes for coal and other fossil fuels means that governments will need to provide incentives for further research into low-carbon energy sources and for the development of affordable technology to utilize these sources.

WHILE YOU READ 8

Look back at this paragraph and highlight the main idea.

19   Some low-carbon energy sources are already being used in a limited way, and others are being studied. Expansion of the use of wind power to generate electricity, for example, is a possibility for the near future. In the more distant future is the prospect of using hydrogen for electricity generation. Scientists are generally optimistic about the effectiveness of such strategies. According to a recent report by the International Energy Agency (IEA), using cleaner, more efficient sources of energy in buildings, industry, and transportation could reduce the world's energy needs in 2050 by one-third and significantly control greenhouse gas emissions.

20   According to most climate experts, forest preservation must be part of the world's response to global warming as well. Recent studies suggest that a halt to deforestation could cut global CO_2 emissions by as much as 3 billion tons per year (about one-third of total fossil fuel emissions). The important role of forests in the mitigation of global warming led to a United Nations initiative that provides developing countries with incentives to protect and use forestland wisely. The plan works by establishing financial values for the carbon stored in trees. Once these values are set, developed countries can make payments, called *carbon offsets*, to developing **countries**. Carbon offsets are a kind of trade. The developing world receives money in exchange for preserving forests. In turn, developed countries do not have to make such large greenhouse gas emission reductions of their own because they are contributing to the global reduction of emissions.

WHILE YOU READ 9

Look back at the two previous sentences to find two reduced relative clauses. Highlight them.

21   The carbon-offset initiative is controversial. Supporters see it as one of the most cost-effective ways to stabilize the concentration of greenhouse

gases in the atmosphere. Critics argue, however, that developed nations will simply use carbon offsets as a substitute for the emissions cuts they should make themselves. Other opponents claim that the initiative hurts people who depend on forest work for jobs, wood for energy, and cleared land for new farms and **settlements**.

22   Some estimates show that stabilizing greenhouse gas emissions at a safe level (350 ppm) could cost the world up to $1.5 trillion. Such high estimates have made cost a matter of great controversy. A number of economists argue that spending so much money would endanger economies around the world. Other experts believe, however, that spending at this level is not out of reach. They conclude that taking action to curb global warming now would cost considerably less than attempting to adapt to damaging consequences in the **future**. (See Figure 4.8)

23   Which countries should be responsible for reducing greenhouse gas emissions? This has also been a subject of much debate. Until recently, developed countries have accounted for most of the world's CO_2 emissions because of their longer histories of industrialization. The United States, for example, was the largest emitter for a long time until it was surpassed by China in 2007. Wide recognition of the developed world as the primary source of the emissions problem led to the Kyoto Protocol (1997), an international agreement requiring major developed nations to meet certain emission reduction targets. However, some developed countries object to the agreement because it does not impose sanctions on developing countries. They argue that burgeoning economic powers, such as China, India,

WHILE YOU READ 10

Look back at paragraph 21. Find three view markers. Highlight them. Then highlight the third point of view.

WHILE YOU READ 11

Look back at paragraph 22 to identify which sentence contains the main idea.
a) The first
b) The second
c) The last

Figure 4.8 Comparing the Cost of Climate Action versus Climate Inaction

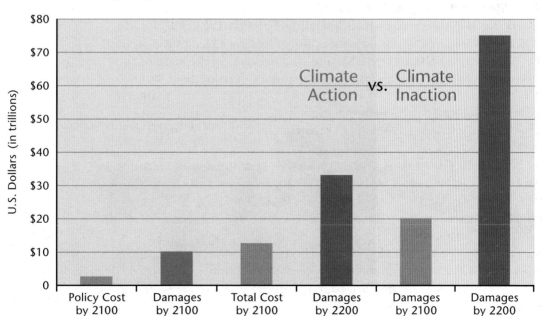

Source: German Institute for Economic Research and Watkiss et al. 2005

and Brazil, are now major contributors to greenhouse emissions. In 2011, the majority of delegates at a global climate conference renewed the Kyoto Protocol for several more years, and they also began plans for a future agreement that will treat all countries equally. However, this has raised concerns among developing countries that the imposition of emissions controls will slow their development.

V. Making Significant Changes

24 Global warming is a serious problem and it is clear that we need to address it in every conceivable way. As more and more greenhouse gases enter the atmosphere every day, people are already experiencing some of the effects in many parts of the world – record-breaking average global temperatures, persistent droughts, severe heat waves, and deadly storms.

25 It is also clear that mitigation of the future effects of global warming depends on individuals as well as governments. Individuals in the developed world, who have the largest carbon footprint, could have a major impact on global warming if they changed some of their usual behaviors. Key changes that would make a difference include reducing business and private travel, often using public transportation instead of driving, choosing energy-efficient light bulbs and appliances, purchasing fuel-efficient vehicles, reducing waste, and reusing and recycling products as much as **possible**.

26 Governments could also influence change. They could create long-term incentive plans and policies that promote the use of clean, non-carbon energy and support the design of energy-efficient buildings, appliances, and vehicles. This will be costly. However, the growing body of evidence makes it clear that the world cannot afford to ignore the threat of global warming. The long-term costs will certainly be even greater if we do nothing now. Most scientists and many political leaders agree that a "wait and see" approach is no longer tenable and that addressing the state of the world's climate must be a collaborative effort and a top **priority**.

WHILE YOU READ 12

Look back at paragraph 25. Which strategy helped you guess the meaning of *carbon footprint*?
a) Context
b) Definition
c) Contrast

WHILE YOU READ 13

Look back at paragraph 26. Highlight the contrast marker that shows where the author's point of view begins. Then highlight two of the author's opinions.

Individuals and governments can take steps to slow global warming.

Main Idea Check

For sections II–V of Reading 5, match the main ideas to three of the paragraphs in each section. Write the number of the paragraph on the blank line.

SECTION II: Facts About Global Warming

_____ A Average global temperatures are rising at a faster pace in recent years than in the past, due to the buildup of greenhouse gases.

_____ B Humans are the primary cause of most of the increase of atmospheric CO_2.

_____ C The rate of greenhouse gas buildup in the atmosphere has been increasing rapidly.

SECTION III: Potential Effects of Global Warming

_____ A If global warming continues at its present rate, we can also expect more exceptional weather conditions on Earth.

_____ B Because of warmer water temperatures and the melting of ice and snow, we can expect sea levels to rise.

_____ C It is likely that farming will be greatly affected by climate variations.

SECTION IV: Responding to the Threat

_____ A Using alternative energy sources that do not exhaust the environment would help to decrease levels of atmospheric greenhouse gases.

_____ B If people stopped destroying forests, it would significantly decrease the amount of CO_2 in the atmosphere.

_____ C One of the controversies related to global warming focuses on the question of which countries should do more to cut greenhouse gas emissions.

SECTION V: Making Significant Changes

_____ A People can help control global warming if they make some changes in their behavior.

_____ B There is more and more proof that ignoring global warming would be an enormous mistake.

_____ C We cannot put off taking action to deal with the already threatening problems of global warming.

A Closer Look

Look back at Reading 5 to answer the following questions.

1 Which statement about global warming is *not* true?
   a The effects of global warming could be very dangerous for life on our planet.
   b All scientists share the belief that global warming is mainly the result of human behavior.
   c Many scientists claim that it will be possible to limit the effects of global warming if we act now.
   d It is possible that global warming will result in more severe weather conditions in the future.

2 This diagram represents the connection between human activities and climate change. Reread paragraphs 6–9. Then complete the diagram with items A–F. Write the correct letter in each box.

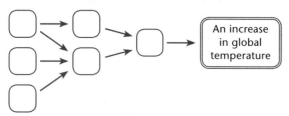

A An increase in emissions of CO_2 and other greenhouse gases
B Reduction in the earth's natural ability to absorb CO_2
C Deforestation by burning
D The expansion of agriculture
E A significant increase in greenhouse gases in the atmosphere
F The expansion of fossil-based industry

3 Why does the writer use the example of coral reefs in paragraph 11?
  a To show that ecosystems have the ability to adapt to temperature changes associated with global warming
  b To show how global warming would affect Australia
  c To show the potential destructive effects of global warming on ecosystems
  d To show how global warming has not yet had an effect on oceans

4 Which two statements best express the potential effects of global warming on agriculture?
  a Some areas will get less rain, so crops won't have enough water.
  b Most crops will be able to adapt to higher temperatures.
  c There could be a damaging reduction in the amount of farmland.
  d Farmers may not be able to grow enough food for the world's people.

5 According to the information in paragraphs 17–18, how can government incentives help solve global warming? Circle all that apply.
  a They encourage consumers to use the appliances they have.
  b They encourage the development of more energy-efficient products.
  c They encourage research on alternatives to fossil fuels.
  d They encourage people to recycle products.

6 The purpose of the carbon-offset initiative described in paragraph 20 is to protect the land that was formerly covered by forests. **True or False?**

7 According to Figure 4.8, what will damages related to global warming cost in 2200 if we don't take action now?
  a $10 trillion
  b $20 trillion
  c $30 trillion
  d $70 trillion

8 Which two questions express controversies related to global warming?

    a Which countries should be responsible for cutting greenhouse gas emissions?

    b Which countries have the longest history of greenhouse gas emissions?

    c How much can the world afford to spend to limit global warming?

    d How can energy-efficient vehicles help reduce global warming?

Skill Review

> In Skills and Strategies 12, you learned that academic writers often use nominalization to concentrate a large amount of information in one sentence. For example, they sometimes create complex noun phrases as subjects. Learning to recognize and understand nominalization will help you become a more efficient reader.

In the following sentences or parts of sentences from the reading, highlight the main verb and underline the entire nominalized subject. Then rewrite the sentence as two simpler sentences.

1 . . . the existence of global warming is an unequivocal fact. (Par. 1)

    _____

    _____

2 The wide use of HFCs by manufacturers since the 1990s was motivated by the need to replace the CFCs that were formerly used in these appliances. (Par. 7)

    _____

    _____

3 In recent years, the accumulation of the heat-trapping greenhouse gases has caused average global temperatures to rise at a much more rapid rate than in the past. (Par. 9)

    _____

    _____

4 The melting of glaciers, ice caps, and large sections of the Greenland and Antarctic ice sheets will also contribute to higher sea levels. (Par. 12)

    _____

    _____

5 The replacement of fossil fuels with clean, safe sources of renewable energy would also be a highly effective way to reduce greenhouse gas emissions. (Par. 18)

    _____

    _____

Definitions

Find the words in Reading 5 that are similar to the definitions below.

1 clear and firm (*adj*) Par. 1
2 people who doubt the truth or value of an idea or belief (*n pl*) Par. 3
3 a building with a roof and sides made of glass used for growing plants (*n*) Par. 4
4 never having happened or existed in the past (*adj*) Par. 5
5 a point at which something starts (*n*) Par. 10
6 the systems of relationships among all the animals, plants, and people living together in particular environments (*n pl*) Par. 11
7 below the surface of the sea or a river or lake (*adj*) Par. 12
8 without weakening in strength or force (*adj*) Par. 13
9 places where garbage is buried (*n pl*) Par. 17
10 fueled with more than one source; made of two or more things (*adj*) Par. 17
11 a reduction in how harmful, unpleasant, or bad something is (*n*) Par. 20
12 a formal international agreement (*n*) Par. 23
13 the establishment of rules that must be obeyed (*n*) Par. 23
14 possible to imagine or think of (*adj*) Par. 24
15 able to be defended successfully (used to describe an opinion or position) (*adj*) Par. 26

Synonyms

Complete the sentences with words from Reading 5 in the box below. These words replace the words in parentheses, which are similar in meaning.

abandon	adversely	contention	induce	substantial
accumulation	attributable	curb	pose	undeniable

1 The question of which nations should cut their greenhouse gas emissions remains a matter of (disagreement) _____.

2 Most scientists believe that it is still possible to (limit) _____ the effects of deforestation if we improve our management of the world's forests.

3 There is (unquestionable) _____ evidence that polar ice caps are beginning to shrink.

4 Some politicians argue that developing countries should share responsibility for the (buildup) _____ of greenhouse gases.

5 Rising sea levels (present) _____ a threat to inhabitants of coastal areas.

6 During the hurricane, many people had to (leave) _____ their homes.

7 The company put their refrigerators on sale in order to (persuade) _____ customers to buy them.

8 The heat wave (badly) _____ affected all the farms in the area.

9 It costs a / an (considerable) _____ amount of money to buy a car that has a gas-electric engine.

10 Many people believe that the recent warm winters in North America are (caused by) _____ to global warming.

Same or Different

The following pairs of sentences contain vocabulary from all the readings of this unit. Write *S* on the blank lines if the two sentences have the same meaning. Write *D* if the meanings are different.

_____ 1 Recently, there has been a **marked** increase in the amount of **greenhouse** gas **emissions** in the atmosphere.

Much higher levels of **atmospheric** gases, such as CO_2 and HFCs, have been released into the air in recent years.

_____ 2 **Excessive** amounts of acid in the ocean may cause the **extinction** of coral reefs.

Oceans are becoming **inhospitable** to coral reef **ecosystems**, but some may survive.

_____ 3 **Mitigation** of future climate changes may be possible if we **tackle** the problems of global warming.

If global warming continues **unabated**, it is likely that it will cause significant climate changes.

_____ 4 One of the ways to **curb deforestation** is to develop **renewable** sources of energy, so that less wood will be used.

One way to ensure the **conservation** of forestland is to develop alternative sources of energy that will not **adversely** affect the environment the way using wood does.

_____ 5 In the 1990s, **hybrid** cars had a **negligible** effect on reducing air pollution because only a small percentage of people drove them.

Hybrid cars had little effect on air quality during the 1990s because a **substantial** number of people didn't choose to drive them.

_____ 6 When people use **artificial fertilizers**, the **runoff** of these chemicals into rivers and streams can pollute drinking water.

The use of chemical **pesticides** can have a **catastrophic** effect on the environment.

_____ 7 When arctic ice sheets **shrink**, it **interrupts** everyday life for polar animals.

When arctic sea ice **recedes**, it makes it harder for polar bears live a normal life.

_____ 8 The last **flood** was **catastrophic** for the town because there was a **staggering** amount of water that **flowed** into people's homes.

The last big storm **interrupted** life in the town because during periods of heavy rain, the people were trapped in their homes.

Academic Word List

The following are Academic Word List words from all the readings of this unit. Complete the sentences with these words. (For more on the Academic Word List, see page 256.)

abandon (*v*)	conceivable (*adj*)	imposition (*n*)	partnership (*n*)	protocol (*n*)
accumulation (*n*)	consensus (*n*)	induce (*v*)	periodic (*adj*)	reversal (*n*)
attributable (*adj*)	emerging (*adj*)	irreversible (*adj*)	pose (*v*)	unprecedented (*adj*)

1 Several businesses and environmental organizations formed a _____ in order to collaborate on climate research.

2 The extinction of plant and animal species is _____; it is impossible to restore them once they disappear.

3 A decrease in rainfall would _____ a significant challenge for farmers.

4 The purpose of the library book sale was to _____ students to read more.

5 By signing the _____, the nations agreed to significant cuts in their greenhouse gas emissions.

6 The day was mostly cloudy, but there were _____ thunderstorms from time to time.

7 The recent droughts in North America may be _____ to global warming.

8 North America recently experienced record-breaking warm temperatures in March, which is _____ at that time of year.

9 There is a/an _____ in the scientific community that we need to act quickly in response to the threat of global warming.

10 As the wildfires got closer, people had to _____ their homes.

11 To encourage healthy living, they voted for a/an _____ of a policy that allowed smoking in restaurants.

12 There was a/an _____ of dust on the floor since it hadn't been swept for weeks.

13 It is _____ that more people will drive cars with gas-electric engines when they become more affordable.

14 The company objected to the _____ of such a large fine for polluting.

15 Because of today's concerns about the environment, there is a/an _____ market in alternative fuels.

Critical Thinking

Reading 5 discusses how human activities can have a
significant effect on global warming. In fact, even our
everyday routines, such as driving a car, using a computer,
and throwing away trash all contribute to greenhouse
gas emissions.

PERSONALIZING

Thinking about how
new information
applies to your
own life can help
you understand a
text better.

A With a partner, think of some of your normal
activities – at home, at school, and at work – that use
energy in ways that contribute to greenhouse gas emissions. Complete the chart
with as many ideas as you can. One example has been done for you.

	ACTIVITIES THAT CONTRIBUTE TO GREENHOUSE GAS EMISSIONS
Home	*I keep the lights on when I leave the house.*
School	
Work	

B Compare your charts with your classmates' charts. Discuss how you could
modify the activities you listed in order to save more energy.

Research

On the Internet, there are several websites that enable you to determine the
size of your carbon footprint by answering some questions about your daily
activities. Locate one of the calculators and answer the questions to calculate your
carbon footprint.

Writing

Write two paragraphs. The first paragraph will discuss some of the activities you
identified and how they contribute to global warming. Include information from
your chart and your research. The second paragraph will explain what you can do
to reduce your carbon footprint.

Exercise 1

Writers may connect ideas between sentences in many different ways. The second sentence may:

a describe a **result** of what is reported in the first sentence
b provide a **solution** to a problem described in the first sentence
c add a **detail** or details to support the more general information in the first sentence

How does the second sentence in each pair of sentences below connect to the first sentence? Write *a*, *b*, or *c* on the line depending on whether it is a result, a solution, or a supporting detail.

_____ 1 There was unprecedented flooding in this fertile river basin last year. Fortunately, the rains ceased and the water retreated before it had reached the level of the 1980 flood, and before it caused any long-term damage to crops.

_____ 2 Removing tropical rain forests to provide farmland disrupts the process by which nutrients are recycled into the soil, which then loses its fertility. Since farmers cut down trees for economic reasons, the only way to address this problem is by developing long-term economic solutions to widespread poverty.

_____ 3 The tropical forests located in the Congo basin in central Africa are known for their rich biodiversity in both plant and animal life. For example, these forests are home to lowland gorillas, forest elephants, and six species of monkeys.

_____ 4 A huge area of Brazilian grassland used to be considered unsuitable for farming because of its poor soil. Recently, however, farmers have added small amounts of fertilizer and found that the land can support crops such as cotton and soybeans.

_____ 5 By exhausting natural resources today and refusing to conserve, future generations are being deprived of their right to use and enjoy these resources. This realization has led some legal authorities to argue that there is a global obligation to include the perspective of future generations in economic planning.

Exercise 2

Make a clear paragraph by putting sentences A, B, and C into the best order after the numbered sentence. Write the letters in the correct order on the blank lines.

1 Approximately 40 percent of the earth's surface is covered by grasslands.

_____ _____ _____

| **A** However, too many cattle results in soil erosion and rapid loss of soil fertility, causing farmers to lose valuable livestock and land. | **B** These lands support rich biodiversity as well as feed humans through the milk and meat of cattle, which are raised there. | **C** If farmers carefully monitor the number of cattle and the condition of the grasslands, these immense areas will continue to be of great human value. |

2 There is a wide consensus among historians that the development of agriculture, approximately 10,000 years ago, was an unprecedented advance for the human race. ___ ___ ___

| **A** However, from an ecological perspective, agriculture also placed immense pressure on natural ecosystems that were susceptible to disruption. | **B** It enabled food to be produced much more efficiently, thereby freeing time for people to study science and thus to achieve gains that would not otherwise have been possible. | **C** When the demands on these systems became excessive and unsustainable, the systems collapsed. |

3 Scientists have warned that catastrophic disruption of a region's ecology can be caused by economic development decisions taken by government authorities that do not appreciate the long-term impact of those decisions. ___ ___ ___

| **A** The story of the Aral Sea basin from 1960 to 2000 proves that such warnings are not exaggerated. | **B** The climate there became much more extreme and the environment deteriorated to a point where it was toxic to the life it once sustained. | **C** The root cause of this ecological catastrophe was the economic decision to convert arid land to agricultural use by irrigation on a large scale. |

4 As the immense rain forests of the earth's tropical zones are destroyed to provide hardwood, fuel, or land for settlement, natural species are becoming extinct at a pace unprecedented since the appearance of humans on the earth. ___ ___ ___

| **A** A resolution of these complex issues will be impossible without an international consensus that so far has proven impossible to reach. | **B** Accomplishing this task, however, will be an enormous challenge for the world community, because it will involve tackling the root causes of the crisis: overpopulation, poverty, and unsustainable development. | **C** Prospects for halting the loss of species are poor, but biologists believe that today's extinction rate can be stabilized if the economic pressures that cause people to destroy the forests for short-term gain are addressed. |

5 Worldwide, the bottled water industry has seen rapid growth, but this has come at a significant environmental cost. ___ ___ ___

| **A** Environmentalists estimate that it takes more than 700 years for these plastic bottles to decompose, or break down. | **B** Fortunately, in 2009, an increased understanding of this environmental problem led to a fall of 2.7 percent in sales of water bottled in plastic. | **C** Each year, Americans throw away approximately 38 billion plastic water bottles. |

Key Vocabulary

The Academic Word List is a list of words that are particularly important to study. Research shows that these words frequently appear in many different types of academic texts. Words that are part of the Academic Word List are noted with an Ⓐ in this appendix.

UNIT 1 • READING 1

The State of the World's Health

account for *v* to explain the reason for something • *Doctors couldn't **account for** the sudden increase in sick school children.*

address *v* to deal with a question or a problem • *Health care workers believe there is an urgent need to **address** the problem of teenage smoking.*

assess Ⓐ *v* to evaluate something • *The scientists needed time to **assess** the new information.*

considerable Ⓐ *adj* very large; a lot of • *The nurse showed **considerable** skill in dealing with the patient.*

contract *v* to catch or become ill from a disease • *The child **contracted** the illness from drinking dirty water.*

correlation Ⓐ *n* a connection between two or more things • *There is a clear **correlation** between an active lifestyle and good health.*

counterpart *n* a person with similar responsibilities in a different place • *The university professor consulted her **counterpart** in England to help solve the problem.*

devastating *adj* terrible; shocking • *The damage caused by the earthquake was **devastating**.*

disparity *n* a great difference • *Although there is more equality today than in the past, significant **disparities** remain between salaries earned by men and those earned by women.*

eradicate *v* to destroy something completely • *Most countries have **eradicated** diseases like polio and smallpox.*

indicator Ⓐ *n* a signal that makes something clear • *A drop in the sale of cigarettes was an **indicator** that the new no smoking policy was beginning to make a difference.*

monitor Ⓐ *v* to watch and check something carefully over a period of time • *The nurse carefully **monitored** the patient's progress throughout the night.*

obesity *n* an excess of body weight; twenty percent or more above a healthy weight • ***Obesity** is a growing problem in many European countries, particularly among children.*

optimistic *adj* hopeful • *The United Nations is **optimistic** that access to clean and safe drinking water can be expanded in the next five years.*

promising *adj* showing signs of future success • *After extensive trials, scientists reported that the new drug looked **promising**.*

statistics Ⓐ *n* a collection of numerical facts • ***Statistics** show that in general, women live longer than men.*

stigma *n* a bad opinion of something because society does not approve of it • *In some countries, there is a **stigma** associated with mental illness.*

target Ⓐ *v* to focus on something • *Doctors say that in order to encourage healthy lifestyles, we need to **target** young children.*

trend Ⓐ *n* a general direction or pattern of changes • *There is a growing **trend** to eat organic food, that is, food that is produced naturally and without chemicals.*

virtually Ⓐ *adv* almost • *After large scale efforts to introduce the vaccine, polio became **virtually** nonexistent in South American countries.*

UNIT 1 • READING 2

Changing Attitudes Toward Cardiovascular Disease

accessible Ⓐ *adj* available; able to be used • *The Internet has resulted in new research being **accessible** to people globally – even those living in remote areas.*

advance *n* an example of progress • *In the last 20 years, there have been a number of important **advances** in the treatment of heart disease.*

aerobic *adj* relating to the increase of oxygen in the blood • *Taking a dance class provides good **aerobic** exercise.*

aim at *v* to intend to do something; to mean to do something • *The new health campaign was **aimed at** encouraging parents to have their young children vaccinated.*

awareness Ⓐ *n* an understanding • *There is growing **awareness** among the public that more emphasis is needed on funding healthcare programs for the poor.*

cholesterol *n* a fatty substance found in the blood • *New medications are successfully lowering **cholesterol** and therefore also decreasing heart disease.*

collaborate *v* to work with someone else for a specific purpose • *The two universities **collaborated** in their efforts to develop medication that better treats HIV / AIDS.*

conduct Ⓐ *v* to carry out an activity or an experiment • *Medical experts **conducted** an experiment to test whether the new medication helped people quit smoking.*

demonstrate (A) *v* to show that something is true; to prove something • *The fact that more inactive people suffer from heart disease demonstrates the importance of a healthy and active lifestyle.*

detection (A) *n* the act of finding or discovering something • *Early detection of cancer is extremely important.*

diagnosis *n* the identification of a disease or illness • *New technology has led to more accurate diagnoses of brain injuries.*

effective *adj* producing intended results • *Providing free vaccines is an effective way to lower the number of childhood diseases.*

enormous *adj* very large; huge • *Dave's parents are very wealthy. They live in an enormous house with 10 bedrooms and 8 bathrooms.*

eliminate (A) *v* to get rid of • *The health care center now requires people to make appointments online, which has eliminated the need to call and speak to a receptionist.*

emphasize (A) *v* to state that something is very important • *The government emphasized the need for all children to have access to clean, safe drinking water.*

initiate (A) *v* to cause something to begin• *The city initiated a new program to educate young mothers about the importance of good nutrition.*

key *adj* essential • *Educating the public about basic health care is now a key component of a doctor's responsibility.*

link (A) *n* a connection • *There is a clear link between education and health.*

outcome (A) *n* a result or effect of an action • *It is too soon to predict the outcome of the new drugs as tests are still being conducted.*

prevalent *adj* existing over a wide area; widespread • *For the last several years, drought has been prevalent over large areas of southern Africa.*

preventive *adj* intended to stop something before it happens • *Preventive medicine includes educating people about the benefits of a nutritious diet.*

project (A) *v* to estimate a number or amount for the future • *The United Nations projects that the world population will increase to 9 billion in the next few decades.*

shift (A) *n* a change in focus or direction • *Greater understanding has led to a shift in attitudes towards people suffering from mental health illnesses.*

strategy (A) *n* a long term plan to achieve a goal • *Preventive medicine is part of the government's new strategy to improve the overall health of the country.*

stroke *n* the result of a sudden change in blood flow to part of the brain • *After his stroke, the patient was unable to move the left side of his body.*

switch *v* to change from one thing to another • *The woman did not like her doctor, so she switched to a new health care clinic.*

Medicine and Genetic Research: Promise and Problems

achievement (A) *n* something good or difficult that you have succeeded in doing • *The scientist's greatest achievement was his discovery of penicillin in 1936.* **achieve** (A) *v* to succeed in doing something difficult • *By reaching the top of Mt. Everest in 1953, the two climbers achieved a goal that many people considered impossible.*

conquer *v* to defeat • *Scientists have not yet conquered HIV/AIDS, but they now understand far more about this disease.* **conquest** *n* when someone conquers a country, region, or person • *In 1979, The World Health Organization announced the conquest of the disease smallpox.*

defective *adj* imperfect; containing a mistake • *Scientists have discovered that some serious illnesses are caused by defective genes.*

emerge (A) *v* to appear; to come out of something • *Information about a new approach to gene therapy is emerging.*

ethical (A) *adj* related to moral beliefs • *There are many ethical questions involved in medical care. For example, do parents have the right to refuse to vaccinate their children?*

immune *adj* protected against something such as a disease • *The body has a natural immune system that fights illnesses such as colds and the flu.*

inherit *v* to receive characteristics from parents through genes • *The boy inherited his dark hair and brown eyes from his father.* **inheritance** *n* money or objects that someone gives you when they die • *The children received equal shares of money as their inheritance when their parents died.*

milestone *n* a significant event in the development of something • *The development of technology that allowed doctors to see which part of the brain controls which function was a huge milestone in neural medicine.*

obtain (A) *v* to get • *The patient obtained information that proved that the doctors had misdiagnosed his illness.*

potential (A) *n* a possibility not yet reached • *The young musician showed great potential; he played better than most people twice his age.*

pursue (A) *v* to follow • *The government is pursuing a new approach to the rising costs of health care. They are emphasizing preventive medicine.* **pursuit** (A) *n* the act of following with the intent of reaching a specific goal • *In pursuit of the truth, the police interviewed dozens of witnesses.*

revive *v* to bring someone or something back to life • *In their biology class, students learned how to revive someone who had suffered a heart attack.* **revival** *n* when something becomes more active or popular again • *The orchestra performed a revival of music from the early twentieth century.*

setback *n* something that causes a temporary delay or stops progress • *The research experienced a **setback** when the project lost funding, but it was quickly started up again when a new source of money was found.*

therapy *n* the treatment to help a patient recover from an illness • *The doctor prescribed exercise and a healthy diet as part of the **therapy** for the patient's heart disease.*

underestimate Ⓐ *v* to think that something is lower or less than it really is • *The government seriously **underestimated** the cost of providing free medical check-ups to low income families.*

UNIT 1 • READING 4

Malaria: Portrait of a Disease

breed *v* to reproduce • *In tropical climates, mosquitoes **breed** in standing water.*

cognitive *adj* relating to or involving the processes of thinking and reasoning • *Research shows a connection between aerobic exercise and **cognitive** ability.*

depress Ⓐ *v* to reduce the value of something • *The weaker economy led to a lower demand for oil which in turn **depressed** the cost of gas.*

disproportionately Ⓐ *adv* too much or too little compared to other similar things • *This particular type of flu is **disproportionately** high among young children and older adults.*

enhance Ⓐ *v* to improve the quality, strength or amount of something • *The city took steps to **enhance** the quality of its drinking water.*

fatigue *n* a feeling of great tiredness • *Common symptoms of flu include headache and **fatigue**.*

host *n* a plant or animal in which another animal or plant lives • *In the 1400s, rats were **hosts** to fleas – tiny creatures that spread serious diseases such as the plague.*

impairment *n* a weakness or inability to do something • *Injury to the left side of the brain can cause **impairment** to the right side of the body.*

insecticide *n* a chemical that kills insects • *It is common practice today for farmers to use **insecticides** in order to improve the quality of their crops.*

leading *adj* most important • *The university invited a **leading** expert in public health to talk to its medical students.*

linger *v* to remain or stay longer than expected • *After the fire, the smell of smoke **lingered** for several days.*

parasite *n* a plant or animal which lives and feeds on another plant or animal • *A **parasite** such as a fluke worm can survive on its host for years.*

perpetuate *v* to cause something to continue • *Many people have **perpetuated** the idea that a person catches the cold virus from cold weather.*

pervade *v* to spread through all parts • *The western approach to dealing with illnesses rather than prevention **pervades** the teaching of medicine throughout universities in developing nations.*

philanthropic *adj* related to helping others through gifts of money • *Most public universities depend not only on funding from the government, but on the **philanthropic** help provided by former students.*

preliminary Ⓐ *adj* coming before an event or before something is completely finished • *Although the testing was not yet finished, the hospital was pleased to announce that **preliminary** results looked very promising.*

primarily Ⓐ *adv* mainly • *Because the disease broke out **primarily** in the north part of the city, health officials were able to quickly find the source of the contaminated water.*

reluctant Ⓐ *adj* not wanting to do something • *Although there are major problems with the United States health care system, the government is **reluctant** to change it.*

remote *adj* far away from somewhere • *A series of local village clinics provides health care to the more **remote** areas of Botswana.*

rural *adj* relating to the countryside rather than city areas • *The government is trying to encourage more doctors to work in **rural** areas by offering free housing.*

spray *v* to send out liquid in very small drops • *The city told the residents to stay inside because they were **spraying** mosquitoes.*

straightforward Ⓐ *adj* simple; clear to understand • *The instructions to install the new software were very **straightforward**.*

thrive *v* to grow, develop and be successful • *Although she works long hours, she seems to **thrive** on the challenge and responsibility of her new job.*

transmit Ⓐ *v* to send, move or pass from one location to another • *Germs **transmit** diseases, so it is important to wash your hands frequently and cover your mouth when coughing.*

vulnerable *adj* able to be easily hurt or attacked • *Very young babies are especially **vulnerable** to illnesses because their immune system is not fully developed.*

UNIT 1 • READING 5

The Health Care Divide

adequate Ⓐ *adj* enough or satisfactory for a particular purpose • *The study questioned whether there was **adequate** safe drinking water available to residents throughout the city.*

affordable *adj* not expensive • *Newly arrived immigrants require **affordable** housing as well as jobs.*

capacity Ⓐ *n* the ability to be able to do something • *The government has the **capacity** to make a real difference in expanding health care to cover all of its citizens.*

commitment Ⓐ *n* a promise to do something • *Both candidates made a **commitment** to lower the cost of education.*

contaminated *adj* to become less pure or poisonous by the addition of something harmful • *The water system was **contaminated** as a result of the heavy use of insecticides on a nearby farm.*

critical *adj* urgent; very important • *There continues to be a **critical** need for education about how to prevent the spread of infectious diseases.*

discrepancy *n* an unexpected difference that requires explanation • *There was a **discrepancy** between the amount of money donated to the hospital, and the money which was actually put into the bank.*

efficiency *n* the quality of working well without wasting time or resources • *The office was able to improve its **efficiency** with a combined approach of more staff training and up-to-date software.*

ensure Ⓐ *v* to make sure • *The doctor ordered several more tests to **ensure** that the patient was getting better.*

evident Ⓐ *adj* easily seen; obvious • *The confusion and panic which occurred after the earthquake made it **evident** that more training was needed.*

expansion Ⓐ *n* the increase in size, number or amount of something • *The political leader argued that the only way to fund an **expansion** to higher education would be to increase taxes.*

expenditures *n* money paid out in return for goods or services • *Buying the newest medical imagers requires large **expenditures** of funds that hospitals in developing countries do not always have.*

facility Ⓐ *n* a building or equipment used for a specific purpose • *The new sports **facility** had a swimming pool as well as a gym.*

hinder *v* to make it difficult for something to happen • *Large crowds of protestors **hindered** the efforts of police to clear the city center.*

immense *adj* huge; enormous • *The United Nations is making an **immense** effort to reduce the number of people infected by HIV / AIDS.*

implement Ⓐ *v* to put a plan or a system into operation • *Mass vaccination programs against polio were first **implemented** in Central America.*

incentive Ⓐ *n* something that encourages a person or organization to do something • *The city reduced its business tax as an **incentive** to bring new companies to the area.*

invest Ⓐ *v* to put money into something in order to make a profit or achieve a result • *The university **invests** a lot of time and money to make sure that its graduates receive a quality education.*

ongoing Ⓐ *adj* continuing • *The **ongoing** discussions between management and workers are about pay and working conditions.*

patent *n* the legal right to be the sole producer of a new invention • *When a pharmaceutical company takes out a **patent** on a new drug, it has the potential to earn huge amounts of money.*

plague *v* to cause someone or something difficulty • *The spread of common germs continues to **plague** even the most advanced hospitals.*

priority Ⓐ *n* something that is given more importance than other things • *Because resources were limited, **priority** was given to families with young children who had lost their homes in the storm.*

prohibitive *adj* too expensive to pay • *The cost of nursing care for the elderly is becoming **prohibitive** in many countries.*

sacrifice *v* to give up something for something else considered more important • *The workers **sacrificed** their vacation in order to make sure the school was finished on time.*

tend *v* to be likely to happen • *Children who grow up around books **tend** to read more as adults than children who have no access to books.*

UNIT 2 • READING 1

The Age of Immigration

abolish *v* to end; eliminate • *The United States government **abolished** slavery in 1865.*

attractive *adj* causing interest or pleasure; appealing • *For many immigrants, the idea of starting a new life in another country is an **attractive** one.*

colossal *adj* huge; enormous • *The family made the **colossal** decision to cross the border and leave their native country for good.*

demanding *adj* requiring a lot of strength, energy or attention • *Nursing is a **demanding** job and requires patience and dedication.*

disintegrate *v* to become weaker or destroyed by falling into small pieces • *There were so many police in the streets that the protest quickly **disintegrated** as the protesters went home.*

endure *v* to experience something difficult, painful, or unpleasant • *Early immigrants from China often had to **endure** difficult working conditions when they first arrived in the country.*

fuel *v* to provide power; to encourage something • *Stories about the cruel actions of the new government **fueled** thousands of people to leave the country.*

hardship *n* a difficult and unpleasant situation • *A lack of clean water and adequate sanitation continue to cause a great deal of **hardship** for people in the poorest countries of the world.*

initially Ⓐ *adv* at first • *The ceremony, **initially** planned for today, had to be postponed because of bad weather.*

interest *n* additional money paid when borrowing money • *Some immigrants borrowed money to travel to the United States, and then were forced to pay it back with very high* **interest**.

option Ⓐ *n* a choice • *When war broke out, my family had only one* **option** − *they had to leave the country in order to survive.*

peak *v* to reach the highest point • *Immigration from Ireland* **peaked** *in the mid-1840s when about half of all immigrants to the United States were Irish.*

persistent Ⓐ *adj* the state of continuing, even through difficult situations • *The newly elected representative was very* **persistent**; *he would not give up until he had reached his goals.*

recruit *v* to persuade someone to become an employee • *There was a shortage of highly skilled computer programmers, so the company went to several universities to* **recruit** *new graduates.*

representative *n* someone who speaks or acts for another person or group • *The employees chose two* **representatives** *to speak to the managers about the poor working conditions.*

source Ⓐ *n* the origin of something • *The computer diagnosis identified why the engine was running poorly. The* **source** *of the problem was a faulty electrical connection.*

stability Ⓐ *n* when something stays the same and doesn't change or move • *The political* **stability** *ended when European countries began to experience unrest.*

starvation *n* an extreme lack of food for a long period • *The drought in southern parts of Africa was so severe that many died from* **starvation**.

subsequently Ⓐ *adv* later • *Many of the Chinese immigrants of the 1870s* **subsequently** *returned to China.*

transition Ⓐ *n* a process of change • *Newtown is a city in* **transition**. *It used to be a manufacturing city; now its economy is more dependent on research and service industries.*

UNIT 2 • READING 2

Who are Today's Immigrants?

authorities Ⓐ *n* a group of people with official power to enforce laws • *Immigrants sometimes waited for hours at Ellis Island while immigration* **authorities** *checked their paperwork.*

case *n* a particular situation or example of something • *The university didn't usually accept credits from courses taken overseas, but in this* **case**, *they made an exception.*

consist of Ⓐ *v* to be made of • *This neighborhood* **consists of** *people from all over the world; it is truly diverse.*

construction Ⓐ *n* the building of something • *Construction of the new bridge came to a halt because of the massive storm.*

contemporary Ⓐ *adj* belonging to the present time • *I don't really like* **contemporary** *music. I prefer the music of the 1980s and 90s.*

deport *v* to send someone back to their native country against their will • *Immigration officials* **deported** *the men because they had entered the country illegally and had committed crimes.*

destination *n* the place someone is going to • *Many immigrants arrived in San Francisco in the late nineteenth century, but their final* **destination** *was to the north, to states like Oregon and Montana.*

domestic Ⓐ *adj* relating to the house, home, or country of origin • *My grandmother was a* **domestic** *worker when she first came to Canada, but she was eventually able to get a better job.*

essentially *adv* basically • *The supervisor talked to the workers about their request for more pay, but he said that* **essentially** *there was no money to increase wages.*

financial Ⓐ *adj* related to the management of money • *The city center, with all its banks and insurance companies, is the* **financial** *heart of the city.*

former *adj* previous; form an earlier time • *Although the current and* **former** *presidents were from different political parties, they came together to raise money for HIV/AIDS victims.*

minimum Ⓐ *n* the lowest possible amount • *The government has just increased the* **minimum** *wage to reflect the growing price of food and housing.*

mobility *n* the ability to move from one place to another • *When borders opened up in Europe,* **mobility** *within the workforce increased dramatically as workers moved to where jobs were available.*

motivation Ⓐ *n* the reason why you are willing to do something • *Knowing there were well-paid jobs available was a powerful* **motivation** *for thousands of immigrants who left India to work in countries such as Kuwait and Dubai.*

prospect Ⓐ *n* the possibility that something will happen • *University graduates have much better employment* **prospects** *than high school graduates.*

range Ⓐ *v* to vary • *The initial stages of culture shock* **range** *from excitement to depression.*

secure Ⓐ *adj* safe • *My grandfather was lucky to have a* **secure** *job throughout the depression; many of his friends lost their jobs.*

status *n* a position or condition at a certain time • *The type of work a person does will give that person a certain* **status**. *Being a doctor, for example, is a high-***status** *job; being a taxi driver is not.*

swell *v* to increase • *After the war ended, the number of refugees* **swelled** *as people looked to start a new life overseas.*

take advantage of *v* to benefit or gain from something • *Many immigrants today* **take advantage of** *the free English courses offered by local libraries and community centers.*

tie *n* connections • *Although my family left Italy many years ago, we still have strong ties to that country.*

unrest *n* disagreements or fighting between groups of people • *The political unrest in the northern part of the country continued as different groups claimed they had won the election.*

unskilled *adj* without needing any skills or training • *Although unskilled employees are paid the lowest wages, society could not function without this group of workers.*

unstable Ⓐ *adj* not strong; likely to change in a negative way • *The current government is very unstable, and everyone is nervous about what will happen.*

wages *n* money paid for work • *Many economies in developing countries depend on overseas workers sending home a percentage of their wages.*

UNIT 2 • READING 3

The Meeting of Cultures

absorb *v* to take in knowledge, ideas, and information • *When you start a new job, it is not easy to absorb all the new information on the first day.*

adapt Ⓐ *v* to adjust to different conditions or situations • *Children of immigrants often find it easier than their parents do to adapt to a new country.*

classify *v* to divide things or people according to type • *The government classifies immigrants differently; some are permanent, some temporary, and some are refugees.*

core Ⓐ *n* the center; the most important part of something • *Language is at the core of culture because it allows the communication of values important to that culture.*

dominant Ⓐ *adj* more important or stronger than something of the same type • *Although immigrants came to the United States from all over Europe, English remained the dominant language.*

embrace *v* to accept something with enthusiasm • *When the war ended, the country embraced the return of its citizens and promised they would never again have to leave the country of their birth.*

harmony *n* peace • *Before the Civil War, African Americans and whites generally lived in harmony in the northern states, but it was a very different situation in many southern states.*

immerse *v* to fully involve someone in an activity • *When I first started university, I immersed myself into university life by joining clubs and making new friends.*

innate *adj* born with; natural • *Culture is not innate; it is something you learn as you grow up.*

interact Ⓐ *v* to communicate; to spend time with other people • *Immigrants need a basic understanding of English in order to interact with people even within an entry-level job.*

mainstream *adj* common, shared and accepted by most people • *The story was widely reported by the mainstream press.*

merge *v* to combine or join together • *The two companies merged into one international business.*

metaphor *n* an expression or a symbol describing one thing by referring to something else • *A metaphor such as a "heart of stone" is often difficult to translate into another language.*

opponent *n* a person who disagrees with something and speaks out against it • *Opponents of the new president complained that his policy toward immigration was too strict.*

poll *n* a study of a group's opinion on a subject • *The latest polls show that more women than men support the president.*

regardless *adv* without being influenced by other events or conditions • *I tell the truth regardless of what other people think.*

segregate *v* to separate people based on race, religion, or gender • *Some religious schools allow girls and boys to study together in some classes but segregate them in others such as sports.*

severely *adv* very badly • *The storm severely affected people living in the poorer areas of the city since many were not able to leave for higher ground.*

tolerance *n* a willingness to accept ideas and behavior different from your own • *The school actively encouraged tolerance within its very diverse student population by teaching the history and culture of many different ethnic groups.*

unjustified Ⓐ *adj* not deserved • *The criticism that new immigrants take away jobs from citizens is unjustified since many citizens do not want to do these difficult and low-paying jobs.*

UNIT 2 • READING 4

One World: One Culture?

alienated *adj* feeling separate or unwelcome • *Some immigrants feel very alienated until they begin to learn the language and make friends.*

bland *adj* not interesting; lacking a strong flavor • *I didn't like the music; it was rather bland, so I left the concert early.*

brand *n* a type of product made by a particular company • *Apple is an example of a brand recognized throughout the world.*

countless *adj* very many • *There are countless examples of immigrants who have arrived with nothing but through hard work have become very successful.*

debate Ⓐ *v* to discuss different opinions about a serious topic • *Right now the country is debating whether new laws are needed to limit the rising cost of university tuition.*

diminish Ⓐ *v* to reduce in size or importance • *As the two leaders got together and began to talk, the threat of war **diminished**.*

dismiss *v* to decide that something is not worth considering • *I was frustrated because my supervisor **dismissed** my idea without even thinking about it.*

distinct Ⓐ *adj* separate; clearly different • *There are **distinct** differences between traditional music from southern African countries and music from West Africa.*

distribute Ⓐ *v* to spread over a large area; to hand out • *The university **distributed** information about free health care to all of its students during the first week of classes.*

dynamic Ⓐ *adj* exciting; full of life • *People love living in the heart of the city because the atmosphere is so **dynamic** with its diverse restaurants and theatres.*

erosion Ⓐ *n* the gradual weakening or wearing away of something • *Some people argue that the popularity of western style music is resulting in the **erosion** and perhaps even the total loss of traditional music.*

icon *n* a famous person or thing that represents something of importance • *The McDonalds sign is an **icon** of American fast food.*

inappropriate Ⓐ *adj* not right for a particular situation • *The politician apologized for her **inappropriate** remarks. She explained she was tired and not thinking clearly.*

incrementally *adv* happening in a series of small steps • *Although I started my job at a minimum wage, my salary was increased **incrementally** over the first two years.*

inevitably Ⓐ *adv* certainly • *Immigrants parents find that, **inevitably**, their children pick up a second language more quickly than they do.*

influx *n* the arrival of a large amount of things or people • *When the conflict finished, there was a sudden **influx** of people returning to their homes and their work.*

intricate *adj* having a lot of small parts arranged in a very complicated way • *The story of the movie was so **intricate** that it was hard to understand what was happening.*

prestigious *adj* respected and admired • *Nelson Mandela is recognized as one of the most **prestigious** figures of the twentieth century.*

profanity *n* offensive, or bad, language • *The movie was classified for adults only because it contained violence and **profanity**.*

profound *adj* felt or experienced strongly • *The father felt a **profound** sense of pride as he watched his daughter receive her degree – the first person ever to do so in the family.*

relegate *v* to put someone or something at a lower rank • *In the past, when African Americans joined the army, their officers **relegated** them to lower jobs such as cooks and cleaners. Now, African Americans are serving in the highest ranks within the military.*

static *adj* not changing; remaining the same • *The price of oil has remained **static** for the past few months, but is expected to increase as winter approaches.*

unfounded *adj* not based on facts; untrue • *The report of the death of the famous actor is **unfounded**, according to the police. He is working on a movie in France.*

value *n* an important principle or idea • *Even though the immigrants came from very different cultures, they shared the common **values** of the belief in freedom, family, and hard work.*

vast *adj* huge; enormous • *There is a **vast** difference between learning a second language in high school and actually using that language in a country where it is spoken as the native language.*

The Challenge of Diversity

allegation *n* a statement, made without giving proof, that someone has done something wrong • *The director denied the **allegation** that he had given his family members high-paying jobs in the company.*

ban *v* to forbid or legally stop something or someone from doing something. • *The U.S. president, Abraham Lincoln, **banned** slavery in 1865.*

bias Ⓐ *n* an unfair personal opinion that influences your judgment • *In court, good judges ignore their personal **biases** and follow the laws as they are written.*

cohesion *n* people being in close agreement and working closely together • *The football team didn't perform well because they lacked **cohesion**.*

compound Ⓐ *v* to make something worse by adding to it • *Illiteracy among girls and women **compound** the economic problems of the country since this important group of citizens cannot contribute fully to the workforce.*

contradict *v* to state the opposite of what someone has said • *The report **contradicts** the claim that bilingual education has a negative effect on children's educational progress.*

detrimental *adj* harmful • *Some people argue that bilingual education is, in fact, **detrimental** to children since it limits their exposure to English.*

disruption *n* interruption • *Bad weather threatens more **disruptions** to the airport, and passengers worry they will be unable to fly for another several days.*

eviction *n* the forcible removal of a person from their home • *When the mother lost her job, the family was threatened with **eviction** since they could no longer afford to pay rent.*

homogenous *adj* having qualities that are the same • *Until the Gold Rush of the 1940s, the small town in California was a **homogenous** white community.*

impede *v* to slow something down • *The sudden slowing down of economic growth **impeded** the government's efforts to encourage more highly skilled workers from neighboring countries to settle in Thailand.*

impending *adj* approaching • *The news warned people of the **impending** storm and recommended that everyone stay inside their homes.*

in favor of *prep phr* in support of • *Polls show that the majority of Americans and Canadians are **in favor of** multiculturalism.*

institute Ⓐ *v* to establish; to start • *In the last few years, the European Economic Union has **instituted** new rules about working throughout Europe. It is now more difficult to get a permit if you are not of European citizenship.*

integration Ⓐ *n* the process of mixing two or more things or groups in a society • *Although many people worried about it, the **integration** of women into the army has gone very smoothly*

irrational Ⓐ *adj* not based on reason or clear thinking • *Even though I know I am safe, I have an **irrational** fear of heights, so I can't go above the third floor in a building.*

massacre *n* the killing of a large number of people who are often defenseless • *The **massacre** of Native Americans is a dark part of U.S. history.*

merit *n* the quality of being good; deserving praise • *The manager was very popular because he evaluated his employees based on their personal **merit**; if you worked hard and did well, you would be promoted.*

remedy *v* to find a solution to a problem or difficulty • *City leaders are working hard to **remedy** the recent increase in crime.*

resistant *adj* to be opposed or reluctant to do something • *At this time, lawmakers are **resistant** to changing the rules about citizenship because these rules are generally seen as working well.*

sanctions *n* an official action taken by a government to force another government to behave in a particular way • *Democratic rule in South Africa came about largely because international **sanctions** had such a negative effect on the South African economy.*

secular *adj* not having any connection with religion • *Although Turkey is an Islamic country, the Turkish government is **secular**.*

stereotype *n* a fixed idea, that is usually wrong, about a group of people often based on gender, age, race, or economic background • *Even in the twentieth century, some Australians believed in the **stereotype** that people native to the country were lazy and incapable of learning skilled work.*

stratification *n* an arrangement of something in a series of layers • *Social **stratification** can be defined as the unequal positions in society based on wealth and power. In some countries it is possible to move from a lower level to a higher level; in other countries, this movement is much more difficult.*

stringent *adj* extremely limiting or difficult • *The rules to leave the country in order to work elsewhere are so **stringent** that many people simply give up trying.*

When Does Language Learning Begin?

accomplish *v* to do or finish something successfully • *I have set goals and now I am working to **accomplish** them.* **accomplishment** *n* something that is successful after a lot of hard work • *Graduating from university at the age of 16 was an amazing **accomplishment**.*

acquisition Ⓐ *n* the act of obtaining or beginning to have something • *The **acquisition** of a second language requires hard work and time.* **acquire** Ⓐ *v* to obtain or start to have something • *I **acquired** my love for animals as a young child.*

auditory *adj* related to hearing • *The stroke affected her **auditory** ability, but she was still able to see.*

decipher *v* to figure out the hidden meaning of something • *Using new x-ray technology, scientists were able to **decipher** the ancient symbols.*

distinction Ⓐ *n* the difference between two things that are quite similar • *It is more difficult for adults to hear a clear **distinction** between two similar sounds than it is for young children.*

expose Ⓐ *v* to create conditions that allow someone to have the opportunity to learn something new • *Students are **exposed** to new ideas and experiences when they go to university.* **exposure** Ⓐ *n* the conditions that allow an opportunity to learn something new • *Vocabulary is related to a child's **exposure** to books at a very young age.*

extraordinary *adj* remarkable; amazing • *The six-year-old child's ability to play classical piano was **extraordinary**.*

fetus *n* a baby before it is born • *Research shows that a **fetus** learns how to recognize its mother's voice.*

novel *adj* new and original; not seen before • *The architect was known for his **novel** approach to design.*

perceive Ⓐ *v* to notice something based on sight or sound • *It was amazing that the baby could **perceive** differences between sounds even at such a very young age.* **perception** Ⓐ *n* an awareness of things through physical senses • *The child had difficulty with auditory **perception** of words, so the teacher introduced more visual aids to help him learn to read.*

prosperous *adj* financially successful; wealthy • *Five years after its launch, the software business was so **prosperous** that it was able to expand into new markets.*

reproduce *v* to copy • *It is amazing that some animals have learned to **reproduce** the sounds of human language.*

retain Ⓐ *v* to keep or continue to have something • *The doctor found that although my father had the ability to **retain** some information, he had problems remembering people's names.* **retention** Ⓐ *n* the ability to keep or continue to have something • *__Retention__ of a second language is more probable when a child is exposed to that language at a young age.*

session *n* a period of time for a particular activity • *The musicians met at a studio and began their recording session.*

utilize Ⓐ *v* to use something effectively; to make use of something • *The Internet allows us to utilize information from libraries all over the world.*

UNIT 3 • READING 2

Learning a Language as an Adult

abuse *v* to treat someone very badly • *The parents abused their son so severely that he was removed from the home and sent to live with his grandparents.*

approximate Ⓐ *adj* almost the same; not quite exact • *I'm not sure of the exact number of international students studying in this city, but the approximate number is around two and half thousand.*

attain Ⓐ *v* to achieve or obtain something difficult • *Children learning a second language attain better pronunciation than adults learning a new language.*

catch up *v* to reach the same place or standard as someone else • *The student missed a lot of class due to illness, but she was able to catch up quite quickly with the other students.*

conflicting Ⓐ *adj* opposing • *In a court, the two sides introduce conflicting arguments and evidence, and the jury and judge must decide which is the truth.*

counterexample *n* an example arguing against a generalization • *The general belief is that children who are exposed to reading at a very young age become more competent readers, but there are many counterexamples to this.*

dispute *n* an argument • *There has been a long dispute among experts as to the influence of environment versus nature upon behavior.*

extend *v* to reach; stretch • *The meeting was supposed to end at five, but it extended into late evening because the managers could not agree on the new policy.*

feral *adj* wild • *The feral cat population is growing, and the city is trying to come up with solutions to deal with this.*

fundamental Ⓐ *adj* the most basic or important thing on which other things depend • *Scientists argue that we need to make fundamental changes in how we approach the production and use of energy.*

hypothesis Ⓐ *n* an idea based on facts but not yet tested • *The scientist presented his hypothesis and then proceeded to present evidence proving that it worked.*

implication Ⓐ *n* a possible effect • *Some argue that a relatively low percentage of students studying a second language in the United States will have serious implications for the country's economic future.*

in the long run *adv* eventually; extending over a period of time • *Many teachers find that although intelligence is an obvious factor in academic success, in the long run, hard work is of equal importance.*

mastery *n* the complete control or understanding of something • *My niece is being raised bilingual and her mastery of both Dutch and English is amazing.*

observation *n* information resulting from a scientific study • *When scientists were studying how babies acquire language, they noted an important observation: a very young baby can recognize the sound of its mother's voice.*

overtake *v* to go past someone or something • *The student began at a disadvantage, but due to hard work and diligence, he quickly overtook other students in his French class.*

phenomenon Ⓐ *n* something that is experienced or felt, especially because it is unusual • *The students discussed the effect language has on a person's view of the world, and then were asked to write an essay on this phenomenon.*

precise Ⓐ *adj* exact; accurate • *Although the science is not yet precise, scientists are getting a much better understanding of how infectious diseases pass from one person to another.*

presumably Ⓐ *adv* most likely • *Presumably, children who begin to learn a second language at a young age and who maintain exposure to this language will retain it more effectively than children who begin to study a second language at a later age.*

proponent *n* a supporter of something • *Proponents of bilingual education argue that this approach allows a student to become proficient in the target language while keeping up with other basic studies such as math and science.*

scholar *n* a person with great knowledge about a particular subject • *Scholars who study language acquisition argue that often too much emphasis is placed on grammar and writing and not enough on speaking and listening.*

species *n* a group of animals or plants that have the same characteristics • *Experts have found that a baby bird learns to reproduce specific sounds of its particular species.*

stimulation *n* something that causes another thing or person to become more active • *Children need to be exposed to lots of new ideas and subjects, which can provide intellectual stimulation.*

superior *adj* better than others • *Although adults can and do acquire a second language, children seem to have a superior ability in attaining accurate pronunciation.*

visual Ⓐ *adj* relating to sight • *I am a visual learner; I understand better through reading rather than listening.*

UNIT 3 • READING 3

Rules of Speaking

breakdown *n* a failure • *The breakdown in talks between management and workers means there is probably going to be a strike.*

call for *v* to need or require something • *The economics course called for an understanding of mathematical concepts.*

compliment *n* a remark that shows admiration or approval • *My teacher paid me a high **compliment** by saying my essay was one of the most interesting she had ever read.*

conform Ⓐ *v* to satisfy the established standards or rules • *In any group, there is pressure on people to **conform** – to dress, act, and think like others in the group.*

convention Ⓐ *n* a way of doing something that is accepted as normal and correct • *Social **conventions** differ from one country to another. For example, in some countries you should take your shoes off when entering a house.*

document Ⓐ *v* to record information in written form • *The researcher carefully **documented** the results from his experiment.*

elaborate *adj* having a lot of details • *The students designed a very **elaborate** computer program.*

empirical Ⓐ *adj* based on data rather than theory • *After numerous studies, we now have **empirical** evidence that fetuses can recognize the rhythms of speech.*

excuse *n* a reason you give when you do something wrong • *The student explained that he had left his homework in the library, but the teacher did not accept his **excuse**.*

govern *v* to have a direct effect or influence on something • *The price of manufactured products is **governed** by the cost of the raw materials and labor.*

gratitude *n* a strong feeling of appreciation for someone or something • *The new president expressed his **gratitude** to the people for offering him the opportunity to lead the country.*

hypothetical Ⓐ *adj* imagined; not based on proven theory • *The instructor provided a **hypothetical** situation and asked her students to discuss how they would act if they found themselves in this situation.*

impose Ⓐ *v* to force someone to accept something • *The government **imposed** restrictions on the number of work permits issued to non-citizens.*

impression *n* a feeling or idea which is produced in your mind by someone or something • *Movies tend to give a rather false **impression** of life in the United States. They make it appear more exciting or more dangerous than it really is.*

interpret Ⓐ *v* to decide on the meaning of something • *Experts are in disagreement about how to **interpret** the latest economic figures.*

minimize Ⓐ *v* to make something seem less important than it really is • *The company tried to **minimize** its role in the accident by blaming the accident on the careless behavior of its workers.*

modify Ⓐ *v* to change something slightly • *The university had to **modify** its admissions policy because of the rapidly growing number of applications.*

sincere *adj* honest; genuine • *When the president of the company resigned, he gave his **sincere** thanks to all of the people he had worked with over the years.*

transfer Ⓐ *v* to move from one place to another • *The Russian student was having trouble making herself understood because she was **transferring** rules of Russian grammar directly to English grammar.*

unconsciously *adv* without thinking • *Children who grow up in bilingual families learn both languages **unconsciously**.*

UNIT 3 • READING 4

Languages in Contact

accelerate *v* to increase speed; make something go faster • *Working in an environment in which the target language is spoken **accelerates** the learning of this language.*

administer *v* to control the operation or management of something • *The local government **administers** many programs to help immigrants learn English.*

advantageous *adj* helpful; beneficial • *When learning a new language, it is very **advantageous** to be able to interact with native speakers of that language.*

cease Ⓐ *v* to stop doing something • *The government reported that fighting has finally **ceased** in the southern part of the country.*

coexist *v* to live or be together in harmony • *In Switzerland, the languages of German, French, and English have **coexisted** for many years.*

contact Ⓐ *n* communication with someone or between groups of people • *In the nineteenth century, New York attracted immigrants from many different countries, but often these groups had little **contact** with each other.*

dictator *n* a leader with complete power • *The Ugandan **dictator**, Idi Amin, wanted to make Swahili the official language of that country rather than English.*

eventually Ⓐ *adv* finally • *After months of negotiations, the countries **eventually** signed a trade agreement.*

exhibit Ⓐ *v* to show something • *By cheating on the final exam, the student **exhibited** poor judgment.*

gradual *adj* changing or developing slowly • *When one language is in contact with another, there are **gradual** changes within both languages as each picks up some words from the other.*

hasten *v* to hurry; make something go faster • *The fact that English is a global language will no doubt **hasten** the decline of less used, local languages.*

literate *adj* the ability to read and write • *Economists argue that a country's economic strength depends on both men and women being fully **literate**.*

longevity *n* a long life • *Happiness, good eating habits, a lack of stress, and exercise are, many believe, the key to **longevity**.*

lose ground to *v phr* to be unable to keep up with something • *Although there was some good economic news today, the Euro **lost ground to** the dollar.*

maintain Ⓐ *v* to keep; to continue • *Said's family came to England two generations ago, but they have **maintained** some of their important cultural customs.*

paramount *adj* most important; essential • *An educated workforce is **paramount** to a country's economic strength.*

path *n* a set of actions that lead to a result or goal • *In most countries, the **path** to citizenship includes a test of the language and history of that country.*

policy Ⓐ *n* a plan or rule followed by a government, business or other group • *Restaurant were concerned they would lose business when the no-smoking **policy** was adopted, but this did not happen; in fact, in many cases, business increased.*

resident Ⓐ *n* a person who lives in a place • *Legal **residents** of Canada have access to low-cost health care.*

sector Ⓐ *n* a specific part of something such as a city or a population • *The industrial **sector** of the city is close to the port and railway.*

suppress *v* to end something by force • *In the early twentieth century, the U.S. government tried to **suppress** native languages by forcing Native American children to speak English at special boarding schools.*

utility Ⓐ *n* usefulness • *The employees questioned the **utility** of the training session since they felt they had learned nothing new.*

vibrant *adj* exciting; full of life • *The Ivory Coast singer and dancer, Dobet Gnahore, is one the most **vibrant** performers in world music.*

vigorous *adj* lively; energetic • *The **vigorous** debate about immigration policies continues among European countries.*

vitality *n* energy and strength • *Ireland has worked hard to maintain the **vitality** of its Celtic language, especially by ensuring it is taught in schools.*

UNIT 3 • READING 5

The Advantages of Multilingualism

anticipation Ⓐ *n* a positive feeling about what will happen soon • ***Anticipation** grew around the city as the opening day of the Olympics approached.*

bond Ⓐ *n* a close or strong connection • *The **bond** between a parent and his or her child is very strong.*

boost *v* to improve or increase something • *The government lowered taxes in order to **boost** economic growth and employment rates.*

candidate *n* a person applying for a job • *The job description called for bilingual **candidates** only.*

compensate for Ⓐ *v phr* to take the place of something useful • *Although the airline paid money to the victims, this did not **compensate for** the terrible experience they went through.*

consistently Ⓐ *adv* always happening in the same way • *Studies have **consistently** shown that being bilingual has significant advantages in the workplace.*

cue *n* a signal for someone to do or say something • *The sound of applause from the audience was the musicians' **cue** to begin playing.*

deficit *n* an insufficiency in or lack of something • *The private school was operating on a **deficit** and was soon forced to close.*

distraction *n* something that takes your attention away from what you should be doing • *Listening to music and texting are **distractions** typical of many high school students who are supposed to be studying.*

domain Ⓐ *n* a specific area or an area where someone has control • *The Internet allows a huge amount of information to be placed in the public **domain**.*

flawed *adj* mistaken; weak • *The argument that bilingualism is a barrier to academic success is generally believed to be **flawed**.*

flexibility Ⓐ *n* the ability to change and adapt to new circumstances • ***Flexibility** is an important skill in most work environments, particularly in the area of technology since this is constantly changing.*

heritage *n* a cultural history • *The government declared the building was part of the **heritage** of the city and therefore should be restored to its former condition.*

ideal *adj* perfect, or the best possible • *My idea of an **ideal** job is one in which I can travel and use my knowledge of French and Spanish.*

ignore Ⓐ *v* to pay no attention • *Babies whose parents **ignore** them are unable to communicate as well as children whose parents give them a lot of attention.*

incident Ⓐ *n* an unusual or unpleasant event • *The police were relieved that the large street protest took place without any **incident**.*

isolation Ⓐ *n* the state of being alone or not connected to anything else • *When James first moved to Dubai, he felt a strong sense of **isolation** because he could not understand Arabic and he knew no one.*

nanny *n* a person who is paid to care for young children • *Many young people apply to be **nannies** overseas because this is an inexpensive opportunity to learn a language and experience living in a different culture.*

onset *n* the beginning of something • *The doctor reminded his patients that at the **onset** of a cold, they should rest and drink lots of fluids.*

personnel *n* the people who work in a place • *The company required all **personnel** to complete a workplace safety course every six months.*

promote Ⓐ *v* to raise someone to a higher or more important position • *When the company realized that Sara was fluent in three languages, it quickly **promoted** her to its international division.*

remedial *adj* intended to correct or improve something, especially skills • *The child was placed in a **remedial** class because she could not speak English very well.*

seek out Ⓐ *v phr* look for • *Employers actively **seek out** multilingual people since this is a huge advantage in today's global economy.*

socioeconomic status Ⓐ *n phr* the position of a person within a society based on such factors as education, income, and type of job • *The **socioeconomic status** of second generation immigrants is generally higher than that of their parents.*

sophisticated *adj* advanced; complicated and made with great skill • *The ability to diagnose diseases has become much more **sophisticated**, allowing doctors to diagnose serious illnesses more accurately and a lot earlier than in the past.*

UNIT 4 • READING 1

Ecology, Overpopulation, and Economic Development

affluent *adj* having a lot of money; wealthy • ***Affluent** countries tend to have low birthrates.*

apparently *adv* according to what seems to be true or likely • *The government's suggestion for helping families have fewer children **apparently** has not been successful as the birthrate in the country is rising rapidly.*

catastrophic *adj* the causing of much suffering or destruction • *The 2010 Chile earthquake caused **catastrophic** damage to the buildings and transportation system of that country.*

counter *adj* opposite • *The data from the experiment surprised the scientists as the results were **counter** to what they had expected.*

deforestation *n* the destruction of forests by cutting down or burning trees • *Today, **deforestation** has spread to many parts of the world, where it is causing serious ecological damage.*

ecology *n* the complex relationships between plants, animals, humans, and the environment in which they all live • *In the 1980s the public became aware of how acid rain could damage the **ecology** of the areas where it fell. It makes the water of rivers and lakes unlivable for many plants and fish.*

emerging Ⓐ *adj* appearing • *Brazil, India, and Russia are examples of countries with **emerging** economies.*

emissions *n* the gases or other substances created by the production and use of light, heat, or gas • *Environmentalists argue we can reduce **emissions** by closing coal-based power plants.*

exploitation Ⓐ *n* the unfair use of someone or something for personal gain • *Nowadays, the public is more aware of environmental damage caused by the **exploitation** of natural resources.*

fertile *adj* able to produce a large amount of high-quality crops • ***Fertile** land requires a constant supply of water and nutrients.*

interrupt *v* to stop something that is in progress • *For thousands of years, water from the river Nile has been used to irrigate farmland on both sides of the river, but drought has **interrupted** the supply of water in recent years.*

irreversible Ⓐ *adj* cannot be changed back to its original condition • *Deforestation is usually **irreversible** since this process destroys the ecosystem necessary for forests to thrive.*

negligible *adj* small and unimportant • *Farmers are becoming increasingly worried because the rainfall so far this year has been **negligible**.*

nutrients *n* the substances that living things needs to live and grow • *Green, leafy vegetables such as spinach and kale are good sources for important **nutrients**.*

obligation *n* something that someone feels morally or legally forced to do • *Countries that signed the treaty are under **obligation** to reduce harmful emissions.*

paradigm Ⓐ *n* a very clear example used as a model • *The ecological disaster of the Aral Sea region is a **paradigm** of the disastrous effects of poor agricultural planning.*

reliant Ⓐ *adj* dependent on something or someone • *Because it lacks its own oil fields, Japan is **reliant** on imported oil.*

sustainable Ⓐ *adj* able to be continued and maintained • *Wind and solar power are examples of **sustainable** forms of energy.*

undernourished *adj* not having enough food to maintain good health • *By the end of the long drought, farmers could not produce enough food and, as a result, their families were seriously **undernourished**.*

vanish *v* to disappear • *Many agree that unless deforestation is halted, many species of animals, insects, and plants will **vanish** in the next decade.*

UNIT 4 • READING 2

The Aral Sea: An Environmental Crisis

collapse Ⓐ *v* to fall apart, or fall down • *The poorly constructed buildings **collapsed** during the earthquake, but the better designed buildings survived.*

conclude Ⓐ *v* to reach a decision after careful consideration • *After reviewing the evidence, the government **concluded** that any further development of the area needed to be carefully monitored to prevent future problems.*

conference Ⓐ *n* a large gathering of people with talks on a specific topic • *The United Nations organized an international **conference** to discuss the future of the South Aral Sea.*

cope *v* to deal with problems or difficulties • *With so many children sick from respiratory illnesses, it was very difficult for the few medical staff to **cope**.*

flow *n* the movement of liquid, gas, electricity, money etc. • *As the second year of drought began, the **flow** of water into the dam began to significantly decrease.*

inhospitable *adj* unfriendly; unwelcoming • *The hot, dry desert is an **inhospitable** area to many forms of life, including humans.*

intend *v* to have as a plan or a purpose • *The farmer intended to plant corn but discovered that wheat was a better option.* **intention** *n* something you want or aim to do • *The government has no intention of developing more land in the already over-developed region.*

irrigation *n* the bringing of water to previously dry land • *Irrigation has enabled humans to turn arid land into productive, agricultural land.* **irrigate** *v* to bring water to dry land • *For thousands of years, water from the Nile River has been used to irrigate vast areas of Egypt.*

marked *adj* clear; noticeable • *There has been a marked improvement in the local economy since some large companies moved into the area and began hiring.*

mean *adj* average • *With a mean rainfall of 460 inches per year, Mt. Waialeale in Hawaii is one of the world's wettest places.*

pesticide *n* chemicals used to kill insects • *Although pesticides improve agricultural productivity, they need to be used with care since overuse leads to serious environmental and health problems.*

rebound *v* to return to an earlier and better condition • *Although the storm caused serious damage, the residents promised that their city would rebound to its former state.*

recede *v* to move further back • *After the terrible 2004 tsunami, more people now know that when the sea suddenly recedes, they need to get to high ground because this is a sign of an approaching tsunami.*

reminder *n* something that helps you to remember • *The student left a note on his desk as a reminder that he had a medical appointment the next day.* **remind** *v* to make someone aware of something forgotten • *Extreme weather systems such as hurricanes remind us of the power of nature.*

render *v* to cause someone or something to be in a particular state • *Technology is changing so quickly that computers are rendered obsolete in just one year.*

reverse Ⓐ *v* to cause something to move in the opposite direction; to move backwards • *The local government worked hard to prevent erosion in that area, but one farmer reversed this progress by suddenly burning a large part of the forest.* **reversal** Ⓐ *n* a complete change of direction, order, or position • *In a significant reversal of earlier trends, people are now moving back to the Aral region.*

salinity *n* the amount of salt in something • *Many ocean-side communities are experiencing increased salinity in their land as a result of rising sea levels.*

saturated *adj* completely full • *After one month of continuous rain, the land was so saturated that floods and mud slides covered the land.*

transport Ⓐ *v* to move something from one place to another • *During the drought, thousands of people survived because the government as well as international agencies transported large quantities of water to the stricken areas.* **transportation** *n* the moving of goods and products • *Public transportation in European cities, such as London and Paris, is extremely efficient; and since it is used by so many people, it cuts down on harmful emissions.*

volume Ⓐ *n* the amount of space with length, height, and width • *Experts continue to worry as the volume of the Colorado River continues to fall due to its overuse by the millions of people who rely on it as their only water source.*

UNIT 4 • READING 3

Biodiversity and Tropical Rainforests

botanist *n* a scientist who studies plants • *Botanists believe that tropical rainforests contain many currently unknown species of plants that might help cure serious diseases.*

catalog *v* to list things in a systematic and organized way • *The graduate student had to catalog all the plants on university property as part of his final project.*

combat *v* to try to stop a particularly serious problem • *The government is trying to combat the growing problem of unemployment by offering tax incentives to companies if they hire new workers.*

consensus Ⓐ *n* a wide agreement; a generally accepted opinion • *Although experts disagree about some of the details, there is now consensus that global warming is the result of human activity and not a natural occurrence.*

conservation *n* the protection of natural resources • *Conservation is not limited to land; many areas of the world's oceans are also in need of protection.*

debt *n* money owed by a person, business, or government • *The company had so much debt that it was forced to go out of business.*

designate *v* to choose something for a specific purpose • *The city designated the area south of the airport as an industrial area.*

excessive *adj* too much; more than is reasonable • *Some people argue that the amount of money spent on conservation is excessive; others believe more money should be spent.*

extinction *n* the state of no longer existing • *Many species of plants, insects, and animals are threatened with extinction.*

generate Ⓐ *v* to create; to produce • *Tourism to the country's beautiful national parks generates a considerable amount of money.*

halt *v* to stop • *After an environmental study, the government stepped in and halted the clearing of forests in that area.*

harvest *v* to bring in a crop from the fields when it is ripe or ready • *Because of a warning that severe storms are on the way, farmers have started to harvest their crops earlier than planned.*

partnership Ⓐ *n* an arrangement in which people, businesses, and organizations work closely together • *The World Wildlife Fund relies on its extremely successful **partnership** between governments and private citizens to save endangered animals.*

preserve *v* to stop something from being damaged or lost • *There was a plan to pull down the old building, but citizens persuaded the government to **preserve** it because of its historical significance.*

properties *n-pl* qualities of something • *This material has two **properties** that make it useful for cold weather. It is waterproof and retains heat.*

renewable *adj* able to be used again or easily replaced • *The sun and the wind are examples of **renewable** energy resources.*

substitute Ⓐ *v* to replace something with something else • *To reduce the amount of fat in daily diets, doctors recommend people **substitute** non-fat milk for normal milk.*

susceptible *adj* likely to be affected by something negative • *Young children are often more **susceptible** to colds and other infections than adults are.*

tackle *v* to begin to solve a difficult and complex problem • *Although the government has begun to **tackle** the problem of pollution in areas around its major cities, this remains a serious threat to the health of people living in these areas.*

unanimous *adj* complete agreement • *Finally, after months of discussion, the vote to preserve part of the rainforest was **unanimous**.*

UNIT 4 • READING 4

The Water Crisis

abundant *adj* more than enough • *Although there is an **abundant** supply of fresh water on this planet, it is not evenly distributed; some areas have more than enough while others have a critical water shortage.*

atmospheric *adj* relating to the mixture of gases that surround the planets • *The **atmospheric** pressure decreases with elevation, so the higher you are, the less pressure there is.*

convert Ⓐ *v* to change something from one form to another • *Desalination plants **convert** sea water into drinking water.*

costly *adj* expensive • *Overdeveloping the Aral region was a **costly** mistake in terms of both human and environmental harm.*

enforcement Ⓐ *n* the action of making sure a law is followed and obeyed • *A 55-mph speed limit was introduced as an attempt to conserve fuel, but its **enforcement** was completely inadequate since the police force ignored speeders.*

exacerbate *v* to make a bad situation worse • *Although bottled water is convenient in areas that do not have access to fresh water, it actually **exacerbates** the problem since it takes pressure off the government from providing piped water.*

filter *v* to remove solids from water • *The government told people that it was not necessary to boil or **filter** the water; it was safe to drink.*

highlight Ⓐ *v* to draw attention to something • *The recent drought in the mid-western United States **highlights** the seriousness of water shortage in areas dependent upon agriculture.*

insufficient Ⓐ *adj* not enough • *The politician explained that there was simply **insufficient** water to allow more development in the desert area.*

moist *adj* damp • *Rice needs a fertile, **moist** environment in order to grow.*

periodic Ⓐ *adj* happening periodically; every so often • *History shows that **periodic** droughts in the southwestern part of the United States forced farmers to leave that area and move elsewhere.*

precipitation *n* rainfall • *As the storm moves in, heavy **precipitation** is expected particularly along the coastal regions.*

prevailing winds *n phr* winds from a specific direction • ***Prevailing winds** are expected to bring rainfall to the area by midnight.*

proximity to *n* the state of being close to something • *People who live in close **proximity to** the ocean expect higher winds and more rainfall than those who live further inland.*

purify *v* to rid something of harmful substances • *Staff from the organization – Doctors Without Borders – regularly teach villages how to **purify** their water so that it is safe to drink.*

rain shadow *n phr* an area protected from rainfall by high mountains • *The eastern side of the Olympic mountains in Washington State is a popular place to live because it is in the **rain shadow** and therefore enjoys a drier climate than the western side.*

resolution Ⓐ *n* a formal statement of a decision or an opinion • *The two countries issued a joint **resolution** that outlined a series of steps needed to ease the water crisis.*

runoff *n* chemicals and animal waste that flow into water • *The sudden death of hundreds of fish was blamed on industrial **runoff** from the nearby factory.*

staggering *adj* shocking because of being so huge • *The amount of water wasted every day by leaking faucets in the United States is **staggering**.*

strain *v* to put a lot of pressure on something • *Raising beef **strains** the water supply in many parts of the world because it takes much more water to raise cattle than to grow vegetable-based food such as wheat.*

subsidize Ⓐ *v* to pay part of the cost of something • *Many countries **subsidize** agriculture because the need to produce enough food is critical to each country's health and economy.*

thereby Ⓐ *adv* because of this; as a result of this • *People continue to throw away plastic bottles **thereby** adding to the problem of landfills. A better alternative is to recycle these bottles.*

topography *n* the natural and physical features of land • *New satellite technology allows everyone to clearly see the* **topography** *of the earth.*

trap *v* to contain, catch, or hold something • *In the 1930s, the U.S. government built many dams across rivers to* **trap** *water to create hydroelectric power.*

underlying Ⓐ *adj* real, but not obvious or easily seen • *The government discovered that the lack of education, was an* **underlying** *problem of the declining economy. They therefore decided to invest in more schools and universities.*

UNIT 4 • READING 5

Managing Earth's Greenhouse

abandon Ⓐ *v* to leave someone or something behind, usually in a difficult position • *If sea levels continue to rise, many people around the world will be forced to* **abandon** *their homes and move inland.*

accumulation Ⓐ *n* a gradual increase • *The weather forecast is predicting more snow today, with an* **accumulation** *of between 10 and 12 inches.*

adversely *adv* badly; affecting something in a negative manner • *The levels of salt began to increase in the rivers,* **adversely** *affecting homes and farms in that area.*

attributable Ⓐ *adj* caused by • *The dramatic rise in respiratory illnesses was* **attributable** *to the overuse of pesticides and insecticides.*

conceivable Ⓐ *adj* possible to imagine or to think • *Some people question whether it is* **conceivable** *to really limit greenhouse gas emissions.*

contention *n* a disagreement resulting from opposing arguments • *Although the cause of global warming is still a subject of* **contention**, *its effects are no longer debated.*

curb *v* to limit • *The government is trying to* **curb** *the use of fossil fuels in manufacturing.*

ecosystem *n* the system of relationships between all living things within an environment • *Many natural* **ecosystems** *are threatened by human activities.*

greenhouse *n* a building made of glass and used for growing plants • *Because spring was unusually cold, growers kept the young plants in the* **greenhouses** *for longer than normal.*

hybrid *adj* fueled with more than one source • *Scientists continue to develop different types of* **hybrid** *vehicles hoping to produce one that is efficient and environmentally-friendly.*

imposition Ⓐ *n* the establishment of rules or laws that must be obeyed • *Some members of the government argued against the* **imposition** *of the new tax on gas.*

induce Ⓐ *v* to encourage or persuade someone to do something • *The government has reduced the amount of tax on gas-efficient vehicles in an effort to* **induce** *people to buy them.*

landfill *n* a place where garbage is buried • *Some of the largest* **landfills** *in the world are the size of small cities.*

mitigation *n* a reduction in how harmful or unpleasant something can be • **Mitigation** *of storm damage includes both preparation before the storm hits as well as clean-up immediately afterward.*

pose Ⓐ *v* to cause a problem or a difficulty • *The lack of housing and basic services such as fresh water* **pose** *a significant threat to the health of people living in settlements around Mumbai.*

protocol Ⓐ *n* a formal set of official rules • *Governments that signed the Kyoto* **Protocol** *have agreed to the reduction of emissions from their countries.*

skeptic *n* a person who doubts the truth, or value of an idea • *Some scientists claim that the recent series of huge storms in the eastern United States is an indication of climate change, but* **skeptics** *argue these storms are a normal part of nature.*

submerged *adj* buried below water • *If the sea levels continues to rise in the Maldives, there is a real danger that this will be a* **submerged** *island nation in the future.*

substantial *adj* large enough to be important • *The new factory will have a* **substantial** *impact on employment in the area since it will create over 500 new jobs.*

tenable *adj* able to be defended • *Knowing that coal releases a significant amount of carbon dioxide into the atmosphere, is it really* **tenable** *to continue to build coal-fueled factories?*

threshold *n* a point at which something starts • *With so many new technologies, we are on the* **threshold** *of a new period in which use of alternative fuels will become normal.*

unabated *adj* without weakening in strength or force • *The hurricane continued* **unabated** *for hours until it finally lost its power and began to weaken.*

undeniable *adj* so obviously true that it cannot be doubted • *It is an* **undeniable** *fact that Greenland and Antarctica are losing ice at an alarming rate.*

unequivocal *adj* clear and firm • *The United Nations announced in 2007 that there was* **unequivocal** *evidence that changes in the earth's atmosphere and ice-caps was the result of human activities and not part of a natural climate change.*

unprecedented Ⓐ *adj* never having happened or existed before • *The cost of gas is increasing at an* **unprecedented** *rate due to increased demand at a time when there is limited supply.*

Index to Key Vocabulary

Words that are part of the Academic Word List are noted with an Ⓐ in this appendix.

innate 2.3
insecticide 1.4
institute (A) 2.5
insufficient (A) 4.4
integration (A) 2.5
intend 4.2
intention 4.2
interact (A) 2.3
interest 2.1
interpret (A) 3.3
interrupt 4.1
intricate 2.4
invest (A) 1.5
irrational (A) 2.5
irreversible (A) 4.1
irrigate 4.2
irrigation 4.2
isolation (A) 3.5

key 1.2

landfill 4.5
leading 1.4
linger 1.4
link (A) 1.2
literate 3.4
longevity 3.4
lose ground to 3.4

mainstream 2.3
maintain (A) 3.4
marked 4.2
massacre 2.5
mastery 3.2
mean 4.2
merge 2.3
merit 2.5
metaphor 2.3
milestone 1.3
minimize (A) 3.3
minimum (A) 2.2
mitigation 4.5
mobility 2.2
modify (A) 3.3
moist 4.4
monitor (A) 1.1
motivation (A) 2.2

nanny 3.5

negligible 4.1
novel 3.1
nutrients 4.1

obesity 1.1
obligation 4.1
observation 3.2
obtain (A) 1.3
ongoing (A) 1.5
onset 3.5
opponent 2.3
optimistic 1.1
option (A) 2.1
outcome (A) 1.2
overtake 3.2

paradigm (A) 4.1
paramount 3.4
parasite 1.4
partnership (A) 4.3
patent 1.5
path 3.4
peak 2.1
perceive (A) 3.1
perception (A) 3.1
periodic (A) 4.4
perpetuate 1.4
persistent (A) 2.1
personnel 3.5
pervade 1.4
pesticide 4.2
phenomenon (A) 3.2
philanthropic 1.4
plague 1.5
policy (A) 3.4
poll 2.3
pose (A) 4.5
potential (A) 1.3
precipitation 4.4
precise (A) 3.2
preliminary (A) 1.4
preserve 4.3
prestigious 2.4
presumably (A) 3.2
prevailing winds 4.4
prevalent 1.2
preventive 1.2
primarily (A) 1.4
priority (A) 1.5

profanity 2.4
profound 2.4
prohibitive (A) 1.5
project (A) 1.2
promising 1.1
promote (A) 3.5
properties 4.3
proponent 3.2
prospect (A) 2.2
prosperous 3.1
protocol (A) 4.5
proximity to 4.4
purify 4.4
pursue (A) 1.3
pursuit (A) 1.3

rain shadow 4.4
range (A) 2.2
rebound 4.2
recede 4.2
recruit 2.1
regardless 2.3
relegate 2.4
reliant (A) 4.1
reluctant (A) 1.4
remedial 3.5
remedy 2.5
remind 4.2
reminder 4.2
remote 1.4
render 4.2
renewable 4.3
representative 2.1
reproduce 3.1
resident (A) 3.4
resistant 2.5
resolution (A) 4.4
retain (A) 3.1
retention (A) 3.1
reversal (A) 4.2
reverse (A) 4.2
revival 1.3
revive 1.3
runoff 4.4
rural 1.4

sacrifice 1.5
salinity 4.2
sanctions 2.5

saturated 4.2
scholar 3.2
sector (A) 3.4
secular 2.5
secure (A) 2.2
seek out (A) 3.5
segregate 2.3
session 3.1
setback 1.3
severely 2.3
shift (A) 1.2
sincere 3.3
skeptic 4.5
socioeconomic status (A) 3.5
sophisticated 3.5
source (A) 2.1
species 3.2
spray 1.4
stability (A) 2.1
staggering 4.4
starvation 2.1
static 2.4
statistics (A) 1.1
status (A) 2.2
stereotype 2.5
stigma 1.1
stimulation 3.2
straightforward (A) 1.4
strain 4.4
strategy (A) 1.2
stratification 2.5
stringent 2.5
stroke 1.2
submerged 4.5
subsequently (A) 2.1
subsidize (A) 4.4
substantial 4.5
substitute (A) 4.3
superior 3.2
suppress 3.4
susceptible 4.3
sustainable (A) 4.1
swell 2.2
switch 1.2

tackle 4.3
take advantage of 2.2
target (A) 1.1

tenable 4.5
tend 1.5
therapy 1.3
thereby (A) 4.4
threshold 4.5
thrive 1.4
tie 2.2
tolerance 2.3
topography 4.4
transfer (A) 3.3
transition (A) 2.1
transmit (A) 1.4
transport (A) 4.2
transportation (A) 4.2
trap 4.4
trend (A) 1.1

unabated 4.5
unanimous 4.3
unconsciously 3.3
undeniable (A) 4.5
underestimate (A) 1.3
underlying (A) 4.4
undernourished 4.1
unequivocal 4.5
unfounded 2.4
unjustified (A) 2.3
unprecedented (A) 4.5
unrest 2.2
unskilled 2.2
unstable (A) 2.2
utility (A) 3.4
utilize (A) 3.1

value 2.4
vanish 4.1
vast 2.4
vibrant 3.4
vigorous 3.4
virtually (A) 1.1
visual (A) 3.2
vitality 3.4
volume (A) 4.2
vulnerable 1.4

wages 2.2

Improving Your Reading Speed

Good readers read quickly and understand most of what they read. However, like other skills, reading faster is a skill that requires good technique and practice. One way to practice is to read frequently. Read about topics you are interested in, not just topics from your academic courses. Reading for pleasure will improve your reading speed and understanding.

Another way to practice is to choose a text you have already read and read it again without stopping. Time yourself, record the time, and keep a record of how your reading speed is increasing.

These strategies will help you improve your reading speed:

- Before you read a text, look at the title and any illustrations. Ask yourself, *What is this reading about?* This will help you figure out the general topic of the reading.
- Read words in groups instead of reading every single word. Focus on the most important words in a sentence – usually the nouns, verbs, adjectives, and adverbs.
- Don't pronounce each word as you read. Pronouncing words will slow you down and does not help you to understand the text.
- Don't use a pencil or your finger to point to the words as you read. This will also slow you down.
- Continue reading even if you come to an unfamiliar word. Good readers know that they can skip unfamiliar words as long as they understand the general meaning of the text.

Calculating Your Reading Speed

After you have completed a unit in this book, reread one of the readings. Use your cellphone or your watch to time how long it takes you to complete the reading. Write down the number of minutes and seconds it took you in the chart on the following pages.

You can figure out your reading speed; that is your words per minute (wpm) rate by doing the following calculation:

First, convert the seconds of your reading time to decimals using the table to the right.

Next, divide the number of words per reading by the time it took you to complete the reading. For example, if the reading is 525 words, and it took you 5 minutes 50 seconds, your reading speed is about 90 words per minute (525 ÷ 5.83 = 90).

Record your wpm rate in the chart on the following pages.

Seconds	Decimal
:05	.08
:10	.17
:15	.25
:20	.33
:25	.42
:30	.50
:35	.58
:40	.67
:45	.75
:50	.83
:55	.92

UNIT	READING TITLE	NUMBER OF WORDS IN READING	YOUR READING TIME minutes:seconds 00:00	READING SPEED (WPM)
Unit 1 Global Health	The State of the World's Health	913	_____ : _____	
	Changing Attitudes Toward Cardiovascular Disease	772	_____ : _____	
	Medicine and Genetic Research	976	_____ : _____	
	Malaria: Portrait of a Disease	1,220	_____ : _____	
	The Health Care Divide	2,018	_____ : _____	
Unit 2 Multicultural Societies	The Age of Immigration	978	_____ : _____	
	Who Are Today's Immigrants?	684	_____ : _____	
	The Meeting of Cultures	1,330	_____ : _____	
	One World: One Culture?	1,227	_____ : _____	
	The Challenge of Diversity	2,217	_____ : _____	
Unit 3 Aspects of Language	When Does Language Learning Begin?	931	_____ : _____	
	Learning a Language as an Adult	843	_____ : _____	
	Rules of Speaking	1,173	_____ : _____	
	Languages in Contact	1,264	_____ : _____	
	The Advantages of Multilingualism	2,353	_____ : _____	

UNIT	READING TITLE	NUMBER OF WORDS IN READING	YOUR READING TIME minutes:seconds 00:00	READING SPEED (WPM)
Unit 4 Sustaining Planet Earth	Ecology, Overpopulation, and Economic Development	1,311	_____:_____	
	The Aral Sea: An Environmental Crisis	1,019	_____:_____	
	Biodiversity and Tropical Rainforests	1,190	_____:_____	
	The Water Crisis	1,153	_____:_____	
	Managing Earth's Greenhouse	2,835	_____:_____	

UNIT 1, READING 1

CVD is Killer Number One. MEP Heart Group http://www.mepheartgroup.eu/facts-a-figures.html

Fact Sheet #339 Tobacco. WHO. 2012. http://www.who.int/mediacentre/factsheets/fs339/en/index.html#

Parker-Pope, T. 2010. Is Marriage Good for your Health? *New York Times*, April 18. http://www.nytimes.com/2010/04/18/magazine/18marriage-t.html?pagewanted=all

Walsh, F. 2012. How India Has Had remarkable Success with Polio. http://m.bbc.co.uk/news/health-17072769

Worldwide HIV & AIDS Statistics. 2012. http://www.avert.org/worldstats.htm

UNIT 1, READING 2

Build A Healthy Base. http://www.health.gov/dietaryguidelines/dga2000/document/build.htm

Earl S. Ford, M.D., M.P.H., et al. Coronary heart disease deaths halved due to treatment & risk reduction. 2007. *NEJM*, June 7. http://ww.natap.org/2007/HIV/060707-01.htm

Reinberg, S. 2011. U.S. Heart Rates Continue to Fall. *USA Today*, October 14. http://yourlife.usatoday.com/health/medical/heartdisease/story/2011-10-14/US-heart-disease-rates-continue-to-fall/50769132/1

Sternberg, Steve. Heart disease deaths plummet ahead of 2010 goal. 2008. *USA Today*, January 1. http://www.usatoday.com/news/health/2008-01-22-heart-disease_N.thm

World Health Organization. Cardiovascular diseases (CVDs). Fact sheet no. 317. 2012, September. www.who.int/mediacentre/factsheets/fs317/en/

UNIT 1, READING 3

BRCA graph: Just ASK: http://www.bracnow.com/considering-testing/hboc-basics.php

Dobson, R. 2000. Gene therapy saves immune deficient babies in France. May 6. http://www.ncbi.nlm.nih.gov/pmc/articles/PMC1117983/ National Institutes of Health.

Gene therapy for Parkinson's disease is safe and some patients benefit, according to study. 2007. *Science Daily*, June 25. http:/www.sciencedaily.com/releases/2007/06/070622101037.htm

Genes and gene therapy. http://www.nlm.nih.gov/medlineplus/genesandgenetherapy.html

Genetic Testing: How it is Used for Healthcare. 2011, February 14. http://report.nih.gov/NIHfactsheets/ViewFactSheet.aspx?csid=43

Kolata, G. 2009. After setbacks, small successes for gene therapy. *New York Times*. February 4. www.nytimes.com/2009/11/06/health/06gene.html

Wade. N. 2011. Treatment for Blood Disease Is Gene Therapy Landmark. *New York Times*. December 11. http://mobile.nytimes.com/2011/12/11/health/research/hemophilia-b-gene-therapy-breakthrough.xml

UNIT 1, READING 4

African Leaders Malaria Conference. http://www.alma2015.org/

Bill and Melinda Gates Foundation: Malaria Overview http://www.gatesfoundation.org/topics/Pages/malaria.aspx

Boseley, S. 2012. Malaria kills twice as many people as previously thought, research finds. *The Guardian*. February 2. http://www.guardian.co.uk/society/2012/feb/03/malaria-deaths-research

Centers for Disease Control and Prevention. http://www.cdc.gov/malaria/about/facts.html

Malaria Atlas Project. http://www.map.ox.ac.uk/

World Malaria Report 2011. http://www.who.int/malaria/world_malaria_report_2011/en/

UNIT 1, READING 5

Capdevila, G. 2011. WHO report: Diseases once linked to rich nations increasingly affect poor. *The Guardian*. May 17. http://www.guardian.co.uk/global-development/2011/may/17/who-non-communicable-diseases-affect-poor-too

Countries without doctors? 2010. *Foreign Policy*, June 11. http://www.foreignpolicy.com/articles/2010/06/11/countries_without_doctors

Flintoff, C. 2012. Like the US, Europe wrestles with health care. *NPR Health News*, March 29. http://www.npr.org/blogs/health/2012/03/28/149564583/like-the-u-s-europe-wrestles-with-health-care

Kaiser Family Foundation Snapshots: Health care costs. 2011, April 28. http://www.kff.org/insurance/snapshot/oecd042111.cfm

The Millenium Development Goals Report. 2011. United Nations Development Program. July 7. http://www.undp.org/content/undp/en/home/librarypage/mdg/MDG_Report_2011.html

National Institutes of Health. 2011. UN meets on chronic non-communicable diseases (NCDs). Fogarty International Center. Vol. 10. Iss. 5. Sept.-Oct. http://www.fic.nih.gov/News/GlobalHealthMatters/Sept-Oct-2011/Pages/un-summit-chronic-disease.aspx

Shah, A. Health care around the world. *Global Issues*. Updated Sept. 2011. http://www.globalissues.org/article/774/health-care-around-the-worldTulenko, K. 2010.

World Bank. Health Data. Updated 2011. http://data.worldbank.org/topic/health

World Health Organization. Report on health workforce. Updated 2012. http://gamapserver.who.int/gho/interactive_charts/health_workforce/PhysiciansDensity_Total/atlas.html

UNIT 2, READING 1

Immigration to the United States. http://eh.net/encyclopedia/article/cohn.immigration.us

Statistics Canada. http://www.statcan.gc.ca/tables-tableaux/sum-som/l01/cst01/demo03-eng.htm?sdi=immigration

U.S. Census Bureau. http://www.census.gov/population/www/documentation/twps0029/twps0029.html

Yale-New Haven Teachers Institute. http://www.yale.edu/ynhti/curriculum/units/1990/1/90.01.06.x.html

UNIT 2, READING 2

Bloch, M. 2009. Immigrations and jobs: Where U.S. workers come from. *New York Times*, April 7. http://www.nytimes.com/interactive/2009/04/07/us/20090407-immigration-country.html#view=allcountries

Epstein, G. 2010. China's immigration problem. *Forbes*, July 19. http://www.forbes.com/forbes/2010/0719/opinions-china-immigration-illegal-aliens-heads-up.html

Migration Policy Institute. http://www.migrationinformation.org/datahub/wmm.cfm

Papademetroiu, D. 2005. The global struggle with immigration. September. http://www.migrationinformation.org/Feature/display.cfm?ID=336

World Migration Report 2010. International Organization for Migration

UNIT 2, READING 3

The Bilingual Education Debate. 2010. *The Los Angeles Times*, July 17. http://articles.latimes.com/2010/jul/17/opinion/la-oew-0717-bilingual-blowbacks-20100717

Canadians Endorse Multiculturalism, but Pick Melting Pot over Mosaic. 2010. Angus Reid Public Opinion. November 8. http://www.angus-reid.com/wp-content/uploads/2010/11/2010.11.08_Melting_CAN.pdf Canadian poll

The Gallup Poll http://www.gallup.com/poll/116431/Research-Reports.aspx

Sclaza, R. 2009. As hosts of the Vancouver Olympics, First Nations are ready to welcome the World. *The Washington Post*, November 1. http://www.washingtonpost.com/wp-dyn/content/article/2009/10/28/AR2009102801479.html

UNIT 2, READING 4

Arango, T. 2008. World Falls for American Media *The New York Times*, November 30. http://www.nytimes.com/2008/12/01/business/media/01soft.html

Roberts, D. 2007. Forbidden Starbucks. *Business Week*, July 16. http://www.businessweek.com/globalbiz/content/jul2007/gb20070716_579557.htm

Subsidy Wars. 2005. Subsidy Wars *The Economist*, February 25. http://www.economist.com/node/3701130

UNIT 2, READING 5

Ball, J., Milmo, D., & Ferguson, B. 2012. Half of UK's young black males are unemployed. *The Guardian*, March 9. http://www.guardian.co.uk/society/2012/mar/09/half-uk-young-black-men-unemployed

Branstein, J. 2006. EU: Netherlands leading trend to more stringent immigration rules. *Radio Free Europe/Radio Liberty*, April 5. http://www.rferl.org/content/article/1067418.html

CBC News. 2004. France's hijab ban. September 7. http://www.cbc.ca/news/background/islam/hijab.html

Euronews: European Affairs. 2012. Reaching Out to Europe's Roma, April 30. http://www.euronews.com/2012/04/30/reaching-out-to-europe-s-roma/

Harlan, C. 2010. Strict immigration rules may threaten Japan's future. *The Washington Post*. July 28.

International Labor Organization. 2011. Racial discrimination and the global economic downturn. *World of Work Magazine*, no. 72. August. http://www.ilo.org/global/publications/magazines-and-journals/world-of-work-magazine/articles/WCMS_165284/lang – en/index.htm

The New York Times: News – Times Topics. Affirmative Action. Updated Oct. 10, 2012. http://topics.nytimes.com/topics/reference/timestopics/subjects/a/affirmative_action/index.html

Polgreen, L. 2011. Scaling caste walls with capitalism's ladders in India." *The New York Times*, December 21. http://www.nytimes.com/2011/12/22/world/asia/indias-boom-creates-openings-for-untouchables.html?pagewanted=1&sq=Dalit&st=nyt&scp=3

Public Broadcasting System. 2006. Native Americans and the Gold Rush. September 13. http://www.pbs.org/wbh/amex/goldrush/sfeature/natives.html

UN News Centre. 2011. Migrants and minorities still vulnerable to discrimination at work. May 26. http://www.un.org/apps/news/story.asp?NewsID=38398&Cr=migrant&Cr1

UN Office of the High Commission on Human Rights. Let's fight racism: vulnerable people. 2012. http://www.un.org/en/letsfightracism/issues.shtml

UNIT 3, SKILLS AND STRATEGIES 7

Lackman, J. 2011. The secrets of twinspeak. *Slate*, August 24. http://www.nidcd.nih.gov/health/hearing/pages/asl.aspx

Machine translation. http://en.wikipedia.org/wiki/History_of_machine_translation

Polyglots have different brains. 2006. *BBC News*, April 26. http://news.bbc.co.uk/2/hi/uk_news/education/4883418.stm

Treffert, D. The polyglot (language) savant. http://www.wisconsinmedicalsociety.org/savant_syndrome/savant_articles/polyglot

UNIT 3, READING 1

Begley, S. 2009. The crying song. *Newsweek*, November 4. http://www.thedailybeast.com/newsweek/2009/11/04/the-crying-song.html

Bock, P. 2005. How do babies learn to talk? *Seattle Times*, March 6. http://seattletimes.nwsource.com/pacificnw/2005/0306/cover.html

Houston, D. 2011. Infant Speech Perception. In R. Seewald and A M. Tharpe (Eds.) *Comprehensive Handbook of Pediatric Audiology*. Plural Publishing.

TED Talks. 2010. http://www.ted.com/talks/patricia_kuhl_the_linguistic_genius_of_babies.html

UNIT 3, READING 2

Secret of the wild child. NOVA. http://www.pbs.org/wgbh/nova/transcripts/2112gchild.html (feral children, Genie)

UNIT 3, READING 3

Pakenham, K. J. 1993. Personal data collection.

UNIT 3, READING 4

Lewis, P. 1998. Too late to say estinct. *New York Times*, August 15. http://www.nytimes.com/1998/08/15/arts/too-late-say-extinct-ubykh-eyak-ona-thousands-languages-are-endangered.html?pagewanted=all&src=pm

Oakland Blog: Native Americans work revitalize California's indigenous languages. 2012. *SF Gate*. July 23. http://blog.sfgate.com/inoakland/2012/07/23/native-americans-work-to-revitalize-california%E2%80%99s-indigenous-languages/

Reyner, J. 1997. Teaching indigenous languages. Northern Arizona University. http://jan.ucc.nau.edu/~jar/TIL.html

UNIT 3, READING 5

Anderson, J. 2010. Looking for babysitters: Foreign language a must. *New York Times*, August 18. http://www.nytimes.com/2010/08/19/nyregion/19bilingual.html?pagewanted=all

Dreifus, C. 2011. The bilingual advantage. *New York Times*, May 30. http://www.nytimes.com/2011/05/31/science/31conversation.html

Maxwell, L. 2012. Momentum builds for dual language leaning. *Education Week*, March 23. http://www.edweek.org/ew/articles/2012/03/23/26duallanguage_ep.h31.html?tkn=UOYFwCZn88e1rEM0d6te%2BOfLl3FuSrmoWNqO&cmp=clp-edweek

Onishi, N. 2008. For English studies, Korean kids say goodbye to dad. *New York Times*, June 8. http://www.nytimes.com/2008/06/08/world/asia/08geese.html

Parlez-vous français? The advantages of bilingualism in Canada. 2008. Canadian Council on Learning.

Watanabe, T. 2011. Dual language immersion programs growing in popularity. *Los Angeles Times*, May 8. http://articles.latimes.com/2011/may/08/local/la-me-bilingual-20110508

Zagier, A. 2012. Early study abroad for US education means split families in South Korea. *Huffington Post*, April 1. http://www.huffingtonpost.com/2012/04/02/early-study-abroad-for-us_n_1396676.html

UNIT 4, READING 1

Conner, S. 2006. Overpopulation is Main Threat to Planet. *The Independent*, January 7. http://www.independent.co.uk/environment/overpopulation-is-main-threat-to-planet-521925.html

Deforestation and Desertification . National Geographic http://www.nationalgeographic.com/eye/deforestation/phenomena.html

FAO. http://www.fao.org/countries/55528/en/npl/

Forest Biodiversity at Risk. FAO. http://www.fao.org/news/story/en/item/45904/icode/

Who Benefits from Deforestation and Who Loses? World Bank http://go.worldbank.org/TQJ206QPT0

UNIT 4, READING 2

Shrinking Aral Sea (08/25/00) NASA http://earthobservatory.nasa.gov/Features/WorldOfChange/aral_sea.php

Walters, P. 2010. Aral Sea Recovering? National Geographic. April 2. http://news.nationalgeographic.com/news/2010/04/100402-aral-sea-story

UNIT 4, READING 3

Conservation Finance. (2012) WWF. http://www.worldwildlife.org/what/howwedoit/conservationfinance/debtfornatureswaps.html

O'Loughlin, Toni. 2009. Number of Earth's species known to scientists rises to 1.9 million. *Guardian.co.uk*, September 29. http://www.guardian.co.uk/environment/2009/sep/29/number-of-living-species

Roles of Forests in Climate Change. 2012. FAO. June 15. http://www.fao.org/forestry/climatechange/53459/en/

Smith, N. J. H., Williams, J. T., and Pluckett, D. L. 1991. Conserving the tropical cornucopia. *Environment* 33.6, pp. 6-32.

Wilson, E. O. 1989. Threats to biodiversity. *Scientific American*, 261 (3).

UNIT 4, READING 4

The Global Water Footprints of Key Crops (2012) National Geographic. http://environment.nationalgeographic.com/environment/freshwater/global-water-footprint/

Vidal, J. 2011. What does the Arab World do when its Water Runs Out? *The Guardian*, February 19. http://www.guardian.co.uk/environment/2011/feb/20/arab-nations-water-running-out

UNIT 4, READING 5

Beinhocker, E., Oppenheim, J., Irons, B., Lahti, M., Farrell, D., Nyquist, S. Enkwist, P-A. 2008. The carbon productivity challenge: curbing climate change and sustaining ecogrowth. McKinsey Global Institute. June. http://www.mckinsey.com/insights/mgi/research/natural_resources/the_carbon_productivity_challenge

Broder, J.M. 2011. Climate talks in Durban yield limited agreement. *The New York Times*, Dec. 11. http://www.nytimes.com/2011/12/12/science/earth/countries-at-un-conference-agree-to-draft-new-emissions-treaty.html?_r=1

The Guardian Environment series. The ultimate climate change FAQ. 2012. *The Guardian*. http://www.guardian.co.uk/environment/series/the-ultimate-climate-change-faq

Harvey, F. 2011. Worst ever carbon emissions leave climate on the brink. *The Guardian*, May 29. http://www.guardian.co.uk/environment/2011/may/29/carbon-emissions-nuclearpower

McGee, M. 2012. CO_2 *Now*. November. http://co2now.org/

Methane gas levels begin to increase again. 2008. *Science Daily*. October 18. http://www.sciencedaily.com/releases/2008/10/081029141043.htm

National Oceanic and Atmospheric Administration (NOAA). 2012. State of the climate global analysis. National Climate Data Center. September. http://www.ncdc.noaa.gov/sotc/global/2012/9

Reay, D. & Hogan, C.M. 2010. *The Encyclopedia of Earth*, May 9. http://www.eoearth.org/article/Greenhouse_gas?topic=60586

Rosenthal, E. & Lehren, A. W. 2012. Relief in every window, but global worry too. *The New York Times*, June 21. http://www.nytimes.com/2012/06/21/world/asia/global-demand-for-air-conditioning-forces-tough-environmental-choices.html?adxnnl=1&ref=world&adxnnlx=1353528409-oBenk3vRmFodSXGks1FWcw

Shah, A. 2012. Climate change and global warming. *Global Issues*, April. http://www.globalissues.org/issue/178/climate-change-and-global-warming

Union of Concerned Scientists. 2010. Global thermometer still climbing. January. http://www.ucsusa.org/global_warming/science_and_impacts/science/global-thermometer-still-climbing.html

US Environmental Protection Agency. 2012. Climate change. November 9. http://www.epa.gov/climatechange/

Art Credits